THE END OF THE NOTABLES

The End of the Notables

by DANIEL HALÉVY

Edited, with Introduction and Notes,
by ALAIN SILVERA

Translated by ALAIN SILVERA and JUNE GUICHARNAUD

Wesleyan University Press
MIDDLETOWN, CONNECTICUT

Library of Congress Cataloging in Publication Data

Halévy, Daniel, 1872–1962.
      The end of the notables.

      Translation of La fin des notables.
            1. France—Politics and government—1870–1940.
      I. Title.
DC340.H313   320.9′44′08   73–6009
ISBN 0–8195–4066–8
ISBN 0–8195–6030–8 (pbk.)

Manufactured in the United States of America
First English edition

Contents

Introduction

Daniel Halévy (1872–1962) holds an honored yet equivocal place among French writers and critics. Neither a man of action nor an original thinker in his own right, he stood out in his day as a guide and interpreter, acting as a prism to his times and epitomizing in his life and work the hopes and illusions of the generation that reached manhood with the Dreyfus Affair. Seen as a whole, his *œuvre*, consisting of some thirty-odd books as well as a vast number of essays, articles, and reviews, marks him out as the chronicler of more than half a century of French national experience corresponding almost exactly to the life span of a political regime whose obscure origins he so skillfully recounted in *La Fin des notables*.

Blessed as he was with a longevity which enabled him to survive almost all his contemporaries, he commands our attention as a living witness of those eventful years stretching all the way from the first great crisis encountered by French democracy through the growing pains of socialism and the agonies of the Great War and extending beyond the trials of the Popular Front to the ultimate collapse of the Third Republic at the hands of Germany. If Daniel Halévy can be categorized at all, it would have to be as that vanishing species of the man of letters, or perhaps more accurately, as what the French call *un politique et moraliste*, for like his friends Georges Sorel and Charles Péguy, he was above all a moralist seeking to explain and to judge the springs of human conduct in public affairs. It is for this reason that his most enduring work will undoubtedly remain *Charles Péguy et les Cahiers de la Quinzaine*, first published in 1918 and reissued in its third version in 1941—an important book recording the transition from the nineteenth century to our own and containing the clue to some of the more elusive trends underlying French political and social thought.

As an essayist and critic, as a biographer and historian, Halévy pursued so very many interests that his name has come to be associated with a bewildering variety of overlapping aspects of the history of his country and times. A leading authority on Nietzsche, whose philosophy he was one of the first to introduce to his countrymen at the turn of the century, he was also instrumental in adapting the ideas of the anarchist Proudhon to the quasi-fascist ideology of the corporate state, which became an integral part of the intellectual climate of Vichy France. Carried away by the socialist fervor ushered in by the Dreyfus Affair, he had started his career by rallying to the *Cahiers de la Quinzaine*, standing apart from the rest of that remarkable literary coterie who gathered around Péguy's *boutique* on the rue de la Sorbonne, and becoming the most persistent spokesman of a libertarian mystique so eloquently incarnated by that maverick champion of lost causes. His intimacy with Péguy led him to explore the rise of syndicalism and the unknown world of the rural masses in such books as *Essais sur le mouvement ouvrier en France* (1901) and the successive instalments of the *Visites aux paysans du Centre* (4th edition, 1935), drawing him closer to the provocative ideas of Sorel, whose *Réflexions sur la violence* he helped to edit in 1911. A central figure in the serious journalism of the interwar years, especially in

Introduction

connection with *Le Journal des Débats* and *La Revue des Deux Mondes*, he gained a reputation for being one of the foremost critics of his day, who will perhaps be chiefly remembered in French letters as the enterprising editor of *Les Cahiers Verts*, published by Bernard Grasset in the twenties.

His position in French historiography is no less secure, and although the works he devoted to modern France cannot be compared either in bulk or in learning with his brother Elie's massive history of the English people in the nineteenth century, they are generally regarded as solid achievements that have greatly contributed to our understanding of the formative period of the Third Republic. *La Fin des notables*, first published in 1930, and its companion volume *La République des ducs* (1937) still rank as minor classics of historical writing which explain the nature of a regime whose difficult beginnings seemed far from clear; indeed, the titles of the books have become household words to subsequent generations of Frenchmen. His editions of the private papers of both Thiers (1920) and Gambetta (1938), to say nothing of his notable efforts to raise contemporary history to the level of a reputable field of academic study, earned him the grudging respect of professional historians. Among his works of a more philosophical nature, his *Essai sur l'accélération de l'histoire* (1961) written in the same vein as his studies of Michelet (1928) and Leibnitz (1940), stands in a class apart as a brief but suggestive speculative essay in the manner of Toynbee.

Somewhat more controversial were Halévy's polemical writings directed against the abuses of the Third Republic, upon which he heaped his disdain with relentless vigor in the late twenties and thirties. During these years his intellectual development was guided by a growing irritation with the parliamentary habits of a regime that had succumbed to sectional interests and Radical demagoguery. Like so many otherwise well meaning but disillu-

sioned Frenchmen, Halévy shared the prevailing sentiment that his country and its institutions were out of joint,
its leaders woefully inept, and its public spirit decadent.
Much of what he published in the decade preceding the
fall of France reveals the extent to which the repentant
Dreyfusard, whose *Apologie pour notre passé* (1910) had
provoked Péguy to reply with a vindication of republican
principles in *Notre Jeunesse* (1910), could react to the
distortion of his youthful ideals by a government no longer
capable of rescuing France from the chaos of party strife
and ministerial instability. To be sure, such diatribes as *La
République des comités* (1934) belong to a respectable
French genre in which, like Albert Thibaudet and Robert
de Jouvenel, Daniel Halévy also excelled. Similarly, his
collection of essays *Décadence de la liberté* (1930) and
1938, *Une Année d'Histoire* (1939)—a spirited attack
against the blunders of the Popular Front—as well as his
more restrained *Les Trois Epreuves* (1942)—a compara-
tive study of the three great defeats suffered by France in
1814, 1871, and 1940—are written in the best tradition of
French pamphleteering. Yet even the books that he wrote
on the spur of the moment, like most of his journalistic
output, illustrate a rare gift for combining polemics with
sound political and social analysis. Dictated by circumstances more urgent than those that inspired his serious
efforts, these tracts for the times, couched in a distinctively
urbane prose, also demonstrate the versatility of Halévy
the publicist.

Yet for all the variety of Halévy's activities and the
very considerable quality of his accomplishments, in none
of them has he proved to be quite distinguished enough to
win an enduring place in the front rank. Lacking the will if
not the ability to attain supreme distinction in any single
area, he developed talents of critical interpretation rather
than creative originality, displaying a predilection for
acting as a spur to the genius of others rather than for
setting out on an independent course of his own. Over-

Introduction

shadowed by his brother as an historian and by his friend Péguy as an essayist, he chose to carry out the auxiliary but invaluable task of clarifying at one remove the broader implications of a cluster of highly original ideas, such as the role of mystique and elites in politics or the relation of nationalism and socialism to parliamentary democracy— ideas that were actively debated among French intellectuals at the turn of the century. And since the general drift of his own thinking was so frequently in tune with the temper of his times, his real interest lies in the way in which he was able to offer fresh insights of his own discovery by drawing attention to the deeper affinities linking Renan's moral pessimism to Barrès's *culte du moi* or Nietzsche's heroic vitalism to Bergson's *élan vital,* just as he later succeeded in shedding light on a recurring theme in his country's tradition of socialist dissent by bringing out the subtler connections that bound Péguy's mystique and Sorel's syndicalist myth to the anarchist ideas of their common ancestor Proudhon. He showed a similar tendency to act as a mediator by advancing the careers of the outstanding crop of postwar writers who were drawn to his *Cahiers Verts,* but in all these endeavors it was primarily as a biographer with a flair for translating ideas into the more tangible form of character and personality that Halévy made his especial contribution to the intellectual history of his time.

The essentially derivative quality of Halévy's thinking can be traced to a youth and an upbringing almost too generously endowed with varied stimulation, for he was brought up in an ambience dominated by some of the most gifted intellectuals of the Third Republic. Born in Paris in December of 1872, Halévy was the scion of a family of German-Jewish descent, which, by connections of marriage with such well-to-do local dynasties as the Breguets and the Berthelots, became part of a cultivated upper *bourgeoisie* that continued to play a leading role in forging French taste and opinion until well after World

War I. The Halévys themselves produced some of nine-teenth-century France's most prolific and versatile musicians and *littérateurs*. Daniel was the grandson of the Saint-Simonian writer and critic Léon Halévy, and his great-uncle Fromental, best known for the once celebrated opera *La Juive*, also taught composition to Bizet and Gounod at the Paris Conservatory. Although his interests were at first almost entirely literary, the ideas communicated by his father, the librettist Ludovic, and by his uncle Lucien Prévost-Paradol, the great liberal journalist and author of *La France nouvelle*, that prophetic book published in 1868, were of considerable importance in shaping the political sympathies underlying *La Fin des notables*.

The illegitimate son of Léon Halévy, Paradol was an outsider of genius, who made his way into the world by transforming a patrician Orleanist tradition rooted in the past into a positive force that continued to weigh upon French politics long after the Second Empire had passed away. Paradol's career was cut short when, as French Minister in Washington, he committed suicide following the news of the outbreak of the Franco-Prussian War, but the principles he had championed for more than twenty years, with steady contributions to the Orleanist *Débats*, survived to become the political credo of the majority of the National Assembly elected in 1871. Emerging as the leading spokesman of a vocal but divided opposition encouraged by the gains of the *Union libérale* in the 1863 legislative elections to press for what Thiers was to call "the indispensable freedoms," he persuaded other liberal politicians, intellectuals, and moderate Republicans to reenter the lists on a common platform, placing parliamentary supremacy above personal rule. Although defeated in 1863 along with the comte Charles de Rémusat, whose disastrous campaign in Toulouse curiously foreshadowed Barodet's stunning victory in Paris exactly ten years later, he pursued his attacks against the regime from the

Orleanist stronghold of the French Academy, where Guizot himself greeted him as its youngest member in 1866. His contribution to the liberal cause, as his colleague at the Academy, the Bonapartist Sainte-Beuve, conceded, was to bring together around a coherent program of institutional reform some of the less intransigent opponents of Napoleon III.

This coalition of provincial and Parisian Notables, whose hour of triumph was to come only after the crushing defeat of the Empire and the quelling of the Commune before being once again swept aside by the voters, was thus able to give permanent shape to a constitutional compromise combining responsible government with representative institutions—a compromise that Paradol had predicted would be far more durable and stable than either a monarchy or a republic. Paradol belonged to the most talented generation of graduates from the École Normale, including such writers as Hippolyte Taine, Jules Simon, Challemel-Lacour, Edmond About, and Jean-Jacques Weiss, all of whom represented an intellectual elite, which, despite shifting party loyalties, shared a dignified hope in the future of their country, and whose works provided Daniel Halévy with much of the source material if not the inspiration for writing *La Fin des notables*. But in a more immediate sense, it was through him that the Halévy's acquired a taste for liberal values, which in turn made it possible for Daniel to penetrate into the heart of Orleanism and to assimilate its spirit.

Ludovic Halévy's name is usually associated with the stage, especially as Offenbach's collaborator and as the librettist of Bizet's *Carmen*. But some of his novels and particularly his memoirs—only brief extracts of which were posthumously published by his son—reveal that he was also a shrewd observer, who kept in touch with many of the political and social trends of his day. His diaries, covering the years 1862 to 1899, contain a copious collection of lively impressions and anecdotes culled from a wide assortment of Parisian circles, ranging from the deputies he encountered as secretary of the *Corps législatif* under the Empire to the salons frequented by the Republic's dignitaries and the more solemn entourage of Taine and Renan, his colleagues at the Academy. A good deal of this material helped his son in recreating the atmosphere of the seventies, and the personal vignettes interspersed with dialogue that abound in *La Fin des notables* are plainly modelled on his father's graceful yet incisive style. Unlike his brother Elie, who after studying at the École Normale embarked upon a life's work that showed little trace of paternal influence, Daniel inherited from his father not only an abiding interest in literature as a commentary on social life, but also a gift for story-telling, combined with a tendency to sacrifice intellectual rigor for immediacy of observation. Moving in much the same world that his schoolmate Marcel Proust was to describe in *Jean Santeuil* or in the early volumes of *A la Recherche du temps perdu,* he showed the first signs of a dilettantism that was to mark his whole career by following Renan's advice to study Arabic and Hebrew as he groomed himself for the writer's craft, and by his own admission his work as an historian was that of an amateur. "I believe that my ideas on history," he acknowledged at the end of his life, "cannot be understood unless one goes back to the life and thought of my father. When I wrote my two books on history I had the feeling that my hand was guided by his voice."

La Fin des notables, like its sequel *La République des ducs,* was written in the form of a narrative, and it is, in effect, a moral tale intended to explain how the political stalemate confronting the Radical Republic of Halévy's day could be ascribed to the origins of a regime that enjoyed the dubious distinction of having provided Frenchmen with the kind of government that divided them least. Filial piety also accounts for Halévy's nostalgic conviction that only an oligarchy of wealth and talent is fitted to rule. But if he deplored the eclipse of the Broglie dynasty and condemned the ravages made on French society by the shallow scientism that passed for Republican ideology, he did make inescapable for the reader the conclusion that the Radicals were bound to exploit the arrogance and the futility of the Notables to establish a new order resting on a partnership between the peasants and the professional middle classes. Taken as a whole, however, Halévy's reconstruction of the three years between 1871 and 1873 is free from the partisanship that one might have expected from the author of *Décadence de la liberté*. Drawn to the personalities of the men who presided over the destiny of the new France, he illuminated the political maneuvering that culminated in the constitutionalist settlement of 1875 by means of character sketches, which gave his narrative something of the grandeur of tragedy. And although his history illustrates the disintegration of the republican mystique by tracing the mediocrity of the Republic to the decline of France's traditional elites in the seventies, his evocation of the halcyon years of parliamentary democracy was written less in anger than with the austerity of a moralist endowed with a rich historical imagination.

The story passes over the events of the Franco-Prussian War and the Commune to describe the tensions pitting the Assembly of royalist and Catholic Notables resurrected from the past by a bewildered electorate yearning for peace and security against the authoritarian ambitions of the "Orleanist" elder statesman M. Thiers and the intransigence of the legitimist pretender the comte de Chambord, whose ideas on divine right were repudiated even by his own followers. But if the deputies who were hastily summoned first in Bordeaux and then in Versailles found it expedient to retain the name of provisional Republic for a government entrusted with the thankless task of negotiating peace with Prussia, their failure to bring about an immediate fusion of the two royalist parties produced a protracted struggle to define the institutions of a new regime, which gradually assumed the shape of a conservative republic rather than of the constitutional monarchy envisioned by the Orleanist majority. Alarmed by the Republicans' triumph in the by-elections in July of 1871, the Assembly reluctantly consolidated the authority of France's national savior in return for arrogating to itself the power of drafting a constitution that would leave the door open to a king (the Rivet law, August, 1871).

Increasing signs that the country was generally prepared to accept "the Republic of M. Thiers" as the best safeguard for democracy and social progress against clerical excesses and the resurgence of Bonapartism made it easier for Thiers to encourage Gambetta's efforts to overcome the peasant voters' suspicions of city radicals by reviving their ancient hatred of Church and nobles. But it also persuaded the Conservative majority, still clinging to the hope of a royalist restoration, that a more reliable president could alone stem the tide of the Jacobin horrors evoked by Barodet's election. As the gulf separating the great rural masses from the worthies of Versailles grew wider, the Orleanists' predilection for parliamentary institutions, placing social conservatism above any monarchical principle, drew them closer to the Center deputies who dreaded dissolution even more than a constitutional deadlock. The overthrow of Thiers in May of 1873, however, merely postponed the formal establishment of the Republic, for the importance accorded to historical memories by all the protagonists reinforced the hostility of the petty *bourgeoisie* against the militant Catholicism and social exclusiveness of a class determined to regain the political ascendancy that had slipped from its hands since the end of the July Monarchy. Yet the conservative constitution devised by the duc de Broglie's precarious majority could not reverse what Halévy describes as "the quiet revolution of the villages"—a revolution that finally enabled the leaders of republican democracy to seize influence and authority and to drive the Notables out of public life altogether.

The End of the Notables has stood the test of time not only because the rise and fall of elites are subjects of enduring fascination to the common reader, but also because Halévy's interpretative essay has led the specialist to investigate more fully an area hitherto neglected by French academic historians. Even today the paucity of regional studies such as Pierre Barral's *Le Département de l'Isère sous la Troisième République, 1870–1940: Histoire sociale et politique* (Paris, 1962) makes it impossible to treat the seventies as authoritatively as André-Jean Tudesq did the July Monarchy in his great *thèse Les Grands Notables en France (1840–1849): Etude historique d'une psychologie sociale* (2 vols., Bordeaux, n. d.).

Roger L. Williams, in *The French Revolution of 1870–1871* (New York, 1969), provides, however, the best and most recent account of the emergence of the Third Republic against the background of the War and the Commune and contains an excellent bibliographical essay. The paramount importance of some local issues is brought out in impressionistic terms by André Siegfried in *Mes Souvenirs de la IIIᵉ République* (Paris, 1946), and more systematically in such articles and monographs as G. Lenormand's "Le Mouvement républicain dans la Somme au début de la IIIᵉ République, 1870–1877" in *Revue Historique* (196 [1946]: 1–30, 129–141); L. Boyer's "Les Elections politiques dans le département de la Loire au temps de l'Assemblée Nationale et du Maréchal Mac-Mahon" in *Annales de l'Université de Lyon* (3ᵉ série, 23, Paris, 1963); J. Lovie's *La Savoie dans la vie française de 1860 à 1875* (Paris, 1962); and G. Dupeux's *Aspects de l'histoire politique et sociale du Loir-et-Cher de 1848 à 1914* (Paris, 1962). Pierre Barral, in *Les Périers dans l'Isère au XIXᵉ siècle d'après leur correspondance* (Paris, 1964), sheds some light on the economic and social ties linking a moderate Republican like Casimir-Périer to his brother-in-law, the Orleanist duc d'Audiffret-Pasquier, explaining how family and business interests brought the upper *bourgeoisie* closer to the old landed aristocracy in an effort to establish a Conservative Republic.

The same author, in *Les Fondateurs de la Troisième République* (Paris, 1968), reprints documents illustrating how the Gambettists' neo-Positivism gained them increasing support among provincial doctors and teachers, and Jacques Goualt, in his analysis of electoral results, *Comment la France est devenue républicaine: Les Elections générales et partielles à l'Assemblée Nationale, 1870–1875* (Paris, 1954), draws on departmental archives to chart the conversion of the peasantry to a republican party regarded as the champion of the economic interests of the little man against the great financial and industrial circles. The latter are vividly described in the first volumes of a relapsed Orleanist, Emmanuel Beau de Loménie, *Les Résponsabilités des dynasties bourgeoises*, (4 vols., Paris, 1943–1960), and in Jean Lhomme's more succinct and less polemical *La Grande Bourgeoisie au pouvoir (1830–1880)* (Paris, 1960), written from a sociological standpoint. These circles' motives for preserving Thiers's Republic against the social disorders that could be unleashed by a royalist restoration are shrewdly dissected in two articles by Jean Bouvier: "Aux Origines de la Troisième République. Les Réflexes sociaux des milieux d'affaires" in *Revue Historique* (4 [October–December 1953]: 209–210, 271–301); and "Des Banquiers devant l'actualité politique en 1870–71" in *Revue d'Histoire Moderne et Contemporaine* (5 [April–June 1958]: 137–151).

The resilience of Orleanism, both as a state of mind and as a set of political ideas, is brought out in Chapter V of René Rémond's *The Right in France from 1815 to de Gaulle* (translated by James M. Laux, Philadelphia, 1966).

Introduction

Louis Girard explains how it drifted closer to Conservative Republicanism in his brief article "Political Liberalism in France, 1840–1875" in *French Society and Culture since the Old Regime*, edited by Evelyn M. Acomb and Marvin L. Brown, Jr. (New York, 1966); but only by sampling Charles de Rémusat's *Mémoires de ma vie* (edited by Charles-H. Pouthas, 5 vols., Paris, 1958–1967) can the reader recapture the spirit of this French counterpart of Whiggism.

The political background is covered by D. W. Brogan in *The Development of Modern France* (London, 1940), with his usual verve. Jacques Chastenet in *Histoire de la Troisième République*, (Vol. I, Paris, 1952), Guy Chapman in *The Third Republic of France: The First Phase, 1871–1894* (London, 1962), and René Rémond in *La Vie politique en France: 1848–1879* (Vol. II, Paris, 1969) go over the same ground, which is admirably summarized in Part III of David Thomson's *Democracy in France since 1870* (5th edition, Oxford, 1969); and which is reduced to a conflict between two rival temperaments—"the party of order" and "the party of movement"—by François Goguel in *La Politique des partis sous la IIIe République* (Paris, 1946). Goguel's bibliography is suggestive; Chapman's comprehensive. The constitutional debates are described in great detail by M. Deslandres in his *Histoire constitutionnelle de la France: L'Avènement de la Troisième République—la constitution de 1875* (Vol. III, Paris, 1937), and by means of some delightful personal vignettes by Frank H. Brabant in *The Beginning of the Third Republic in France (February–September 1871)* (London, 1940). R. A. Winnacker confirms that the Notables owed their electoral victory to the national desire for peace in "The French Elections of 1871" in *Papers of the Michigan Academy of Sciences, Arts and Letters* (XXII [1936]: 477–483). And Robert I. Giesberg recounts the protracted peace negotiations leading to the early withdrawal of the

The End of the Notables

German occupation forces in 1873 in *The Treaty of Frankfort: A Study in Diplomatic History* (Philadelphia, 1966).

The most thorough study of the impact of the defeat on French intellectuals is Claude Digeon's *thèse La Crise allemande de la pensée française, 1870–1914* (Paris, 1959), which supersedes André Bellessort's antirepublican tract, *Les Intellectuels et l'avènement de la IIIe République: 1871–1875* (Paris, 1931), and Michel Mohrt's more sober *Les Intellectuels devant la défaite, 1870* (Paris, 1942). The influence of such republican thinkers as Emile Littré and Charles Renouvier is the subject of a dry but useful work by John A. Scott, *Republican Ideas and the Liberal Tradition in France, 1870–1914* (New York, 1951). The career of Gambetta's enigmatic adviser was traced by Edouard Krakowski in *La Naissance de la IIIe République: Challemel-Lacour, le philosophe et l'homme d'état* (Paris, 1932).

There is no satisfactory biography of Thiers, although the reader may want to consult Henri Malo's *Thiers: 1797–1877* (Paris, 1932) or Jean Lucas-Dubreton's *Aspects de Monsieur Thiers* (Lausanne, 1966). For this period there are two well documented studies by Robert Dreyfus: *Monsieur Thiers contre l'Empire, la guerre et la Commune, 1869–1871* (Paris, 1928) and *La République de M. Thiers* (Paris, 1930). Gaston Bouniols has published selections from his surviving political correspondence in *Thiers au pouvoir, 1871–1873* (Paris, 1921), and Halévy wove them together with some shrewd comments in his edition of *Le Courrier de M. Thiers* (Paris, 1920).

In collaboration with Emile Pillias, Halévy also edited the *Lettres de Gambetta* (Paris, 1938). Gambetta himself is the subject of competent biographies by Paul Deschanel (English translation, London, 1920), H. Stannard (London, 1921), and Jacques Chastenet (Paris, 1968). The first chapters of Samuel M. Osgood's *French Royalism under the Third and Fourth Republics* (The Hague,

1960) explain the rivalry between the Orleanists and legitimists, and *The Comte de Chambord: The Third Republic's Uncompromising King* (Durham, 1967) by Marvin L. Brown, Jr., contains rich insights into this phase of the Pretender's life. For the duc de Broglie we have his own memoirs, published in instalments in *La Revue des Deux Mondes* (1929). The literary critic Emile Faguet has written a sympathetic portrait in *Mgr. Dupanloup: Un Grand Evêque* (Paris, 1914).

ALAIN SILVERA

THE END OF THE NOTABLES

On the Origins of Our Confusing Times

My purpose here is to investigate the history of our times, which are so little known and, indeed, so difficult to grasp. I have often thought how clearly I was able to discern my country's recent past when I was about fifteen years old, in around 1885. Listening to the tales of my parents and grandparents, glancing through such papers as the amusing *Charivari* or the more solemn *Monde illustré*, I felt as if a lively storyteller, some great and diverting invisible Homer, were guiding me from war to war, from revolution to revolution. But if a youngster of fifteen, or a young man, or even an adult were to question his elders today about the presidency of M. Grévy or of Félix Faure, what kind of an answer would he get?[1] They first give their attention to the Great War—that massive stumbling block which casts its shadows in every direction. What happened before the Great War? How do the elders perceive the fifty- or sixty-odd years that slowly led up to it? Those years weigh so heavily upon them that the sheer weight is virtually all they know about them. The general obscurity might, I fear, be diverting and even discourage curiosity. I am inclined to believe that the reason our children display such a lack of interest is that they are in the habit of knowing nothing about a past which neverthe-

3

less seriously concerns them and, in spite of themselves, even determines their lives.

All this makes for woeful ignorance, and it would be a pity to allow it to persist and to grow. For my own instruction I tried to learn what I could, thereby undertaking this work.

When do our confusing times begin? The first problem is: When precisely should we start our tale?

The period in question is called the Third Republic, but it is merely a label: it encompasses too many years and too many diverse movements. The first shadows can surely be detected in the wake of the War of 1870–1871. Yet they did not suddenly darken our history. They were preceded by a certain sparkling development of minds, customs, and events which, later on, dimmed. After 1870, the men of the heroic and romantic nineteenth century were still with us: the voices of princes, statesmen, and orators could still be heard, dominating the scene, and their tone of grandeur still heightens and illuminates the course of events. These early years have, in fact, been quite adequately covered by historians. Hanotaux's lucid book covers the first decade, which stretches from 1871 to 1879 and corresponds to the Conservative Republic.[2] We also have some good eye-witness accounts left by contemporaries, such as the memoirs of the vicomte de Meaux, the duc de Broglie, and Charles de Freycinet, as well as Littré's *L'Etablissement de la Troisième République*, Renan's *La Réforme intellectuelle et morale de la France*, and J.-J. Weiss's *Combat Constitutionnel*. All these works do throw some light on the period—or at least some twilight.

But what then? Jacques Bainville, author of a brilliant sketch of French political history, notes quite rightly that "after 1880 there is a void"—nothing to feed or direct a curious mind.[3] Clearly, 1879 marks the final year of that twilight zone. We can even be more precise and set the date on January 9, 1879. On that day one-third of the senators were replaced, and republicans won almost every one of the seats. Thus the Conservative majority, which in 1875[4] had disappeared from the Lower Chamber, now disappeared from the Higher Chamber: Marshal MacMahon resigned; Dufaure, a Catholic republican, withdrew as prime minister; and Grévy entered the Elysée,[5] appointing a cabinet made up of such people as Ferry, Cochery, Tirard, and Freycinet—all men of the new France, leaders during the "confusing times" which had just begun. Should this date, then, have been the starting point for our tale? We didn't think so. What followed was too closely linked with what came before. We must first try to explore that twilight zone where all the bitterness, hopes, wrath, plans, and complex thinking that were to form the future were beginning to take shape. It is therefore necessary first to come to grips with Thiers, Broglie, MacMahon, and Gambetta (whose short career was almost over by 1879).

But at what point should we take up their story? At what point in the careers of Thiers, MacMahon, Broglie, and Gambetta should we begin? With the Republic itself and the September 4th Revolution? If so, we should have to tackle the entire war—the war against the Germans resumed by the republicans, the siege of Paris, Gambetta in Tours, rallying and arming the provinces . . . All of this, however, would only lead us astray: the War of 1870 is not our main concern; it does not belong to our times; it marks the dramatic conclusion of the Napoleonic wars. Gambetta belonged to the same tradition as Danton; Moltke avenged the humiliation of Jena; and both of them were well aware of it. Let us therefore set aside the siege of Paris and the battles waged along the Loire.

What happened afterward? Paris capitulated; Thiers encountered Bismarck. In those days Thiers was France's elder statesman, and recalls the striking early years of the nineteenth century. The war was followed by peace. What were Thiers's credentials in negotiating that peace? He spoke in the name of a vanquished people and an almost crumbling state; the defeated Empire had collapsed; the Republic, defeated in turn, was a mere façade kept alive by a group of men who had rallied round Gambetta in Bordeaux and by the revolutionary fidelity of a few large cities: Paris, Lyons, Toulouse, Bordeaux, and Marseilles. Refusing to acknowledge those subversive rebels, Bismarck wanted France to elect an Assembly and appoint representatives to negotiate. We would do well now to examine the origins of that Assembly.

Never had elections been held so hastily: they were announced on February 2, and on the 6th the voting booths were opened and the entire Assembly was elected in a single day.[6] Poor, bewildered electors! Artisans, peasants, wood-cutters from the depths of the forests, and fishermen on the high seas—all were summoned to express their views on momentous issues which they could hardly grasp: war and peace, wiping out the past, and paving the way for the future, the question of the Monarchy, the Republic, and the Empire. Although they had exercised the right to vote for twenty years—ever since the Revolution of 1848—they had been constantly in the habit of paying mind to the *préfets*, the mayors, or the priests. Now, when events were moving fast, the *préfets* had lost all their authority, the mayors were bewildered, the civil service was a shambles. The past had collapsed, the present was in ruins. How and for whom were they supposed to vote? The Bonapartists, who were responsible for the disaster, were discredited. As for the republicans, almost no one wanted any more of them: they had lost the war a second time round, and they were proclaiming war to the bitter end at a time when the country sensed an urgent need for peace. New leaders were needed. Yet what was the alternative to the Bonapartists and the republicans? Paradol[7] observed in 1870 that for a deputy to be elected, he had to meet one of three conditions: he had to be a government official, a Red, or a big landowner. Since the civil servants and the Reds had been discredited, all that was left were the landowners, the patrimonial families. The new Assembly was all theirs. What a surprise! Here were the La Rochefoucaulds, the Noailles, the Broglies, the Haussonvilles, the Harcourts, the Tocquevilles, and along with those nobles, the old *bourgeoisie:* the Guizots, the Bochers, the Ernouls, the Anisson-Duperrons, the Casimir-Périers; there were even the princes: Aumale and Joinville.[8] In short, the Old Regime—indeed, all of France's old regimes—emerged almost miraculously from the native soil torn asunder by disaster.

These events occurred in the midst of chaos. Several of the newly elected deputies were still serving in the army when they were notified by the same mail that they had been simultaneously nominated and elected. They all rushed to Bordeaux and discovered to their joy and astonishment that they had been returned in such overwhelming numbers. Many were legitimists—over a hundred of them.[9] As members of the gentry serving under the colors, they had retained a kind of lofty prestige in rural areas which had renewed the courage shown during the war; all of them had rallied to fight in Gambetta's militia; even the peasants had asked to be led in combat by the grandchildren of the *émigrés,* and led by them they were. J.-J. Weiss has vividly described the arrival in Bordeaux of those hastily elected members of Parliament—provincial landowners and nobles, several of them old men who had never left their castles since 1830—a colorful lot who were greeted with laughter by the citizens of Bordeaux as they marched down the Cours de Tourny shouting "Long live the King." They thanked the Good Lord for their unexpected victory. "France may now speak; God will decide," wrote their prince, the comte de Chambord. God, through France, had spoken.

That sense of exhilaration, however, was not universal. The liberal Orleanists—still cautious, even a bit reticent—as well as such thoughtful legitimists as Falloux and Kerdrel, were there to restrain the "Ultras" and to warn them about the men and the times. Who were they after all? Totally unknown vestiges of a bygone past who, in deference to the wishes of an exiled and aging Bourbon prince, had remained on the periphery of national affairs. It was only a fortuitous and hasty election, an almost desperate election, that had thrown them into a hostile, ardently republican city, whose armed population was threatening them. What might be their fate? Probably brief and sorrowful. They would be signing a disastrous peace. A sad fate! The country which had yearned for peace and had elected them precisely for that purpose was to fire them, insult them, sweep them out.

They were fortunate, however, in having Thiers by their side, for Thiers possessed authority and experience. He had served as prime minister under Louis Philippe; he had played a prominent part in the bourgeois reaction of 1849; as an historian and leader of the Liberal opposition under the Second Empire, he had succeeded in making his voice heard; in July 1870, with remarkable foresight and indomitable courage, facing up to the Bonapartist Chamber, he had warned of the dangers that would result from a declaration of war against Prussia; and his conduct during the war had further contributed to enhancing his prestige, for in spite of his age he had undertaken the task of pleading in favor of the French cause in European courts. Although he had failed, he had succeeded in earning everyone's admiration and gratitude. News of his electoral triumphs reached Bordeaux from every corner of France: nominated in twenty-five departments, he was elected twenty-five times.[10] Endorsed by what amounted to an unexpected plebiscite, the old Liberal monarchist was willingly accepted by an Assembly dutifully responsive to the national will. What a stroke of luck that he was there, at that tragic moment, to guide it and to share its burden, assume responsibilities, and point the way to the future. With Thiers at the helm, the Assembly might even resume

8

the good old safe policies pursued by the Assemblies of 1849 and 1850.

Perhaps: there was a possibility, a glimmer of hope. The most pressing need was to make peace. By unanimous consent, all the Orleanists, legitimists, and republicans voted to appoint Thiers Chief of the Executive Power. Since the title seemed somewhat modest, two words were added at his friends' request and Thiers became "Chief of the Executive Power of the French Republic," whereas Grévy, a moderate republican, was elected President of the Assembly.

Does this mark the beginning of our tale? Does the atmosphere seem familiar? At times one can live and breathe it. When Thiers asked that all the political parties rally round "la noble blessée," we can vaguely discern in the applause that greeted those simple and moving words a certain tone lacking in the Old Regime, as well as a solidarity in the face of disaster, which was to recur later on. Yet, no, our story has not yet really begun. The cruel days that were to follow—the German peace demands presented in Bordeaux; Alsace and Lorraine sacrificed by a vote of the Assembly; Victor Hugo prophesying on the rostrum—all that lies outside our scope; it marks the end of an era, the disappearance of a certain France, of that insolent nation which for the past three centuries had laid down the law in Europe.

Suddenly the drama shifted: Paris, the armed capital, refusing to surrender its rifles and cannon, rose in revolt against the Assembly, against the nobles and monarchists of Bordeaux. "Long live the Republic!" shouted the people. Never before had that cry been uttered with such force and conviction. The Republic was then beloved. Many had earnestly awaited its advent throughout the eighteen years of the Empire. "Now that we have it . . . ," said an enthusiastic workman as he shook Thiers's hand on the night of September 4. "But we had it," that Republic of our founding fathers; we had nearly and finally obtained justice and fraternity, and there were many who stubbornly believed that only through complete justice and fraternity would the country be truly strong; such a dearly bought prize could not be given up.

But Thiers, succumbing to the pressure not only of Bismarck, who wanted him at Versailles, but of the Bordeaux Assembly, and harassed by events, had neglected Paris. When he arrived there on March 17, he decided to act swiftly in order to regain control of the situation. The Parisians had kept three hundred cannon on the heights of Montmartre. Thiers decided to recapture them by surprise. But three hundred cannon cannot be maneuvered through the narrow streets of a working-class district by surprise. Montmartre rioted; the troops were surrounded by the rebels, and two generals were captured and massacred. Whereupon Thiers came to another swift and unreasoned decision: he ordered the evacuation of Paris, even the forts, and the Army was withdrawn to Versailles, where the Bordeaux Assembly had been convened.

What a turn in fortune yet again: the wandering deputies settled down in Louis XIV's palace; they camped there as the Army was doing outside, surrounding and protecting them. The halls of the château were turned into dormitories; the theater was reopened for their sessions. Who would win, the Red city or the Assembly, the people of Paris or those provincials insulted from the platform by that young Jew Crémieux[11] as "an assembly of country bumpkins"? At that particular moment Crémieux was leading a revolt in Marseilles. He was soon to be shot, but he is still remembered for that memorable phrase which divides France—on the one hand, the large cities, armed and threatening, if not in a state of outright revolt; on the other, the rural population. War broke out between the two adversaries. Shall I tell the tale of the Parisian uprising (the first example of a dictatorship of the proletariat), and the second siege of the capital, and the bloody week of May, the thirty thousand dead, the palaces in flames?

No, I shall not deal with those major events, for here again they mark the end of an era, the catastrophe of a rebellious and romantic century. On the other hand, perhaps they constitute a new beginning. Yet what had begun developed so slowly that they scarcely affect our story. When young Nietzsche, during those days in May, closed himself in and wept over the destroyed monuments and the threat to the Louvre, what did he glimpse? What is the meaning of those tears that were never forgotten by the conscience of Europe, no more than was the detour made, in July 1789, by Immanuel Kant in order to hear the latest news about the French Revolution? What Nietzsche had foreseen was not the future of the Third Republic, but rather, looking sixty years ahead, Moscow and its fanatical hatred of Western civilization.

June 1871

How did Frenchmen feel in June 1871? Germany was occupying their country from the border all the way to the Parisian suburbs of Saint-Denis and Vincennes; and their disgraced capital still smelled of blood and smoke. Lyons, Marseilles, Toulouse, Bordeaux, Limoges, and Périgueux, still under arms, bid fair to rise once again in revolt. Sorrow, silence, and stunned bewilderment prevailed throughout the land.

How could forcibly imposed order be made stable and permanent? The precarious state of affairs inspired fear, and mixed in with the general atmosphere of fatigue and anguish was a feeling of contrition. This was without precedent. Throughout the nineteenth century Frenchmen had, with the encouragement of the European people, remained proud of their turbulent and fated vocation for putting on grand revolutionary performances. Even the sad reversal of June 1848 had not diminished their prestige. Wasn't it only natural to expect that Mount Sinai would attract storms, dark clouds, and lightning, and wasn't France after all the Mount Sinai of modern times? But directly following June 1871 everything had changed. The rest of Europe, still gazing upon this constantly amazing country, now did so with pity or disdain. English tourists, gathered on the terrace of Saint-Cloud,[1] turned their field glasses in the direction of Paris in flames, and their scathing curiosity was an additional cause for sorrow. The French were weary of giving performances, and perhaps weary of their past glory. Their one and truly humble wish was to return to those old routines which other countries had never forsaken. But how? Old routines have their own ways of persisting, and France had lost the key to them.

What about monarchy? In those days there were still a great number of noble and bourgeois families who had never lost their feeling for the Old Regime, which was faithful to the King and to the King's Church, and much of the Assembly were members of those families. Disasters had come and gone, but the Assembly was still there, as busy and active as ever and, contrary to expectations, still in a position to determine the future. Would the fragile Republic sanctioned by Bordeaux be allowed to survive? Out of the 650 deputies who gathered at Versailles, some 500 were said to be monarchists. To be sure, they were very divided: there were the legitimist and the Orleanist factions; the ultramontane legitimists and Gallican legitimists; the Catholic Orleanists and Voltairian Orleanists— all of which made up a rather unstable coalition. Yet loyalty to the Monarchy prevailed in the end. How would these royalist deputies go about restoring the king's authority? One can imagine their families in the background, their wives and children who reminded them at table or in bed that their duty was to take the initiative. But the vanquished nation remained silent, and its silence was not a clear enough sign that the people—except for those in the Vendée, Anjou, Mayenne, and Brittany—considered the principles of monarchy dead.

First of all, the princes were recalled: the law which had exiled them was repealed on June 8. This gave rise to a debate during the course of which Thiers, after unexpectedly displaying some opposition, finally gave his consent.

When the phrase "The Royal House" was uttered on the rostrum, it was greeted with cheers and applause from the nobles sitting on the extreme right. They were as "happy as grown-up children," noted Le Temps,[2] which had been an Orleanist paper only shortly before, but was now ironic and hostile.

"The Royal House," however, was no more than a label for a divided family, and the monarchists' most urgent need was to put an end to the civil war which, by dividing Orleans and Bourbons since 1830, had been undermining their cause. Since it was the Orleans who had been the rebels, it was up to them to return to the fold: they were ready to, and they made it known—a great event, or so it seemed, to the dwindling circles of loyal legitimists.

Would France once again become a monarchy? If the Royal House appeared united before the Assembly, the main obstacle was overcome and the way was clear. Thiers let them hope and let them talk. Actually, having long been on intimate terms with both legitimists and Orleanists, he did not believe in any genuine reconciliation, in any fusion of the two branches. The Orleans were invited to his residence in Versailles, where both groups showed great courtesy to one another. Since the princes remained standing, everyone remained standing. And Mme. Thiers, perhaps somewhat annoyed, asked the duc d'Aumale to be good enough to set an example by sitting down. "Madame," replied the Duke, "I have not forgotten that I am in the presence of the Chief of State," whereupon a legitimist remarked: "The only one missing here is the comte de Chambord," to which Thiers eagerly replied, "He would be most welcome."

The comte de Chambord was not present at Thiers's reception; he wasn't even in France. He was lingering in his castle in Austria. Now that it was no longer necessary, why did he stay in exile? Why, like the Orleans, didn't he come to Paris to mingle with the crowds, or at least return to Chambord, to his peasants, to his people? Was he hesitating? Was he thinking? If so, what was he thinking? When the comte de Paris, the head of the Orleans branch, had requested an audience, he had been told: "Not yet." The reply was interpreted as a bad sign. What was Chambord waiting for? Now that he was the sole leader of the French royalists, it was up to him to take complete control, to talk to them, to rally the rest of France to their cause. Yet he was singularly ill-prepared to assume such a task. Ever since the age of nine he had spent his life in castles on the Rhine or the Danube, constantly surrounded by courtiers who had taken turns in preserving, with almost heroic obstinacy, the authentic spirit of the old court, with its rounds of entertainment, its religious and hunting practices, and its ancient rituals of work and leisure. Did he have any notion of that new France matured by so many industrial, political, and moral revolutions during his years of exile? He undoubtedly still regarded her as guilty, as being stained by his family's blood. With a grandfather who had been guillotined and a father who had been assassinated before he was born, he had been hailed as "the miraculous child," and the women and priests who had brought him up had never failed to remind him of that legend. He had listened to it all; he had believed it all. His mind had been shaped by fanatical *émigrés*. As a young man he had married a princess of Modena—the most reactionary court in all Europe. And so he had gone on living, paying no heed to his times, advising his supporters to follow his example by withdrawing, keeping aloof, and waiting, as he himself did, for God's appointed hour, the miraculous return that had been prophesied by his miraculous birth.

He was kindly and well liked by everyone; but his gentleness concealed the obstinacy of a lonely man and a mystic. Of all French writers his favorite was Veuillot, whose splendid and violent prose and radiant soul helped provide him with comfort during his sad years in exile. And during that same month of June 1871, it was Veuillot alone, in his perturbed country, who proclaimed that restoration was imminent. To be sure, in addition to his newspaper *L'Univers*, there were *L'Union* and the *Gazette de France*, to say nothing of some twenty-odd provincial papers in the hands of aristocratic and clerical cliques. But they failed to reach the public, and it was Veuillot, with his ultramontane sympathies, who suddenly emerged as a writer of national stature. The language he used was astonishing: he prophesied a miraculous, mystical event—the restoration of the French throne along with the papal throne in Rome, both of which had crumbled as the result of the atheist conspiracy. But this White Revolution in opposition to the Red Revolution—this challenge to ever-vigilant and quick-to-react Italy—ran counter to the wishes and yearnings of an exhausted France. France wanted to find a refuge; Veuillot proposed a policy of adventure. The republicans were quick to seize upon every foolhardy remark, while the Orleanists (we should bear in mind that their prince's request for an audience had been turned down) reacted with icy silence.

Chambord kept his plans to himself. On July 2 he arrived in Paris. It was a Sunday, an election day. As a result of deaths and numerous resignations in the Assembly, by-elections were due to be held in fifty departments. Was Chambord giving any thought to them? No, universal suffrage was no concern of his; he did not even deign to acknowledge it. Escorted by two noblemen, the comte de Monti de Rézé and the comte de Vanssay, he arrived at the Gare du Nord early in the morning. Who was this man whose voice and eyes revealed a pride in his ancestry and in his power to command and to be loved—this fifty-year-old man who walked heavily with a slight limp—was he a French prince, was he an elderly Austrian nobleman? Everything that caught his eye was foreign to him.

To begin with, he asked to be driven to the cathedral of Notre-Dame, where he knelt down and prayed. Then, to the Sainte Chapelle to meditate for a while in memory of Saint Louis, his ancestor. Then, to the Pont Neuf and a bow to Henri IV. As for the Louvre and Louis XIV, not so much as a glance or a tribute. For according to pure royalist doctrine, which in those days was strictly aristocratic and Christian, the Sun King stood condemned as a despot and a Gallican. Finally, the Tuileries, where he was born and had spent his childhood, and which was the only place in France that brought back memories to him. All that remained were dreadful ruins—a blackened façade and hollow window-frames: he recognized the one that had shed light on his games.

Since it was time for mass, he asked to be taken to the nearest church. It was Saint-Roch. Did he intend to devote all his time to such prayers and pilgrimages? Since the news of his arrival had been discreetly announced, many royalist noblemen had requested an audience with their prince. And he knew it. But, as in the case of the comte de Paris, his reply was: "Not yet." Still accompanied by the two noblemen, he left Paris in the afternoon to visit the château that bore his name, Chambord, which had remained empty for the past half-century. What did he mean by the words *Not yet?* What action was he contemplating? A few had guessed; rumors had spread in the Assembly in Versailles: Chambord, with splendid loyalty, wanted above all to warn the French that he would return to France only under the aegis of the white flag.

But the white flag had almost been forgotten. It was under the tricolor that all the legitimist nobility had just fought with the defeated Army; and the papal Zouaves[3] had borne it in their well-known charge at the battle of Patay,[4] during which six of them had perished, one by one, keeping it aloft. Was giving up the tricolor conceivable? Even the prince's most loyal supporters were stupefied:

what he asked was impossible. They decided to warn him, to speak to him harshly before he issued a public statement. Five dignitaries of the royalist party were entrusted with that task: the comte de Maillé; the duc de la Rochefoucauld; the vicomte de Gontaut-Biron; Laurentie, editor of *L'Union*; and finally, the Bishop of Orléans. That small delegation of Frenchmen who, on the morning of July 4, took the train in the direction of the Loire, where their ancestors had held such renowned gatherings in the sixteenth century, constituted the last meeting of the States-General: three nobles, a bourgeois, and a clergyman—the last vestiges of a regime that had vanished.

They were received by Chambord, who put them at ease and asked them to speak their mind. First Maillé and La Rochefoucauld. "It is absolutely essential to maintain the tricolor," they said, "for what is at stake is the French crown." Then Gontaut. "It was under the white flag," he said, "that our forefathers died behind yours. It commands our favor, our memories, and our love. But your forefathers, like our own, gave up their lives for France, and once again France demands a sacrifice." Chambord remained attentive and inscrutable. As for Dupanloup,[5] few Frenchmen possessed that bishop's keen sense of France during the seventeenth and eighteenth centuries; no one, for forty years, had spent as much energy trying to preserve the old Gallican Church's tradition of charity and caution; and perhaps no other Frenchman at the time had that strong and that keen an apprehension of the other France, the unknown France which was then emerging. Dupanloup believed that Chambord alone, supported by all the judicious elements in the land, was capable of stabilizing the nation and saving it from collapse. But Dupanloup did not belong to the ultramontane faction; Veuillot vied with him constantly; and Chambord didn't like him. Indeed, Chambord had seen him privately, after the rest of the delegation, and had warned him that all political matters had already been discussed and were not to be brought up again. Dupanloup yielded and spoke of the Church and its urgent need for a monarch who understood it. He spoke to the best of his ability, and his words were fiery. Finally, he stopped, and Chambord, without answering, asked him to withdraw. The five remonstrant petitioners left together. "That man is incredible," murmured Dupanloup. On July 5 the royal Letter was published in *L'Univers*. "Henri V," declared the Count, "cannot forsake the white flag of Henri IV. I received it as a sacred trust from the old King, my ancestor, while I was dying in exile; I have always regarded it as inseparable from my distant country; it waved above my cradle, and I wish it to throw shade on my grave."

"O God of my cradle, be the God of my grave," young Lamartine had written in 1820. It was the same thought, in the same tone of sentimental loyalty. But in echoing a poet's lines, was the prince doing his duty as a king? The Germans were occupying Saint-Denis; the treasury was empty; every minute counted. All Capetians would have understood. His Letter was a farewell; France interpreted it as such. Not even deigning to wait for a reaction to his words, Chambord made his way back to Austria.

Should this celebrated episode be relegated to the past? At first sight it would seem understandable only in terms of the past. But beware, that is merely an illusion. Chambord did not belong to the Old Regime; his gesture was not at all in keeping with the realistic tradition of the French Monarchy. Chambord was a child of the *émigrés*, a reader of Chateaubriand. His Letter was the last, and perhaps one of the more beautiful, of the great Romantic odes. Thus, being Romantic, it was also revolutionary. Indeed, and on its own terms, the comte de Chambord's decision was a revolutionary act: it undermined one of the most solid foundations of the old ruling classes, thereby hastening their final collapse during the succeeding ten years. It also marked the end of the French Monarchy, which became a myth and a legend, and which, as such, was to have some curious and passionate revivals in the years to come.

CHAPTER 3

That Same Month of June

Since we must pursue several threads to find our way through the maze, let us change viewpoints. After Chambord, let us turn to Thiers, one of the keenest Frenchmen who ever lived and one of the best prepared for battle. This time, using him as my guide, I shall return to, and reexamine, the same month of June 1871. And using him, we shall probably be able to catch a glimpse of the emerging future.

But we must first know him well. Thiers belonged to the past; he was rooted in the century now drawing to a close. Whereas Chambord, steeped in Veuillot, was a disciple of Bonald and Joseph de Maistre,[1] Thiers belonged to the tradition of the National Convention and the Consulate, a follower of the Emperor, the heir of Napoleon. A member of the Carbonari[2] as a young man, he had sworn the death of all kings and performed the ritual act of regicide by stabbing a straw dummy. Few Carbonari had kept their word that faithfully, for Thiers had spent his whole life stabbing kings and princes. His first moment of glory was at the age of twenty-five, when he wrote the first historical work devoted to the French Revolution, thus giving it new life; his second moment of glory came in 1830, when he led the vigorous and triumphant campaign against the Bourbon King. What success for a man of thirty: one crown toppled, another bestowed! For it was he who had led and propelled Louis Philippe to the throne. But having made him King, Thiers had wanted him to reign but not to govern; indeed, Thiers had wanted to rule in his place. Since that shrewd prince, Louis Philippe, had ousted him, Thiers had plotted to bring about his downfall. He still called himself a royalist, however; the label pleased him. Since the word *Republic* still had fearful overtones, it terrified the European courts, which Thiers was careful to treat with caution. Still, deep down, and whatever the circumstances, he dreamed of becoming the leader, and throughout the turbulent century his goal was some exalted presidency, some Caesarean dictatorship. After coming up against a bit of resistance from Louis Philippe in 1840, he exclaimed: "I shall sleep in the Tuileries!" displaying, in typical fashion, how immoderate he was in his rather mad ambitions and his use of words. Until the end, Thiers dreamed of sleeping in the Tuileries. The very first day in Bordeaux, calculating his chances of success, he had told his friends that the Monarchy would be restored in two years. He thus would have two years to himself. He should have liked the National Assembly, the residual legatee of the 1851 Assembly, to pass a resolution adopting the Constitution of 1848. His motives were clear: the Constitution of 1848 gave the people back the right to choose the head of state. Louis Bonaparte (soon to become Napoleon III) had been elected President in 1848. In 1871 Thiers was certain that he himself would be acclaimed.* Although the Assembly had decided otherwise, Thiers had nevertheless exercised dictatorial powers, imposing the Assembly on a Paris in revolt, and imposing himself, his own policy, and his secret

---

* On August 10, 1871, he wrote to Girardin: "When we got out of the war-to-the-finish party last February, the wisest course would have been to revert to the Constitution of 1848. It would have been wiser and also more convenient." The letter was printed in *Le Rappel*, May 2, 1874.

plans on a worried Assembly. For like Chambord, he too had his secret plans, and those plans were to establish the Republic, as he had promised the republicans.

The event took place during the first few weeks of the Parisian insurrection. The whole of France had then turned to Thiers. What was the significance of that tragic adventure to which Paris was committed and in which Thiers was against Paris? At the cry of "Long live the Republic," the city swiftly took up arms. Did Thiers, elected as representative of the monarchist Assembly, mean to crush the Republic itself in Paris? A delegation of mayors representing the strongly republican South was sent to ask him precisely that. They were ready to give him their help if it meant putting an end to revolution and civil war. But in return, they wanted the Republic; if not, they would support Paris. The matter was pressing: the *préfets'* reports were unanimous in pointing that out. In the South and even in central France—in other words, directly to the south of a line drawn between Tours and Besançon—the people no longer supported the deputies they had elected in February and in many places seemed ready to join the Parisians in their revolt against the Assembly. The *préfet* of Besançon wanted the military forces stationed there to remain; the *sous-préfet* of Valence wanted his army to occupy the town's railway station in order to cut all communication between the revolutionary cities of Lyons and Marseilles; Limoges, Mâcon, and Le Creusot were in a state of open revolt. On the other hand, the northern provinces remained quiet. But unlike June 1848, there was no sign of volunteers marching on Paris to restore order. Thiers had called for them, had hoped they would come; but the weary country had left him alone with the remnants of a defeated army. The daily reports that he received from small towns and villages seemed to confirm, in humble language, the wishes expressed in a threatening tone by the delegates from the

23

cities: everyone was asking him to restore order and national unity in a republican form. There was no positive reference to the monarchy; the old word was invariably interpreted pejoratively or used as a term of reproach.*

Thus, whether by way of petitions or threats, demands for the Republic came to Thiers from all parts of the country. This delighted him, since he had never liked kings and was now in a position to exercise his own sovereign authority. He had therefore given his promise to go along with the cities' delegates. He might have confined himself, without in any way betraying his commitments to the Assembly, to reassuring them that he would not tamper with the republican institutions he had inherited. It is clear, however, that he went even further and promised to work to establish the Republic. That promise was given in an undertone, in secret. At a time when Lyons was regarded as the capital of republican regions in the South, it would appear that Thiers committed himself to the people of Lyons, to the city's mayor, Hénon, and to the Freemasons who had accompanied him. In fact, Hénon was himself a Freemason—that is, a man sworn to secrecy. Thus a sort of pact was made: Promise us the Republic, said the provincials and Freemasons. Hand the Parisians over to me, replied Thiers. And the provincial Radicals, agreeing to the pact, washed their hands of the blood they caused to flow in exchange for their reward.

Nothing can be kept secret. Rumors of the deal began to spread, and the National Assembly demanded an explanation. Thiers had received the republicans; what had been the result of their talks? Resorting to insolence, which was the best way of being evasive, Thiers retorted: "Wait a few weeks before attacking me. Then the events will be up to your ability and your courage." No one had attacked him. A friend, Mortimer-Terraux, had merely questioned him discreetly. But Thiers had a great gift for

* See Appendix I regarding these petitions.

manipulating his rages. If need be, he even contrived that they be sincere and irresistible. It has been said that Mortimer-Terraux was so stricken by Thiers's storm of abuse that he was taken ill. "Wait a few weeks . . . Then the events will be up to your ability and courage." That unprovoked insult hurled against the Conservatives created a resounding stir that echoed long and loud. It rang out like one of Mirabeau's celebrated phrases, which was clearly Thiers's intention. The weak and incompetent were men of the royalist party! Thiers despised them, loathed them, just as his hero Napoleon had despised the legitimists. And by openly publicizing his feelings, he was sure to joyfully reawaken the French people's old hates and old jealousies.

Master of Paris after a two-month siege and a week of battle, and having enhanced his prestige by his frightful victory, Thiers had gone on pursuing his tactical maneuver. Now that Paris had been handed over to him, he seized the opportunity in order to rid himself of the working-class elements that had always been against him, of that "vile multitude," as he had once unforgettably and insultingly called them. Keeping their part of the bargain, the provincial republicans and Freemasons had allowed the massacres to continue and the survivors to be outlawed.* Now that the revolutionaries had been crushed, the only obstacle that stood in his way were the princes. There, he had to be cautious, and as we have seen, he was quite capable of it. Thoroughly familiar with the royalist cause and knowing well that it was hopeless, he had played the game—a game involving no danger—of flattering the princes and holding those receptions in their honor at the presidential palace. Legitimists and Orleanists had about

---

* The demonstrations of the Paris Freemasons, who set up their banners and called for a truce at the Neuilly Gate, were repudiated by the Masonic hierarchy. At their 1871 Convention a resolution demanding amnesty for the convicted outlawed Communards was rejected as being political in nature.

as much in common as fire and water; they were not
merely two parties but two incompatible breeds, and the
Orleanists, deep in their hearts, were closer to a certain
kind of Republic than to the Bourbon King.

The Republic, therefore, was the only solution. But
what Republic? There were many types. The republican
experiment of 1849 had been dominated by the *grande
bourgeoisie*, the nobility, and the clergy. Thiers himself
had backed that regime; along with the *grande bourgeoisie*, the nobility, and the clergy, he had championed
parliamentary institutions against the opposition of the
urban and peasant masses, which had been converted to a
vague form of radical Bonapartism. That precedent was
uppermost in people's minds, and the Liberal bourgeois of
the *Débats* agreed to adopt a common social program
with the Catholic Liberals of *Le Français*, in spite of
differences on religious issues, both groups believing that
the republican experiment should be revived. Thiers was
far from raising any objections; indeed, he endorsed those
views, even putting forward such brilliant formulas as
"The Republic without republicans." But at bottom, he
favored an entirely different course of action. He was
looking, and had hopes, elsewhere.

Thiers was not likely to forget that the republican
Conservative scheme of 1849 had come to a sorry end:
early in the morning, on December 2, Louis Napoleon had
ordered him to be taken from bed, led to Mazas,[3] and
then out of the country. Along with the *grande bourgeoisie* and the nobility, Thiers had been beaten. And he did
not want to be beaten again: he was getting on in years,
and time was running out. Preferring to have no further
dealings with his unlucky allies of 1849, he sought out and
acquired new ones. In 1852 the masses had rejected the
grande bourgeoisie and the nobility, and had hailed an
emperor. Although Thiers did not expect a revival of
Bonapartist demagoguery, he now felt that the French, in
keeping with their old traditions, were likely to espouse

some form of authoritarian Republic with a dictatorial president. He had always been a gambler and this was his trump card. Who, if not he, would be the leader? Wasn't he already? He never tired of reading the numerous petitions that poured into his office, expressing gratitude and requesting the Assembly to consolidate his power by elevating his title to: Thiers, President of the Republic. Such repeated demands accurately reflected the country's need for gratitude and some form of authority. Responding with delight to all the hints, and accepting both truth and falsehood, Thiers looked forward to a republican regime with himself as Consul.

It so happened that the same month of June 1871 provided an opportunity for gauging national sentiment and being acclaimed yet again. On July 2, 117 vacancies in the Assembly were to be filled through by-elections. The Conservatives had no doubt that victory would be theirs: they themselves had set an early date for the election. Hadn't they, along with the man of their choice—Thiers —just defeated the Reds in Paris? With Thiers at their side, they would triumph. Feeling quite confident on that score, they turned their attention to their princes, to their quarrels and reconciliations, to the festivities honoring their return, to their petty social and family intrigues. Allowing them to agitate, Thiers concentrated all his energies on the 117 vacancies in the forthcoming elections. Many concerned him directly: having been returned in 25 constituencies in February, he was due to be replaced in 24 of them. Although he had been elected as a monarchist, he was determined that 24 monarchists would not be elected to the Assembly under his name and patronage. Behind the scenes he was carrying on secret negotiations with the republicans and endorsing their candidates. He wanted to be all things to all parties. Thiers is ours; he maintained law and order, the Conservatives would claim. Thiers is ours; he established the Republic, the republicans would claim. Although Thiers did not underestimate the

Conservatives' strength, he was determined to win over the passion and enthusiasm of the republicans. He was admirably suited to conduct that type of subtle campaign. Defying the majority of the Assembly, he had formed a cabinet made up to a large extent of republican ministers who had served in the insurrectionary government of September 4th. Jules Simon headed the Ministry of Education, and Jules Favre, the Foreign Office; the Ministry of the Interior had been awarded to Picard, who had contrived to furnish him with a remarkably loyal body of *préfets* and *sous-préfets*.[4] About ten ministers who had served in the September government had remained, as well as many of the mayors of small towns and villages. Thus, despite the disastrous reversals they had suffered in the February elections, the republicans succeeded in holding onto much of the power they had gained in a single day of revolution. The Assembly had forced Picard's resignation, but his service director, Calmon, had remained. Calmon, a former civil servant under Louis Philippe, later to become a senator under the Republic, was altogether devoted to Thiers and to his cause. Without the weak Conservative minister's being aware of it, Thiers ran everything along with Calmon.*

So much for his activities behind the scenes—or at any rate, all that can be known about them (Thiers surely had other dealings with the Freemasons and Gambetta). All those petty details did not overwhelm Thiers: he was gauging public opinion. With a remarkable sense of timing and a flair for the dramatic, he managed to stimulate the masses' pride and confidence by staging two public displays on the eve of the election—one financial,

---

* The following extract from a letter to Picard, dated March 11, 1871, illustrates Thiers's free-and-easy way of dealing with his ministers: "I want to apologize both for myself and on behalf of the Cabinet for the appointment of two *préfets*, for Toulouse and Saône-et-Loire, which you will perhaps come across in *le Moniteur*." In other words, Picard's signature had been used without his authorization.

the other military. On June 27, with the support of high finance, which sensed that the population's savings were plentiful and available, he dared ask the country for two billion francs. The loan was oversubscribed beyond the wildest expectations: five billion were raised within six hours. Next came a military display on June 29. Thiers had decided to show the Parisians an army filled with new life: a hundred thousand men were on parade at Longchamps.[5] On his reviewing stand Thiers stood and watched the march of battalions, squads, and artillery batteries—contingents from that old army which had once besieged Antwerp, liberated Belgium, conquered Algeria, liberated Italy, and twice, by its victories at Sebastopol and Solferino, avenged the defeats that Napoleon I had suffered at the hands of Russia and Austria. The crowds, gripped by the spectacle, too moved to cheer, contemplated the display of military might, which they had thought had been crushed—a mere shadow, a memory, a promise of future greatness. Doffing their hats in silence, they greeted the vanquished decimated forces—the Algerian riflemen of Wissembourg, the infantrymen of Saint-Privat, the cavalrymen of Reichshofen and Sedan. Their charge brought the parade to an end as they lowered their thousand swords before the motionless old man. Stepping down from the reviewing stand, Thiers walked over to MacMahon, who was mounted on his horse, and warmly shook his hand. On the way back, along the avenues of the Bois, Thiers was hailed with cheers of "Long live France", "Long live the Republic!" His friends drew his attention to the frequency of the second cheer.

On the evening of the 28th, on the eve of the parade, Thiers had given a reception at the presidential palace. The ambassadors, all the members of the corporate bodies of the state, the Institut, and all of Parisian high society had come to pay their respects, gathering round him like courtiers; and mingling with that new court could be seen the princes of the house of Orleans—Aumale, Joinville,

Chartres, and Nemours, the sons of King Louis Philippe under whom Thiers had once served. How reassuring for France's future! What a comfort! And for the Carbonaro of 1820, what a triumph!

CHAPTER 4

The Approaching Twilight

Results of the elections: out of 117 seats, the republicans gained 112. What a sudden turn-about! In May 1870 seven million Frenchmen had voted in favor of the Empire; in February 1871 they had elected 500 Catholic and monarchist deputies; on July 2 the same electorate, voting in fifty departments representing an accurate cross-section of the country at large, had switched to the republicans and crushed the very same Catholics, the very same monarchists, the great landowners, and the Notables of bygone days. All of which showed how steadfast was universal suffrage, henceforth to become the absolute master of France.

To be sure, political issues had hardly been at stake in February: the electors had voted not for the monarchist ticket but for the "peace ticket." In July political considerations had revived and become the determining factor. But what did the popular choice for the Republic mean? How is one to understand that resounding word which no longer terrified the country? Was it the Radical Republic that the voters had just rallied to? Yes, in a few large cities (Marseilles, Limoges, Toulouse, Lyons, Paris) and in a few southern regions (the area around Narbonne, and the valleys of the Durance and the Var). All told, this represented an extremely limited domain. But elsewhere? Had the people voted for the patriotic and bellicose Republic incarnated in Gambetta during his three-month dictatorship? Yes, in the East, along the bleeding frontiers of Alsace and Lorraine, in those areas occupied for what seemed an indefinite length of time by the German army. But in the rural districts of the North, the Center, and even the West, whose vote had just been so clear-cut, the popular reaction had been altogether different. There, no doubt, the population had merely accepted the *fait accompli* and expressed their desire to maintain the kind of Republic which, under Thiers's presidency, had given the country peace, put an end to the revolution in Paris, and restored law and order. Surely it was not as a result of divine grace that seven million electors who, only fifteen months earlier, had said "Yes" to the Empire had now been converted to republicanism. They were endorsing the new regime and its new leader just as they had endorsed its predecessor. The Conservatives, being extremely cautious, had vainly refrained from challenging the existing institutions, and had vainly taken pains to back Thiers. Their very caution seemed to conceal some ulterior motives with regard to the royal interests, so that the country had voted against their princes and their Monarchy, whose strength had once lain in their guarantee of stability, although the Monarchy now seemed likely to lead to a policy of adventure. The nation had also voted against the priests, against the bishops, and against the defeated Pope, remaining indifferent to his appeals for help.

There was probably something still deeper and more permanent that accounted for the population's reaction. The French people have never liked the nobility to have power; if they liked their kings, it was only when they had stood for justice against the nobility. Under the Empire they had shown no interest in the opposition led by Liberal aristocrats and bourgeois. This had been confirmed by the results of the recent elections of 1869:

while electing some thirty-odd republicans, they had turned down the Broglies, the Audiffret-Pasquiers, the Bochers, and the Decazes, who had been defeated everywhere. By some fluke, those same aristocrats and bourgeois had been carried to victory in February 1871. If they were once again defeated, it was perhaps a sign that all was back to the status quo, the status quo of the State, of French bureaucracy.

The elections had been held on the 2nd; Chambord's manifesto had been issued on the 8th. Thus the news of the two events—the prince's refusal and the republican victory—was announced in a single week.

The prince's refusal was received with astonishment and dismay by the Right. Veuillot stood alone in greeting the manifesto with enthusiasm. It was even likely that he had drafted it and that Chambord had merely endorsed and signed it. That otherworldly flag, those fleurs-de-lis, that whiteness displayed as an act of defiance against the brutal splashes of color—the red, blue, and white—of the flags of a revolutionary and nationalistic century, all that delighted Veuillot, and cheers welled up from the bottom of his heart. Such a heroic assertion, such royal insolence, perhaps augured a divine revolution—that parousia of which no Christian should ever despair. And behind Veuillot, in the vestries, in the convents, and in pious circles, arose unknown prophets, who, in low voices, counted the signs foretelling that the last days, divine or satanical, had come. The Pope, a prisoner in Rome, and the Savoyard and Prussian victors were signs of Satan's triumph. The signs of God: the Virgin appearing twice on French soil, once at la Salette and again at Lourdes—a prophecy that France, only apparently defeated, would once again emerge victorious; and Chambord's heroic fidelity. Quite different was the tone of the newspapers and that within the ranks of the old party. *L'Union* and *La Gazette de France* merely obeyed, neither approving nor criticizing. The reaction within the Assembly was something else again: all discretion was cast aside, and much of the rural gentry, who were accustomed to speak bluntly, now used sharp words to say what they thought of their prince's scruples, his poetic prose, and his defection.

Among the members of the Center the two events were greeted more with sadness than surprise. The vicomte de Meaux, a moderate legitimist, explained the electoral defeat in a short sentence. "We were monarchists," he said; "the rest of the country were not." It could not have been better expressed. As for the Orleanists, they had never believed in the Bourbon prince and never fervently wished for his return. The dramatic Letter merely confirmed their fears. They had always thought that they should be ready to come to terms with a Conservative Republic. Now this had become all the more necessary: it was an ordeal, and it was inevitable. Thureau-Dangin,[1] in his paper *Le Français*, expressed this view in religious terms:

> Is it possible not to see the hand of God everywhere these days? Would He be responsible for the proliferation of so much destruction and disappointment, and would He thus strike down the noblest souls, if His purpose was not atonement and instruction? It would seem to us that what He wishes above all is to punish the country for giving up hope, and that by thrusting aside the arm which several people dreamed of entrusting with the work of salvation, He wishes to remind us that it is up to us alone, with the help of the Almighty, to save ourselves from the abyss into which we fling ourselves.*

Both the Left and the Extreme Left rejoiced. They rejoiced over the royal Letter. "Chambord," exclaimed Thiers with glee, "is France's George Washington!" They

---

* Since the article was not signed, it is difficult to be absolutely sure who wrote it. But it was Thureau-Dangin who was responsible for articles in *Le Français* expounding its doctrine.

rejoiced over the electoral triumph: to have secured 112 seats, 80 of which were won, meant tolling the knell for those elected in February. And the most fervent among them concluded that the Assembly was now worthless: it had fulfilled its mission, which was to make peace; it should now be dissolved and make way for a Constituent Assembly that would establish the Republic.

The word *dissolution* was being heard for the first time and was soon to be repeated with growing urgency. Yet for the moment it was no more than hastily mentioned, a vague murmur. A hundred other tasks called for immediate attention—countless private tasks that are hard for the historian to grasp, but which are reflected by history: the resettling of families, the reopening of workshops, the resumption of trade. As the last hay was being brought in and the first grains of wheat were being harvested, France gave its undivided attention to the newly found peace. There were tasks for the State: At Satory, only a short distance from the new capital of Versailles—where, at the château, the Assembly held its sessions—the rebels of May were being tried and executed. And the Germans were still standing guard at Saint-Denis, waiting for payment of the balance of their ransom before evacuating the Ile de France. They would probably be paid. The success of the first loan raised hopes, but those hopes were clouded by uncertainty, for the Germans were to occupy Nancy, Verdun, and Belfort for a long time. Did they not have the ulterior motive of holding on to those last remaining fortresses, thereby making it necessary to again take up arms to get them back? There were other causes for concern: the presence of the German army in one-fourth of the country gave rise to acts of violence, to assaults and murders—painful problems to solve, dangerous pretexts that had to be averted. More than anything else in the world, the country yearned for the repose of a long period of peace, both at home and abroad, but no one really dared to expect that much. The historian, that late-comer, is a fortunate man: he knows everything and does not waste his time on unwarranted apprehensions. His objective detachment distorts his accounts, for the riddles and unknown quantities of the moment are lacking. Nations come and go, says the prophet, and the future hangs before them in tatters . . . This violent biblical metaphor, still so true and yet so rarely sensed, would not have come as a surprise to Frenchmen in the year 1871. Dissolve the Assembly: what a daydream! With the exception of some editorial offices and a few cafés, the watchword had no echo; no one took it seriously. Besides, the Germans would have objected: it was the Assembly that had negotiated the treaty and the Assembly that had pledged to carry it out. The Germans would not have allowed its dissolution.

"Reorganizing the country," Thiers had told the Assembly, "will be our one and only concern." In a stiffer and more noble tone, the vicomte de Meaux said the same: "By toiling in silence, we must restore strength, and not illusions, to this country." The Assembly had applauded them both and agreed to carry out its task in that spirit.

Yet the vicomte de Meaux had demanded somewhat more than any French Assembly could give: the National Assembly was not silent; still, it certainly toiled, and despite the illusions that were tempting and sometimes irresistible, it did restore the nation's strength.

During those first months in power the Assembly was an amorphous body. The parties had not yet shaped its character, and they themselves needed time to emerge from it as separate entities. Between the royalist Right and the radical Left floated a few hundred men who were groping for certainty and loyalties. They were noblemen and bourgeois of all sorts, more or less liberal, more or less favorable to religion—a few were even anticlerical—but all were Conservatives. Moreover, they were all well-educated and cultured men, a genuine elite, the type one could encounter only in a hastily elected parliament. What they lacked was any parliamentary experience and a seasoned leader. Perhaps the duc d'Aumale might have been able to lead them, but this patriotic Orleans prince-soldier wished above all to regain his army commission, and he had promised Thiers to withdraw from his seat in the Assembly, to which his Oise constituents had elected him. Albert de Broglie also showed signs of leadership, but Thiers, perhaps deliberately, had asked him to serve as French ambassador in London. Thus Thiers remained in sole command, dominating the inexperienced masses, whose muddled opinions were conveyed by way of such people as Dupanloup, de Meaux, Ernoul, Wallon,[2] Lucien Brun, even Belcastel and Francslieux—knights of the crown and the fleur-de-lis.

The few hundred Centrists were perplexed: as parliamentarians, they had no guide; as royalists, they had no king. Would it be accurate to say that what drew and held them together as a group was a common doctrine? The word would be an exaggeration; rather, they had common leanings—the same habits and preferences, the same dream. Elected after the debacle of the authoritarian Second Empire, they pursued a liberal dream whose traditions went back to the aristocratic unrest of a very ancient France. Old nations, like old dwellings inhabited by successive generations, are haunted by ghosts. Out of that tradition represented by the French Liberals, the Fronde and its chroniclers (first of all, Retz, who had been one of the guiding lights of the eighteenth century) had constructed a vivid legend. Fénelon and his friends—the Saint-Simons, the Chevreuses, the Boulainvilliers, all of them nobles at odds with the royal bureaucracy, had given it its initial form, and then Montesquieu, its memorable and final form. In the course of the eighteenth century the dream had lingered on and been magnified as the aristoc-

racy became fervently interested in the doctrine of "inter-
mediate bodies": *Parlements,* provincial estates, chambers
of agriculture, and Assemblies of Notables. Among those
dreamers was the hapless Louis XVI: he had tried everything—the *Parlements,* the Notables, the States-General
—and the Revolution had at first been regarded as a
large-scale expression of aristocratic liberalism. The same
aristocratic liberalism had served as the inspiration for the
monarchical constitutions of the nineteenth century, and
in the course of the struggle against the Bonapartist
Empire, the tradition had been revived. A fine book that
was published at the time, Prévost-Paradol's *La France
nouvelle,* which all members of the National Assembly
had read, took up the same theme and revived its spirit.

Now the members of the National Assembly bore a
striking resemblance to their grandfathers, who had belonged to the Constituent Assembly of 1789. Men such as
Broglie, de Meaux, and Gontaut faithfully followed in the
same tradition as La Rochefoucald-Liancourt, Lally-Tol-
lendal, Cazalès, and Mounier, so that when Chambord
wrote, "Together, we shall renew the great movement of
the last century," he was still expressing the same thoughts
that Fénelon had inculcated in his ancestor, the duc de
Bourgogne, two centuries earlier. On this matter the
legitimists, including Veuillot himself, were sometimes at
one with the Orleanists. "We must spread social con-
sciousness everywhere" wrote Veuillot in *L'Univers,* "so
that the country be preserved everywhere, and so that she
beget all that is necessary and outlaw all that is sterile and
dangerous. In short, we must restore France to herself, and
see that she is not slaughtered or on the point of dying yet
again as a result of receiving a single blow. The only way to
obtain that result is to revive the liberties of the provinces
to the greatest possible extent."

However, it was not liberty in the abstract, but
scattered and specific liberties—the type which (it was
earnestly hoped) would be influenced by local and tradi-

tional forces. Such was the political ideology of the liberal Conservatives in the Assembly. They put it into practice by quickly passing some laws. First of all, the municipal law: in reaction to insurgent Paris, which demanded its franchises and accused the Assembly of having dictatorial designs, they granted the communes all the liberties they retain to this day. Great landowners, both bourgeois and noble, they prided themselves on being thoroughly familiar with the villages, and it was through the villages that they wished to begin France's regeneration. There they still had rank and influence; traditionally, they were their leaders, and many of the town halls were located in the châteaux themselves. Thus a substantial vestige of ancient France had survived intact. The short-lived Republic of 1848 had made the mayor's office elective; the Second Empire had restored to the *préfets* the right to appoint the mayors. Without any hesitation, the Conservatives in the National Assembly provided for the election of mayors, hoping thereby to win the peasantry by that act of confidence.

In the month of August a second law was passed, extending the rights of the *Conseils Généraux*[3] and investing them with more permanent authority by means of standing committees designed to serve as advisory bodies to the *préfets*. Some Conservative southerners, in a good position to predict the future, objected to the reform, pointing out that it would work to their disadvantage. The councils established by them, they said, would be taken from them and turned against them. But those futile warnings went unheeded.

Thiers had raised objections to both those laws. "I am less a liberal than you are," said he, testily. Indeed, he was not a liberal in any sense; he was born to be a consul. But the liberal Conservatives in the Assembly were overjoyed not only to institute liberties but to do so in opposition to Thiers. The mayors were civil servants, affirmed Thiers; they represented the State and should therefore be appointed by the State. And he had been so insistent that, in cities and towns with a population of over 6,000 inhabitants, he was granted that the *préfets* would retain the right to appoint mayors. As for the *Conseils Généraux*, the same dispute arose. Thiers wanted to keep a tight control over the *préfets* and disliked having them controlled by anyone else. He protested harshly: "Your commission is like a syringe shoved up the backside of my *préfets*." The National Assembly, in a lively mood and once again emphasizing its liberalism, stipulated that the *Conseils Généraux* should be entitled to express political opinions. This led to a new clash, but Thiers won the day.

Irked by that elegant and *frondeur* liberalism which stood in his way, Thiers continued to turn to the Left for support. Another ideology, another dream—the authoritarian dream that had inspired, and was still inspiring, the Revolution—prevailed in that group, setting the State against the nobles and the priests, and fanning the embers of a cause, the strength of which had touched Thiers as a young man. The Left lay in wait for him. We prefer the *préfets*, they whispered, to the vestries and the châteaux . . .

The Conservatives, suspecting such a move, had not yet calculated its scope. As they knew, Thiers was not a monarchist; but they believed he was resolutely opposed to popular radicalism. That proved a mistake, and some astonishing discoveries were soon to put them on their guard.

In order to understand the first discovery, we must explore the intrigues right down to their most petty details. It appeared that one of the deputies elected on July 2, a radical Freemason by the name of Testelin, had been able to produce a letter from Barthélémy-Saint-Hilaire, Thiers's, private secretary, clearly endorsing his candidature. Barthélémy-Saint-Hilaire was a republican, and Thiers used him as a go-between with the Left (this was later confirmed). Was it thus possible that the same candidate could rely on the votes both of Thiers's friends and of those who were friends of the Commune? Testelin had succeeded in doing so. It seemed incredible. The Assembly demanded an explanation, but none was forthcoming.

The second discovery was more serious. This time Lyons was involved. Everything that originated in that city was sure to receive prompt attention from the Assembly. Anticipating Paris, Lyons had espoused republicanism in September. At a time when Paris was still flying the tricolor, Lyons had hoisted the Red flag and had kept it flying from its city hall throughout the war. During the Commune it was with great difficulty that Lyons had been kept in check, and on July 2, whereas a submissive Paris had appointed moderates, Lyons had appointed Reds to the Assembly. The radical South turned to Lyons for guidance and leadership. From the very beginning, everyone sensed that Lyons was destined to become the political capital of the Third Republic.

Now, in the month of August, the city observed a holiday celebrating its secular schools in a manner which the Conservatives found intolerable. Their indignation was justified: a street riot would not have had such consequences. In Lyons, the mother city of the Virgin Mary, the 15th of August was a traditional holiday, both popular and religious; it was celebrated with great pomp and circumstance in the cathedral, as well as in the streets, at Fourvière.[4] But the city council prohibited all processions on that day, and, replacing them by an entirely different type of festivity, proclaimed that Sunday, August 13, would be celebrated in honor of the city schools. In violation of the law of 1850, those schools had already been secularized and the teaching orders of priests expelled. The holiday was meant to express the real meaning of that expulsion and give it revolutionary significance. The children were marched in procession to a public park where a meal awaited them (26,000 francs, a considerable sum in those days, having been voted for the purpose). The deputy mayor, Barodet (we shall encounter him later, for this obscure individual's election as a deputy in Paris was to be a real event), made a speech to the children in which he advocated Positivist ethics as a new gospel. Had the Beaujolais wine on that hot day gone to a few people's heads? Had a few schoolmistresses been so affected by it that they had to be escorted home? Since clerical slanders are ingenious, they should be discounted. As for the incident itself, it called for the most serious consideration. On that Sunday in August 1871, on the morrow of mishaps which called for a truce among all parties, the municipality of Lyons took the initiative of launching a religious and educational policy which was to become the guiding policy of the Third Republic: the outlawing of Catholicism in all its visible forms—its public and popular holidays; and the establishment of a counter-Church to control children's minds—all of which foreshadowed the kind of tactics that were to be rigorously pursued long into the future.

Who had authorized the Lyons festivities? Someone was responsible, and the Assembly wanted to know who. Was it Jules Simon, the minister of Public Education? Known as a Radical directly before the incident, and still a Freemason, he was regarded with suspicion. But he protested vigorously: the initiative had been taken by the city administration, over which he had no control. Speaking for himself, he expressed his disapproval and condemned the sectarian propaganda that was influencing children. Was it, then, Lambrecht, Minister of the Interior, who was responsible for it? That was difficult to believe: Lambrecht was a resolute Conservative who, much to the Assembly's satisfaction, had been chosen to replace the republican Picard. Nevertheless, they wanted to question him. Since Lambrecht was away, they had him summoned. And they waited a long time. What was keeping him? He was said to be ill. He came at last and, like Simon, protested his innocence, apologized, and placed the blame elsewhere: he had been neither warned nor consulted by the *préfet*. Was the *préfet*, then, responsible? The festivities could not have been organized, nor could the funds have been voted, without his consent and approval. The *préfet* of Lyons was that same Valentin who, having been appointed to Strasbourg by the government of National Defense, had been able to slip through the German lines, swimming across the ditches in order to reach the besieged city and represent the new Republic. He was therefore a man of the 4th of September. Thiers had kept him in his administration and had entrusted him with the most difficult of posts: Lyons. Had Valentin acted without permission? It seemed unlikely. Jules Simon kept silent; Lambrecht kept silent; and the Assembly understood at last: only Thiers, they surmised, could have been responsible. Every morning he conferred with the *préfets* and *sous-préfets*, and reached decisions with them, but never condescended to inform his ministers, whom he was invariably disposed to treat as under-secretaries of state. Sometimes Calmon replaced him at these meetings, and Lambrecht, an honest and weary man, was unable to control the overflowing energies of a chief whom he was accustomed to serve and obey.* Still flirting with the Red city, Thiers had decided to tolerate the holiday instituted by the free-thinkers of Lyons. That was, in any case, the likeliest explanation. Having discovered more than enough, the Assembly prudently called off the investigation.

The third surprise was concerned with the disarming of the National Guard. A serious matter: in Paris it had taken a tragic turn and had precipitated the insurrection of the Commune. In Lyons, Marseilles, Toulouse, and Bordeaux it had still to be settled: in those cities the

---

* "Lambrecht, Thiers's lieutenant . . ." wrote Emile Ollivier concerning the 1869 elections. Cf. *L'Empire libéral*, 11:549.

National Guard had kept the weapons they had vehemently demanded during the war and which Gambetta's government had shipped them by the wagonload, while the Breton recruits about to be sent to the front line from the camp of Conlies had been left unarmed. Those weapons had merely contributed to the civil war: the Bordeaux Assembly had deliberated in February under the threat of them; in Lyons and Saint-Etienne they had been used against officers and civil servants. Yet they were allowed to remain in the hands of those who had done the shooting and killing. "I have no confidence in Thiers," wrote Victor de Laprade in June 1871. "He wasn't able to do anything in Lyons, which, next to Paris, is the most throbbing center of communism; he has not even dissolved and disarmed the National Guard."

This had finally to be done. On a committee appointed by the Assembly, General Ducroc, a monarchist, and General Chanzy, a republican, agreed in favor of disarmament. The vicomte de Meaux, the Committee's *rapporteur*, went up to the rostrum to set forth the measures that had to be taken. He spoke forcefully, with moderation and caution. (He had been warned by Falloux that Thiers, speaking to him the night before on the very same subject, had strangely lost his temper: the southern cities wanted to remain armed, and Thiers seemed anxious to treat them tactfully.) Once de Meaux had spoken, Thiers climbed up to the rostrum at a fighting pace. The Assembly was calm; he blew up a storm. "Why are you sounding the alarm and spreading panic?" said he to de Meaux, questioning him heatedly. Then, addressing all the members of the Right: "Here you are, protected by 120,000 men, and you still don't feel reassured." Now his rather tart voice rang through his harshest words. Again, he was being insulting: it was his way and his tactics. The Right, duly insulted, shouted and turned against Thiers, who became, or pretended to become, enraged. "It has been alleged that there is dissension between the Assembly and myself. That's true, that's true," he exclaimed; and *L'Officiel*,[5] which had been checked by him before publication, made known throughout the country that phrase he had just repeated. The Left, overcome with pleasure, cheered him on, while the Right and even the Center, which spilled over into the Left, watched the incomprehensible performance with stupefaction. "Nobody listens to me. I know what I now must do," declared Thiers, and returning to his seat, he gathered up his papers and briefcase.

All the deputies rose to their feet. In those calamitous times Thiers was the incarnation of France—in the minds of everyone, the Germans as well as the French; it was he who was responsible for order and for peace. "I know what I now must do," he had said. Would he withdraw? Would he resign? That was how his outburst was interpreted. But it was inconceivable that he resign . . .

Nor did Thiers have any such intention. All the gesticulations and shouting were merely fits of temper, the coquettish tricks of an old man putting on an act. Ducroc, Chanzy, de Meaux, and Broglie had no trouble reaching a compromise: the government, entrusted with the task of dissolving the National Guard, would carry out the law at its discretion and was asked not to precipitate matters. The keeper of the seals, that useful Dufaure (who, like Thiers, had served as minister under Louis Philippe), endorsed the policy of appeasement.

It was obvious that Thiers was playing a game. On the one hand, he was seeking the support of the masses, of that "vile multitude" he had so mistreated in the past. He had always been the insulting type, and now directed his insults against others. But here there was something more; his rage concealed a calculated design.

At that point, Thiers's status was in the hands of the Assembly. He wanted it to alter the functions of his office, to give it a fixed term, to enhance its power and prestige.

His modest title, "chief of the executive power," was not enough for him. "*Chef! Chef!*" he protested, "that's what they call a cook. Do they take me for a cook?" Numerous petitions had requested that he be named President of the Republic; it was his wish as well, his most fervent wish. There was no fixed period of time for his authority; he wanted one established. There was nothing to protect him from the changing moods of the Assembly: he wanted a constitutional text as a guarantee. Rivet, one of his deputy friends, had introduced a bill that conformed to his wishes. It was that same Rivet who, at Bordeaux, in February, had had the words "French Republic" inserted in the motion that had established Thiers's power. "On that day," he said "I hammered a nail into the monarchists' shoes; now I want to thrust a fish bone down their throats." That new law was to be the fish bone.

The leaders of the majority made speeches about it. Consolidating Thiers's power meant consolidating the Republic and putting it into the hands of a rather untrustworthy man, which they were reluctant to do. It also meant establishing a dictatorship: according to the bill proposed by Rivet, the Assembly would cede all its rights to Thiers. Although he could not dissolve the Assembly, it, in turn, could not overthrow him. Appointed both President of the Republic and Premier for three years, he would be in a position to control all the levers of power, and by virtue of the principle of presidential irresponsibility, ministerial responsibility—the basis of any parliamentary regime—would cease to exist. This was a lot to ask of a young and active Assembly, of such men as Buffet and Broglie, who for the past twenty years had, under Thiers's own leadership, struggled against the Second Empire, demanding those very rights which Thiers now wanted to sacrifice. It was generally conceded that some concentration of power was required to restore peace and order. But did such a temporary measure have to be made into a permanent institution? Thiers's ambition ran counter to the liberalism which was the political creed of the Assembly. The leaders of the majority did not refuse to enhance the dignity and authority of Thiers's power, but on the other hand, they wanted to limit it by separating the functions that were centered on him—the functions of Chief of State and of Minister. That irritated Thiers: he wanted at the same time both power and stability, the right both to speak from the rostrum and to be irresponsible. That lively outburst of his just recounted above, that threat of his to resign, had been a feint designed to impress the Assembly. What could it do without him? Who could it find to succeed him?

The bill that Thiers requested so urgently had to be seriously looked into. It was supported by a very strong wave of public opinion. The provisional and precarious nature of the State's institutions shocked the instinctive dogmatism and beliefs of the masses. They wanted a text—one word. If Thiers were proclaimed President for a specific period of time, it seemed that that should alter the circumstances and satisfy the masses. It was said that the Germans refused to accept long-term bonds in payment of the ransom because Thiers's power was not guaranteed; all that was needed, then, was to ensure that guarantee in order to facilitate the negotiations with the Germans. In any case, the country was deeply inclined in that direction. The parties of the Right resigned themselves to the situation. An incident which arose in the course of the debate suddenly made their position easier: Gambetta, who seldom dared to speak in an Assembly still obsessed with memories of his defeat, climbed onto the rostrum and declared that he was against the law. He denied the Assembly any right to vote or to decide in any way whatever the political future of the country. "I shouldn't want a Republic established by an incompetent Assembly," he boldly exclaimed. He was challenging the Assembly. In opposition to Gambetta, it voted in the law as an assertion of its powers. Thiers was granted his wish, and once again the Assembly inserted that word it didn't like—*Republic*—in a constitutional text. But it did not yield on the principle of irresponsibility, and did not want to extend his powers beyond its own: the President of the French Republic, stipulated the first article of the new law, would exercise his functions under the authority of the National Assembly and only for as long a time as the latter had not completed its task. Thiers and the Assembly were linked to each other, as if in marriage. In fact, the text had little significance, and the marriage was to be short-lived. But the country was pleased. One phrase uttered in the course of the debate was not forgotten: the Assembly, said the Orleanist Vitet, had pledged to make an honest effort to implement republican institutions.

The law was voted on August 31, 1871, after which the deputies left for vacation. They were in need of a rest. The session had lasted for seven months, during which they had confronted the problems of a war they had brought to an end, of a peace they had negotiated and concluded, of a rebellion they had crushed. And in the course of all the confusion and hazards, they had voted in three fundamental laws, had established such institutions as the French commune and department as we know them today, and willy-nilly had steered the country in the direction of its republican destiny.

CHAPTER 5

Autumn Observations and Conversations

With the recess of Parliament, there fell a sudden calm. Elections for the *Conseils Généraux* were held in October. Many voters, weary of being summoned and consulted, and of casting their ballots for unknown candidates who were expected to resolve obscure problems, abstained. The official statistics, very carelessly kept at that time, do not show the proportion of actual votes to registered voters, but the small number of ballots cast is quite revealing. The results at first seemed confusing, and so, indeed, they were. Since the parties were not organized, candidacies reflected the moods of people and places, and their political character was not clearly defined. After some time, it became possible to decipher the riddle—the equation with two thousand unknown quantities: the July election response was confirmed. In the cities the Republic prevailed. In rural areas the aloof and reticent lords of the manors, hoping for a monarchy without daring to say so, continued to lose ground. The Empire had instilled the notion of authority; since the Republic existed, people felt it should last and that, like its old leader Thiers, whose obstinate zeal was so heart-warming, it would prove to be active and confident. Actually, a Red or Reddening Republic in the cities, and a Republic cast in Thiers's image in the rural areas, was what the nation clearly wanted. Moreover, the expression of that desire was very moderate in nature: on October 23 the *Conseils Généraux*, meeting for the first time, elected their presidents, 56 of whom were Conservatives of various shades as against 18 republicans and 12 Radicals. The breakup of the Center, thus confusedly divided between the Orleanists and the followers of Thiers, makes it difficult to interpret those figures with any accuracy. Great prudence was shown during the sessions that began forthwith: it was forbidden by law to take any political position, and the law was respected even by the Radicals, who were drawn to their Conservative colleagues by a common feeling for hard work, and who made it almost a point of honor to emulate them in that respect. I might add that they were also guided by prudence.

Since politics were in abeyance, we must look elsewhere and investigate the few eminent thinkers who, then as now, stood for France; it would be well to explore their thoughts. Their ranks were decimated by recent deaths: Proudhon, still a young man, died in 1864; Sainte-Beuve, in 1869; Montalembert, Mérimée, and Lamartine, in 1870. None of them had witnessed the national disaster. Three great Romantics survived—Hugo, Michelet, and George Sand. And right behind them, occasionally forming part of their circle, were younger men who had already achieved fame—Renan, Taine, and Flaubert.

Let us first turn to Hugo. Elected to the Assembly in February 1871, he had almost immediately withdrawn. He refused to accept the humiliating peace, he refused to honor by his presence those who had ratified it. He had returned to Brussels and then to Guernsey, where he welcomed to his home and to his table the Parisian revolutionaries who were fleeing the Versailles army and Thiers's justice, thus resuming what amounted to an exile in the company of those new outlaws. "I am leaving," he told Lockroy;[1] "I can't stand the sight of all this." After twenty years of solitude, he had lost his perspective on human events. He did not acknowledge as his own a Republic inaugurated by the sacrifice of 1,500,000 Alsatians and Lorrainers and the slaughter or proscription of 50,000 French republicans.

Michelet also withdrew. After having been generous in words and in facile advice, encouraging all revolutionary initiatives on the eve of the war, he now seemed to have been transformed by the disaster into quite a different man and reverted to silence. When the republicans asked for his backing, he refused: "For the moment I can't contribute to any newspaper or even lend my name . . . The domestic situation is still unclear; *it is in a state of flux*, but things are still so nebulous that writing might only deepen the wounds and increase the difficulties." He went far from Paris, which had been devastated by fires, resolved never to set eyes on the havoc that was wrought, and he sought solitude on the coast of Provence, there to begin writing his gloomy history of the origins of the nineteenth century. Every age, he wrote, is reflected in its monuments—its temples, cathedrals, or palaces. Our age is reflected in its own monuments—its barracks and factories. The barracks are French, the factories, English. The barracks and factories have spread over the last century to the point where they now embrace all peoples, forcing them to submit and adapt to a dismal form of discipline. The eighteenth century rose toward the light; the nineteenth kept descending, and its history is the record of a gradual and distressing decline. Michelet's friends kept cautiously silent regarding his three-volume *Origines du dix-neuvième siècle*, and the general public was unaware of his ideas, which it would have found unbearably depressing; indeed, even today, they are still virtually unknown.

Unlike the others, George Sand refused to let herself be cut off by sadness, greatness, or old age. Her splendid female courage was not crushed by the pressure of events.

A friendly maternal woman, she took up with her juniors—
men such as Renan and Flaubert (and, through them, she
could approach Taine). Remaining loyal to her native
province of Berry, she corresponded with Flaubert, that
stubborn Norman, so that we know the ideas they
exchanged. What was being written and said in such
quarters is of great interest. George Sand listened willingly;
we would do well to follow her example. Further on, we
shall hear what she had to say.

Flaubert, Taine, and Renan had been the new
guiding spirits of the Second Empire: what a gulf separated them from their elders, the Romantics. It would
seem that the gulf separating them from us is less painful,
less profound. Hugo and Michelet turned away from a
France that had been stripped of her dreams and her glory:
they were baffled; they no longer recognized her. But
Flaubert, Taine, and Renan were not baffled. They had
never known the century in full bloom. The Restoration,
with all its vigor, its wit, its courtesy, and its grace, the
enduring resplendence of the year 1830—all that had
existed before their time. The popular Revolution of 1848
suddenly brought down, before their very eyes—indeed,
almost upon them—a liberal and bountiful social order
which had preserved a great deal, perhaps even the best, of
ancient France. They saw France sacrificed by riotous
rebellion to the tyranny of universal suffrage, then by
universal suffrage to a Bonapartist dictatorship, then by a
Bonapartist dictatorship to the materialism of big business, as well as to frivolous tastes and deeds. Finally, they
saw France being led down the road to enormous disaster,
the very enormity of which, alas, failed to astonish them.
The fact that they were not astonished is the saddest thing
about them. Renan, Flaubert, and Taine, even before they
were thirty, had lost the power to hope.

"Renan's book is very good," wrote Flaubert to
George Sand in December 1871, "very good, in the sense
that it conforms with my own ideas." The book he had

recommended to his friend was *La Réforme intellectuelle et morale de la France*, such a sad book and, underlying the serenity of its style, such a cruel book. "Let us remember," wrote Renan, "that sadness alone is capable of producing great things, and that the only true means of reviving our country is to draw its attention to the abyss into which it has fallen." Renan drew attention to the abyss; as for any hopes of reviving the country, he considered them in such limited terms that, if one reads him carefully, one realizes that he eliminated them all. Revolutionary fervor, he wrote, which is fatal to all peoples who have ever succumbed to it, has gripped France and is killing her. Her recovery is bound up with the traditions she had forsaken. Could she go back to them? Renan sketched out fully the guiding principles for an aristocratic and royalist policy—a restoration of the princes and nobles who had served to endow France with the power and greatness she had lost. Did this merely satisfy Renan's desire to think and to write? Or was it meant as a piece of advice? If it was meant as advice, then it would remain a dead letter, and Renan, more than anyone else, knew that. "The handful of people whose politics followed the line of argument I have seen fit to adopt," he wrote, "are those who are the most utterly defeated in the fatal crisis which is unfolding before our very eyes." Utterly defeated—that much was clear. Unperturbed, with haughty intellectual satisfaction, Renan drew up the balance sheet of his own disappointment. "The rights of the nation," he wrote by way of conclusion, "are inalienable, and the fact that the nation makes light of our advice ought not keep us from giving it." In discharging his obligations in that way, was he doing his duty to his fellowmen or to his own intellect? To the latter, it would seem. And he described briefly the despicable future that France, according to him, could hardly escape. "All that the future holds out is the prospect of a series of unstable dictatorships, a Caesarism similar to that of the late

Roman era." His concluding word was: "*Laboremus*"—
"let us work." Indeed, he himself was to work, but so far
away! It was in Rome, during November and December
1871, that he concluded his account of the age of Nero by
writing his *Antéchrist*. But regarding France, not another
word. He refused to pursue obstinately an impossible task.
His book had been published; he considered that he had
done his duty.

This was the book in which Flaubert discovered his
own point of view. Renan's polished and concealed
nihilism appealed to his own more brutal and outspoken
nihilism. Like Renan, Flaubert despised the revolutionary
cult which inflamed the masses, deified their collective
opinion, and placed the future of State and society at the
mercy of universal suffrage. To his mind, universal suffrage
was "a disgrace to the human spirit." The first thing to do
was to eliminate it. This meant that an attack had to be
launched. He did, for a while, contemplate such a course
and wrote *Le Candidat*, a political comedy condemning
all parties, but it was mediocre and it failed. From then
on—like Renan, who disregarded his country—he went
back to antiquity: he again turned his mind to and
completed the tragedy of Saint-Antoine, that bitter farce
on human aspirations.

Taine was a man of a different stamp. Although a
philosopher, a friend of Renan's, and an admirer of
Flaubert's, he was stubbornly and instinctively attached
not only to his country but even to the *bourgeoisie*, and
his advancing age, along with the pressure of events,
reinforced his instincts. Like Renan and Flaubert, Taine
was struck by the almost vertical collapse of the traditional
social order, the ancient French hierarchy. The nobility
had lasted for a thousand years, but the *bourgeoisie* had
lost its prestige in a single century, and now the masses,
ruling unchecked, would exert all its still untried pressure
on the State. Although he reacted strongly to that
possibility, Taine, unlike Flaubert and Renan, did not

allow himself to be distracted from it. Rather than persist in merely denigrating or scorning universal suffrage, he wanted to try and study that formidable phenomenon, that enormous craving for power which threatened to destroy those states that did not learn how to curb it. Universal suffrage was indeed a formidable phenomenon; we are so accustomed to it that we have some difficulty in weighing its impact. We must recall that in 1872 Europe was hardly attuned to it. Although prepared for it by two centuries of parliamentary experience, England was still reluctant to adopt it; it was unknown in Austria; and in Italy 500,000 electors made up the entire electoral body. Only two countries had adopted it: one of them was Germany, where it had been introduced by Bismarck, but Bismarck was there to keep it in check by means of his disdain, his vetoes, and his brutal dissolutions of Parliament. The other was Spain, a country constantly torn by bloody upheavals. If it were suddenly to dominate France, where the revolutionary tradition was so strong and the State so apparently crippled, what form would the upheavals take? "Is it possible," wrote a fine essayist, Dupont-White, "to predict the impact of a pressure group still unconscious of its power, one that is destined to play such a great role and that is still harboring such formidable memories and grudges?" It was safe to expect a catastrophe.

Everyone, however, was not that pessimistic. Taine reported that the reputedly witty Picard, formerly a member of the Government of National Defense and then, for a few months, Thiers's minister, had said: "Universal suffrage will not be abolished; it will be conjured away." But Taine showed no sympathy for Picard's skeptical quip; he failed to note how prophetic it was. Honestly incapable of making any allowance for conjuring tricks, he sought to discover the principles governing the new force. Even at that time, the various forms of universal suffrage, which are still put forward

occasionally, had already been proposed: election in two
stages; the right to vote based on legal qualification, with
education considered an advantage; the right to vote
based on domicile, with vagrants, the unemployed, and
bachelors being granted a restricted suffrage or denied it
altogether; and finally, multiple election, which would
work to the advantage of families.* Yet how futile were all
these safeguards! The simple and barbaric formula—one
man, one vote—was deeply rooted in peoples' minds and
imaginations, and magnetically attracted Europe. In an
effort to investigate and choose among all those safeguards, Taine published a brochure in which he recommended an electoral system in two stages which, according
to him, was best suited to bring out local talent and
establish the basis for an educated and well-informed
political body, which France had always lacked. This
brochure was not the only example of Taine's preoccupa-
tion with political matters. He also wrote an article in the
Débats on the means and usefulness of circulating Conservative and Liberal newspapers among the people; and
he took part in launching the École Libre des Sciences
Politiques, which was destined to have such a long life. It
was he who drafted its statement of purpose: the new
school was to provide the realistic and precise scholarly
training that the university was incapable of furnishing—a
type of training that would be especially useful in preparing for high positions in industry and the civil service.
Oddly enough, sixty years after its foundation, the school
still quite satisfactorily fulfills the purpose for which it was
established: it has molded generations of diplomats and,
to this day continues to train the administrative, financial,
and economic elite of the nation.

It would therefore appear that Taine had decided to
take an active part in public affairs. Yet his direct

---

* Among the many excellent books published at the time, those by
Naville, for example, or Castellane are still useful.

intervention soon came to an end. We shall no longer find evidence of his actions; we shall no longer hear his words of advice. Like Renan and Flaubert, Taine was to devote himself entirely to writing his great work. It was to be neither an *Antéchrist* nor a *Saint-Antoine*. In contrast to Renan or Flaubert, Taine, with almost desperate energy, launched into the problem of French society. Setting aside (somewhat to his regret) a comprehensive and strictly analytical study that he had already begun, he undertook to write his *Origines de la France contemporaine*. It was to prove a powerful work and would have its impact, but not for another fifteen years, and in order to write it, Taine went into strict isolation.

Was writing that work the only reason for his decision to keep aloof and silent? "The best of all things is silence," he said, "and, from time to time, a page by Marcus Aurelius." Those words contain a bitter secret that must be understood. Flaubert's seclusion was not surprising, and Renan's somewhat less so; but Taine's silence was so unexpected and so sudden that it poses a problem. Thiers was to be overthrown; the comte de Chambord almost seized the throne; the National Assembly was to vote a republican constitution; the crisis of the 16th of May was to stagger the country; yet neither Taine nor Renan* were to utter a single word. Both of them continued to opt for silence and Marcus Aurelius. An explanation is needed, and here is the one I propose: Taine and Renan kept silent because they had lost all hope and belonged to no party. The conflicting forces drew their inspiration from two

---

* It was not until 1878 that Renan was to publish *Caliban*, his second political work after *La Réforme intellectuelle et morale de la France*. But what a gulf between the two! By 1878 the republicans had emerged victorious, Broglie had been defeated, and Renan, under the cloak of fantasy and using irony to muffle the impact, rallied to the winning side. "What has just happened," says one of his characters, "bears out what I had foreseen and what no one wanted to believe: that Caliban was capable of making progress . . . The narrow-minded Conservatives dream of possibilities for regaining the power they lost. More enlightened men accept the new regime, allowing themselves nothing more than the right to indulge in a few harmless jokes."

sources: on the one hand, radical humanitarianism; on the other, Catholicism. And both Taine and Renan were equally repelled by each of those dogmas. Sainte-Beuve would surely have been quite as repelled. All of them regarded radical humanitarianism as nothing more than an absurd intellectual temptation, and they considered the Church a pernicious influence on French society and the masses. The Church had not only accepted but blessed the *coup d'état* of 1851; if she had parted company with Napoleon III, it was only to rally to Pius IX's absolutist policy, supporting his *Syllabus*[2] and his acts of defiance. This, Taine and Renan did not forgive. In their view, piety, superstition, and frivolity had tarnished modern Catholicism. A different sort of Catholicism probably continued to exist and had its loyal followers. Dupanloup, of course, had not bowed down to a reckless Emperor, and at the Vatican Council in 1870 he had objected to the *Syllabus*; Broglie and his friends at the *Correspondent* had agreed with Dupanloup and had given him their support; so that men like Renan and Taine might have sought a compromise with them on the basis of a moral concordat. But Dupanloup and his friends did not represent the Church—far from it; they were considered as defeated and were held in suspicion by the Church. Besides, Taine and Renan, during that momentous year of 1871, were simplistically but resolutely opposed to the Church. Young family men at the time, they entrusted their children to the Protestant Church. To them radicalism was the plague, and clericalism was leprosy. Hence not only their embarrassment in the face of the conflict, but their silence. Even John Lemoinne,[3] the great journalist of the *Débats*, had said: radicalism is scurvy; ultramontanism is leprosy. If one had to choose between the two, scurvy was preferable.

It appears certain that French intellectuals shared the feelings of Taine and Renan. The same embarrassment can be sensed in *La Revue des Deux Mondes* and *Le*

Journal des Débats, to which they contributed, as well as at the French Academy, to which they would soon belong. In those circles everyone was conservative and attached to royalism, but did not accept Catholic domination. This was clearly demonstrated by the four elections to the Academy held on December 30, 1871. The French Academy had not filled its vacancies since July 1870. Montalembert, Villemain, Paradol, and Mérimée had died. The duc d'Aumale had been elected to Montalembert's seat by 28 votes out of 29. In the place of Paradol and Mérimée—one an Orleanist, the other a Bonapartist—two royalist historians were elected, Camille Rousset and Loménie, one an Orleanist and the other a legitimist. For the fourth vacancy there was a scramble. Littré had submitted his candidature. Not only a philologist, the author of a dictionary which, after sixty years, is still being consulted, Littré was also a philosopher, a disciple of Auguste Comte, whom he had succeeded as master of that Positivist school whose powerful systematic ideology had impressed so many thinking people. He had already been a candidate in 1863. His rival on that occasion had been Mgr. Dupanloup. As a bishop, Dupanloup refused to concede that the leader of an ungodly sect should be welcomed and honored by a state body. Dupanloup was not an ultramontane. He respected the State, but in return he expected the State to respect the Church and to ensure respect for it. In 1863 it was he who had won the election. Thiers, who at first was hesitant, had rallied to him, and Littré had been defeated and kept out of the Academy for ten years. He now again submitted his candidature. A man without the slightest vanity, he was motivated by a concern altogether contrary to the Bishop's: he refused to admit that the doctrine he professed should disqualify him from playing a role in State affairs. One principle stood opposed to another. The Academy was to arbitrate. By 17 votes to 13, Littré was elected.

The event had considerable moral significance. Aumale and Littré had been elected on the same day—on the same day and by the same men: 17 members of the Academy had cast their votes both for a prince and for a Positivist. In other words, the conservative elite of French society was deeply split; a group of powerful minds, remaining neutral with respect to the parties, had perceived something seriously wrong in each of them, and therefore had no trust or hope in either one. And that dual rejection resulted in the pessimism which lay behind their silence.

Let us now return to George Sand, in whom everyone confided. By way of conversations and letters she was familiar with all the bitter thoughts, yet her ever maternal heart kept her from pronouncing any irrevocable judgments. Flaubert was sometimes irritated by that indefatigable gentleness, which was perhaps more profound than the sour mood that had taken hold of him. "You don't understand," he would tell her. "In spite of those large sphinx's eyes of yours, you have seen the world through a haze of golden light. It came from the sun in your heart, but such darkness has loomed up over you that you now no longer recognize things for what they are." Indifferent to sermonizing, George Sand persevered in her gentleness and her hopes. "Let us die without cursing our race!" was her answer to the cold, harsh judgments of Renan and the virulent harsh judgments of Flaubert. And Flaubert, who generally replied so curtly, remained silent for once and refrained from answering her reproaches. "Let us die all warm and alive," she again wrote him. This was a shrewd concession, conceding no more than a word which was no sooner conceded than it was retracted, so that in the end nothing had been conceded. George Sand knew that to have a great virile mind is often unfortunate. Because of its very energy, it detaches itself from instincts and is thus denied their humble and sustaining certainties. Hence the sadness, which is probably more a sign of weakness than of strength. Because of one false principle, France was lost, contended Renan, Taine, and Flaubert. A mere daydream, thought George Sand—the daydream of melancholy thinkers who had had no contact with the well-springs of life and no idea of the resilience and permanence of people and nations. Sainte-Beuve was right to say that pure intellect was a dead moon, for it is pure intellect that devastates the countryside it illuminates.

With no doubts about France's future, how did George Sand conceive it? What did she envision? For four months in 1848—from February to June—she had been an ardent republican. The flame was short-lived; it died down, leaving little more than sparks. And I believe that it was not the republican woman but rather the sensible woman, truly mingling with the masses and capable of listening to them, who came out strongly against the princes. "It's true; we want no part of them," she wrote, "and that, I am convinced, is the prevailing sentiment: a terrifying weariness with dynasties, an instinctive distrust of all those who have wanted to conduct our affairs in our place." So she accepted Thiers's authority: "Let it be our wish that he remain in power long enough to teach us how to discuss without resorting to revolution." On that point, Taine, Renan, and Flaubert agreed with her. "If only the *status quo* could last," wrote Taine, "it would provide the country with a liberal and parliamentary education." *If only it could last*: from the winegrower dressing his grapevines to Renan writing his *Antéchrist*, all Frenchmen yearned for that lost blessing—permanence.

George Sand, then, accepted Thiers, but without liking him. "It is sad to have to admit that we must go through this phase of great moderation, which is a *slow and cold* method, instead of being able to rely on the young and vigorous forces of public opinion! What a lot of potential and vigor we shall have to curb to avert madness and disorder." That remark harked back to the memories of 1848: George Sand was unable to forget those bygone years when souls were so impassioned, when good intentions and hopes were so forthcoming. At times, she did confess her nostalgia and some regret: "I feel as if great loyalties have slackened—have, as it were, been sundered," she confided to Flaubert. She was wrong. She had never lost those heartfelt loyalties that were lacking in Renan, Taine, and Flaubert, or that were so weak as to distort their thinking.

CHAPTER 6

Parliament and
the Salons

WHEN the Assembly reconvened in December, the country was still smarting from its wounds. In the occupied departments there were some painful incidents—even murders. Four German soldiers were killed by peasants who, after being arrested, were acquitted by a jury. Germany protested, and Bismarck, not satisfied with apologies, began fulminating and publicized a letter he wrote to his ambassador:

> The fact that the feeling for law has so utterly died out in France should serve to remind Europe of the difficulties encountered by the French government in trying to free the feeling for law and order from the pressure put upon it by the impassioned masses . . . The high moral training of the German people, as well as their feeling for law and honor, preclude any possibility of similar behavior on our part . . . In the future, if we are denied the right of extradition, we shall be compelled to carry out arrests and take French hostages, and in case of extreme necessity, we may even have to resort to harsher measures.

Did Bismarck contemplate resorting in peacetime to the hasty executions and the burning of villages by which the German General Staff had ensured the security of its men during the war? He had made himself understood, and it provoked indignation.

Both the insult and the threat were serious, which perhaps accounts for the great calm that marked the opening session of the Assembly. Thiers welcomed the body with a most cautious and restrained statement. "Since the aim of politics," he told the Assembly, "is to establish a permanent form of government, all this is principally your concern, and we should be impinging on your rights if we were to act hastily in this matter." He added:

> Speaking for myself—in a state of utter weariness, and sometimes pain, when I turn aside from my constant work to reflect for a time on our woes—I personally have accepted but one task: to reorganize this country, which has been shattered by defeat, by re-establishing her relations abroad and her administration, finances, and army at home, maintaining strict order while carrying out this task, and always standing ready to hand over the mandate with which you have entrusted me in a form that has been scrupulously and faithfully preserved.

The republicans did not care for those words, whereas the royalists, quite to the contrary, approved them. Had they at last found in Thiers the leader they had elected? For a short time they had hopes of it. Yet the winter turned out to be one long quarrel.

Disputes, reconciliations, crises, or imminent crises— each week had its difficulties. "Every night one has the impression of being on the eve of a revolution," wrote an English observer who was amazed by the spectacle, "but every morning one realizes that it was nothing at all." During the reign of Louis Philippe, between 1830 and 1848, French parliamentary life had frequently given that impression; it was to do so even more frequently in the future.

Yet all that was merely on the surface. Behind the din produced by rather futile turmoil, the nation was diligently and vigorously shaping its destiny. Ever since 1872 it has been obvious that the only way to untangle all the elements involved is to observe them simultaneously on two levels: on one—the level that first strikes the eye—the French are impelled by a partisan spirit which splits them apart; on the other, which is not as conspicuous, quite a different spirit grips them and leads them to accomplish their tasks. One might say that never had a statesman been confronted with a nation that undisciplined and that difficult to guide as the divided France which Thiers had to guide in 1872; or, what was equally true, that never had a statesman been backed by a nation that disciplined and that easy to guide as that very same France during the very same year. It all depends on the level one chooses to consider, assuming that one is willing to settle for a single point of view. While Thiers needed men and money in order to rebuild the country's finances and its army, the new taxes and the army law were by no means adopted without debate. Yet Parliament always agreed to grant Thiers more men and more money than he requested, which may be attributed to a common fervor and a common determination to restore the country's tottering strength and past glory. From 1871 to 1898, wrote Charles Maurras[1] thirty years later, "La Revanche" was to be Queen of France: it is an illuminating formula when applied to the years we are considering. "La Revanche," the invisible Queen, governed the tumultuous debates and was always obeyed. And *Revanche* is indeed the right word. For a moment we thought of correcting it, of toning it down, and of writing "Restoration" instead. But no, *Revanche* is indeed the right word. Almost no one had any doubt that it was necessary, and the whole drift of politics and of national life was to prepare for it.

Always obeyed, yes—but through crisis after crisis. So it would be well to examine the naïve and untried

Assembly, to mingle with the crowd of men which composed that body and which was constantly perplexed by the course of events. Except for basic principles, for which, out of patriotism, they felt a sense of duty, everything seemed to baffle them. In addition to their lack of experience and their ignorance of matters they should have known about, they were hindered by the stubborn memories, more embarrassing than useful, of outmoded regimes and customs. All their leaders, whether leftist or rightist, belonged to the past. Louis Blanc, Edgar Quinet, Jules Simon—revolutionary republicans and spiritualists— as well as Broglie, Decazes, Audiffret-Pasquier, and their leader Thiers, belonged to bygone days. Despite their determination to understand and to adapt, they were incapable of fathoming the new age, yet they persisted in chattering and dreaming about it.

The Radicals dreamed of a Convention elected by the people; the liberal Conservatives dreamed of sharing sovereignty; old Thiers dreamed of being consul. Just as those dreams had vied with one another during the first months of the Assembly, they again emerged and vied with each other. Every statement provoked a quarrel. A quarrel, for example, in connection with the *Conseil d'État*. That venerable institution of Bourbon origin had gained considerable power under the Second Empire, and since it was discredited, like the regime it had served, the National Assembly decided to reform it. Placing it under its own strict control, the Assembly deprived the government of the right to appoint its members, arrogating that right to itself, so that henceforth the councillors of state would be elected by the Assembly. For Thiers it meant less power and was therefore a false principle. He felt the blow, gauged the margin of error, got angry, protested, but ultimately yielded.

On the question of finances—further quarrels and, this time, a violent debate. The Assembly, in a spirited and generous mood, was inclined to vote in favor of an income tax. Thiers could easily have pushed it through, but he didn't want that kind of tax; he preferred a duty levied on imported raw materials. Hence there was a dual conflict: the National Assembly, favoring free trade, did not want what Thiers wanted, and, on the other hand, favoring an income tax, it wanted what Thiers didn't want. Thiers thus ran counter to it on two issues, and the Left, even more than the Right, was against him.

Thiers confronted everyone, altogether indifferent to the taunts provoked by his obstinacy, and no one realized that by stubbornly opposing those two issues, the old man was expressing the deep feelings of the French peasantry and *bourgeoisie,* and was in fact the man of a future that would long prevail.

For forty years France under the Republic preserved the fiscal regime that Thiers championed against the reformers of 1872, and she was to raise the import duties that had been lowered by the Second Empire. Free trade opens doors: France wanted to keep hers shut; the French wanted to be left alone, to eat their own bread, drink their own wine, be clothed with the wool of their own sheep, be shod with the leather of their own cattle, and live on the fruits of their perfect country—in short, to protect themselves from the outside world. The French had the same aversion to the income tax, and for similar reasons: Was the treasury to know what every family earned? But every family wanted to keep its secrets and be left alone, secluded within its walls and behind closed doors. The French countryside is the most rigidly divided in the world—strictly parceled out by ditches, hedges, and walls. Thiers would not yield. The Lyons industrial interests, earning large profits in the raw silk market, were aghast at the proposed tax and suggested instead that the necessary funds be raised by means of a tax on turnover. This angered Thiers, who considered it outrageous that industrialists express their views on State matters and lobby in the Assembly. The general welfare came first, he believed, and private interests should have no say. He flamed up; any discussion of his plans seemed to him a lack of consideration. Every argument presented against him drew sparks. "It is annoying," a member of Parliament remarked sadly, "not to be able to make a move without having the sun in one's eyes." Finally, lightning struck. Thiers handed in his resignation and withdrew. He was implored to reconsider, but in vain. He would hear nothing of it.

What a scandal! Did Thiers intend to impose his authority on the Assembly and act like a dictator? The Assembly had thought that by appointing him President of the Republic at his request, it had raised him above and set him apart from the responsible ministers. But Thiers was insatiable: he wanted to be both President and minister, cumulating and mixing up all the issues, and then making his own decisions on them all. M. Thiers, wrote Chateaubriand in 1835, could become a great minister if only he would stop being a muddler. But Thiers never stopped being a muddler. The Right was indignant and accused him of blackmail. The Left was equally displeased, but reacted cautiously, expressing the hope that some compromise could be reached. It was not easy; Thiers remained unshakeable.

Neither free trade, he insisted, nor an income tax! A minor issue like that, he was told, should not become a question of confidence. It was a basic issue, he replied, and he would not yield an inch. Finally, they had to give him his way.

Three hundred deputies went and handed him the Assembly's submission.

The jolt provoked a climate of uneasiness which was not easily dispelled. What a fragile shelter protected France as she tried to recover, catch her breath, and renew her spirit! She was at the mercy of an old man's whims. "The clearest consequence of the latest crisis," wrote

Arnim, the German ambassador in Paris, to Bismarck, "is that it once again indicates the state of disorganization in which this mob, once known as the French nation, is dragging along."

What had been Thiers's motives—all his motives? Once the crisis was over, everyone sought him out; they were concerned, especially the Right, which, always prone to be skeptical and alarmed, was now excessively so. When Thiers withdrew, had he meant to precipitate the inevitable dissolution of the Assembly itself and thereby the election of a new Assembly that would be more obedient and unanimously in favor of him? It was surely one of his motives later on. Perhaps he was already contemplating it at the time, and it tempted his friends and close associates. "Nothing can be done with this Assembly!" exclaimed the vivacious Mme. de Rémusat at a dinner at the Reservoirs the very night of the crisis. And Christophle, one of Thiers's loyal and intimate friends, had declared that everything must be interrupted in order to restore the Constitution of 1848. That Constitution, it will be recalled, provided for the election of the President by universal suffrage. Perhaps those words revealed the old man's secret thought and his boundless ambition: he would have been delighted to end his political career with popular acclaim, a triumph, and a principate.

Here again we come up against that "muddler," so described by Chateaubriand: under circumstances which, given their simplicity and grandeur, seemed to have almost called for simplicity and grandeur, Thiers went on being an irritable and irritating schemer.

If the Chief of State, who was always a gambler, kept dreaming up one scheme or another, then everyone was free to dream up similar schemes for the future! At the reopened aristocratic *salons*, new ideas were excitedly exchanged. The Faubourg Saint-Germain[2] had known two great eras: the first had lasted fifteen years, from 1814 to 1830; the other, a very short one, had lasted from 1871 to

1876. All the French nobility, delighted to have recovered their prestige, gathered round the duchesse Pozzo di Borgo, the duchesse d'Avaray, the comtesse Duchatel, and the duchesse de Galliera. The old diplomatic house of the duchesse Pozzo di Borgo was frequented by ambassadors and the international, well-traveled European aristocracy. Pure legitimism was predominant at the duchesse d'Avaray's (her son-in-law was bound by contract not to serve any government other than the Bourbon king's). On the other hand, it was pure Orleanism that prevailed at the comtesse Duchatel's, where Thiers was still invited and regarded as a hopeful possibility, so that efforts were made to win him over with kindness. In the spacious drawing-rooms at the duchesse de Galliera's, and in the gardens that stretched all the way from the rue de Varenne to the rue de Babylone, the French peerage would gather and the followers of both the Orleans and Bourbon branches would meet, sometimes chat, and sometimes avoid each other. One evening the duchesse de Mouchy caused a scandal when she had quite naïvely sat on a couch that the comtesse de Paris, wife of the Orleans leader, had just vacated. It was careless of me, she explained by way of apology. Yet the incident had been greeted with great joy in legitimist circles. To avoid such distractions, the duchesse de Galliera thereupon set aside one of her drawing rooms for her friends the Orleans princes so that they might be free to gather and entertain there. The legitimists never entered it.

What a lot of talk took place in those four *salons* and the ten or twenty lesser ones, where everyone babbled about the Bourbons. "We are people who have recovered our health after all the doctors had given us up," said the duchesse de Noailles. "We need to prove ourselves to ourselves at the top of our lungs." They did prove themselves to themselves by resuming as best they could all those plots and schemes which, so often in the past, had burned out and wasted the French aristocracy's fervor.

And what could they be plotting together if not some new royalist adventure? They were accustomed to royalty alone, and they believed that royalty alone would completely restore their fortunes. Six months had elapsed since the day Chambord, by refusing the tricolor, had struck the mortifying blow that had broken their spirit. Six months— a long time, given their patience and frivolity. Did that doom them to despair? No, for the temptation was too strong; it overcame everything. It would have been vain to remind them that in August the National Assembly had pledged to make a sincere effort to try out the Republic. The King came first: no promise could stand in the way of the allegiance they owed him.

Thiers believed he was indispensable—hence his self-assurance and his insolence toward the Assembly, which the nobles in the majority impatiently tolerated. But was he really indispensable? Why not have the duc d'Aumale as President? Aumale was a splendid and able prince: the Army still remembered his feats of valor in Africa; the French Academy had invited him to be a member on the basis of his historical work; his proud bearing was familiar to everyone; he was universally liked and respected. How rich in men was that vanquished France, that ancient France which had just been fatally stricken! She suffered not from poverty but rather from abundance, from a surfeit of individuals and traditions, of beliefs and loyalties—a cumulative vitality derived from historical events, each of which had been glorious and had kept its prestige. Aumale would make a perfect leader. In reply to overtures he let it be known that he was ready; if Thiers happened to falter and if the Assembly appointed him, he would answer the call. For a time Thiers seemed in danger; would he be overthrown and replaced by a prince? The majority of the Assembly seemed to favor that. But the Bourbons' hatred for the Orleans put a stop to the maneuver. Before committing themselves, the legitimists wanted to consult their prince. How would he react to such a scheme?

Actually, Chambord had just left far-off Frohsdorf,[3] where he had presided over his faithful nobility for so many years, and moved to Antwerp for a few weeks to give a hearing to his friends. How odd that a French prince who was no longer legally exiled should nevertheless continue to live beyond the frontiers as though forced into banishment by years of habit. Delegations from all the provinces came to greet him in Antwerp, bearing good wishes, homage, and gifts (Lille presented him with a white flag made of a marvelous silk fabric on which the emblems of the Church, the keys of Saint Peter, were intertwined with fleurs-de-lis). He was asked whether he would allow the duc d'Aumale to replace Thiers and be elected to the presidency. "No," he replied. "The royal house is one and indivisible and there is no room in the Republic for any of its members." Someone suggested that the title of the office might be changed and the duc d'Aumale be named Lieutenant General of the Kingdom. But Chambord would hear nothing of it: he did not find the Duke's rise in station appropriate. With a single word, he had put an end to the parliamentarians' plots.*

Now it was the Bonapartists' turn to plot. With many of them in the Army and in high positions in the civil service from which they had not been dismissed, they too

---

* Actually, his stay in Antwerp came to a sorry end. The Belgian anticlericals, probably tipped off by their French friends, organized protest demonstrations in the streets, and all their shouting and jeering made it difficult for him to entertain visitors and to hold receptions. The inhabitants of Lille followed suit and prepared a most unpleasant welcome for the returning royalist pilgrims, who had presented the Count with that white flag in which they took such pride. The *préfet* of Lille, although very amused by the idea, decided to avoid any brawls by stopping their train outside the city and having them brought home by bus rather ingloriously.

That most efficient *préfet* named Hendlé, who was to end his career in high administrative positions, was a Jew and apparently the first of the Jewish *préfets* of the Republic.

It would be interesting to have details on the careers of all Thiers's *préfets*, and all the sources necessary for such a study may be found in the personnel files in the National Archives. Unfortunately, it is difficult to obtain access to them.

had houses in which they could meet and await their chance. Although they were somewhat discreet about it, their self-confidence had not been shaken by defeat. They despised the Republic as futile anarchy, and the Monarchy as weak and antiquated. Only the Empire, they stubbornly believed, was capable of being accepted by the people and gaining the allegiance of the rural areas and the working-class suburbs: they were certain that the future was theirs. The Bonapartes alone knew how to go about it. There were rumors that Napoleon III had not given up; he would soon mount his horse and be greeted at the gates of Geneva by Bourbaki,[4] who was in command of Lyons; from Geneva to Paris, with drums beating and flags flying, it would be a pleasant stroll . . . All this was whispered about with the kind of total seriousness that the most frivolous remarks assume in *salons.* And once again the cry of alarm went up at the duchesse de Galliera's and the comtesse Duchatel's; and once again the name of Aumale was put forward. Would it not be possible to appoint him—with the Left Center's backing—not President perhaps, but Vice-President of the Republic, so that a soldier be there, by Thiers's side, prepared to mount his horse, take up arms, and oppose Bonaparte's return?

Thiers was aware of those plots and flouted them; he felt no need of a deputy vice-president to protect him. *"The Republic . . . ,"* he would say, with emphasis from the rostrum of the Assembly. It was his policy and it was his pleasure. The word never failed to be challenged. *"Provisional, provisional . . ."* was the direct reply and rectification of the *Chevau-légers,*[5] seated on the extreme Right. The two conflicting words composed a kind of refrain as they were repeated over and over, precipitating an uproar during the course of which the Left, always on the alert, would support Thiers with their applause, while the moderate Right, even the Center Right, would finally overcome their reserve and irritably join in. One day, echoing from the seats of the Extreme Right, came the

73

insult: "You old bastard!" It was meant for Thiers. Once the meeting adjourned, everyone rushed to catch the trains from Versailles to Paris; and in the crowded compartments, filled with elegant ladies who had been watching from the galleries, the quarrels and the deadly chatter continued. "Versailles is still a hornets' nest that turns the best of all people sour," wrote Picard. "No true passion, but quarrels, spite and jealousy."

In early spring, before adjourning for its Easter recess, the Assembly conceived the idea of setting up a "permanent commission." Its purpose was to keep an eye on Thiers during the intersession. Defying the commission, Thiers took advantage of the lull to reopen the Elysée and entertain in Paris. Nothing could have been more unwelcome to his Conservative opponents. Stubbornly attached to the idea of Versailles as a permanent residence, they were hostile to Paris, which Thiers, on the other hand, was trying to conciliate, to appease, and to flatter in every way. So Thiers invited Paris to his drawing rooms. He sent no invitations, but merely inserted a note in friendly newspapers, announcing that Thiers would hold open house for all those "who, because of their duties or positions, are likely to be connected with government." Ladies were accepted "on equal terms with their husbands, and needed no invitation either." Those evening parties were a great success. Ambassadors, members of the Academy, generals in full-dress uniform, industrialists, and bankers—in short, *le tout Paris*, except for those who frequented the far-off *salons* of the Faubourg—came to the rue Saint-Honoré to pay their respects to the President and hear him hold forth in small groups, and to partake of the buffet, with liveried butlers serving stingily buttered sandwiches and a few dry (very dry) cookies, and pouring out generous quantities of gooseberry juice. Theirs had never been a spendthrift. As far as expenses were concerned, he had maintained the traditions of the July Monarchy. At 11:30 P.M. the candles were blown out: to comply with the law, Thiers had to return to Versailles by the midnight train. He never failed to comply with that regulation, and he never left without a few witticisms, some taunts directed at Versailles, and some kind words to the happy Parisians; indeed, the whole affair—the open doors, the gossip, even the modest buffet—met with great success. The Parisian *bourgeoisie* was delighted with the President's visits and with the sulky reaction of the Faubourg Saint-Germain. It all seemed to hark back to the divided Paris of the Restoration years, which revived memories, made the old feel younger, and amused the young. In those days the Parisian bourgeois had backed Orleanism against the Bourbons, and they had remained Orleanist in opposition to the Empire. Thiers was their man, and they subscribed to his policy and his Republic as the most natural thing in the world.

With the opening of the spring session, the battle began where it had left off: it was still chaotic, but this time it was fiercer because of the issue at stake: the serious question of the military law.

France wanted to be armed. Her 400,000 professional soldiers had just confronted the 1,200,000 well-disciplined men who formed an integral part of a country perfectly trained and mobilized for war, and she had been defeated. She wanted to be in a position to withstand another shock and face her conqueror on equal terms. This entailed revolutionizing her institutions and customs, becoming the same as the conqueror, sending all her youth to the barracks, mingling all her children together, the rich and the poor, the mass of artisans and the university elite, and subjecting all of them to the same discipline.

The Radicals fervently championed the reform: it suited their own doctrines, and in the same breath they demanded that egalitarian military service and egalitarian education be made compulsory. They even took pleasure in thinking that the Conservative majority, reluctantly following their lead, would thereby become more unpopular. It was a recurring theme in their newspapers: the Conservative Assembly was incapable of taking the strong measures necessary for providing France with an army. On this score they met with total disappointment. Patriotic feelings and a taste for military matters, to which the parties of the Right were strongly committed, prevailed over the sense of aristocratic privileges and liberties. Indeed, the aristocratic families did not object to having their sons forced into a career which they took to instinctively and for which they themselves would have volunteered. They had all served in Gambetta's militia, and now, by joining the cadres of the new army, they would perhaps succeed in bridging the gap which for the past half century had separated them from the masses.

The guiding spirit and spokesman for the parties of the Right was the duc d'Audiffret-Pasquier. A great noble, a scholarly jurist, and a forceful orator, he had served during the Empire as president of one of the tribunals of the *Cour des Comptes*,[6] and the Imperial government had dreaded the independence of his rulings. He was the last of the *parlementaires* of the Old Regime; he carried on and honorably embodied a tradition representing a breed of men who had been altogether stifled and ostracized by democracy. It was by the remarks with which he concluded a speech devoted to the subject of business operations conducted during the last war that the Duke won over the Assembly:

> When we see before us this sad procession of heartless and unscrupulous merchants who took advantage of the country's misfortunes in order to grow rich, we wonder: Who is responsible for those people's education?
>
> When we see peasants oblivious to the fact that one does not by choice hand over one's provisions to the invader, we wonder: Who is responsible for those people's education, and what could they feel in their hearts?
>
> And when, compared to this, we see the example set

today by our restored army; when we see it working hard and silently outside the political arena; when we recall that it was this army that saved us in 1848, that it was this army that saved us in 1871, that it is this army that still stands ready to save us yet again, if necessary, from our dissensions and our folly, then we wonder if this army is not the school to which we must send all those who need to be reminded how to serve and how to love their country.

May all our children, then, go to it, and may compulsory military service become the great school for future generations!

The whole National Assembly, the Right mingling with the Left, cheered the Duke's words. But the enemy was still on French soil; France was not fully liberated. And the Germans became alarmed. They had not expected that quick a restoration of the France they had crushed; they had not expected that "this mob once known as the French nation," overcome by financial burdens and almost deprived of government, would find the energy to reform itself so radically and to completely re-arm itself. The German press, reflecting Bismarck's thinking and obeying his orders, took on a menacing tone. Here is what was printed in the *Gazette de Cologne* published in May:

We ask you, good Frenchmen and misguided politicians, not to get excited. The fact of the matter is that under the terms of the treaties, even if France paid, for example, two billion and 999,999,999 francs between now and February 28, 1876, the army of occupation would still be entitled to occupy Rheims, Epernay, Toul, Verdun, Nancy, Belfort, etc., in order to guarantee payment of the balance. As we stated earlier, we have no idea what the government's reaction will be to the French government's proposals. But if it consented to evacuation only on the condition that France pledge herself not to raise an army or build fortifications in the six departments to be evacuated, and if it reserved the right to keep its garrisons in Belfort, Toul,

\and Verdun until the indemnity has been paid, it should be perfectly free to do so! Above all, Frenchmen must not forget that we are committed to nothing.

This article was written by the ambassador himself, Count d'Arnim, whom Thiers used to meet in Paris. Bismarck, moreover, clearly expressed his government's position: the German government would consider it unsuitable for France to adopt compulsory military service.

Torn between French public opinion, which favored the reform, and Germany, which objected to it, Thiers found himself in a delicate situation. He managed to maneuver skillfully, exploiting his very own failures or, unintentionally, being served by them. Availing himself of the massive backing of French public opinion to resist the Germans, he did resist and wrote to Gontaut-Biron, France's envoy to Berlin:

> Obviously, they will not ask us to give up our independence! Never was such a suggestion made to me, either during the painful peace negotiations at Versailles or during the various other negotiations that ensued. To be sure, it was regarded as doubtful that we would be able to meet our commitments by paying the exorbitant sum of five billion. It was regarded as doubtful. Well, *we can!* We want to pay it and we shall pay it. And they would try to pick a quarrel with us because we want to restore our country, morally, materially, and politically! This had never been attempted before; no such suggestion had ever been made, and I should hope that it will not be made today!

Then, using the same wiles on the Germans that he had successfully used on the Assembly, he told d'Arnim: "If, as a result of your demands, you make my task impossible, then I resign." Whereupon d'Arnim and Bismarck raised cries of protest, for they were relying on Thiers for the payment of those billions that were indispensable to them, and his withdrawal would have seriously concerned them.

Thiers nevertheless succeeded in giving them some satisfaction without any loss of dignity. This can be attributed both to his good luck and to his skill. For the system of the well-armed nation to which the Germans supposedly objected did not really appeal to him; he himself, out of personal conviction, did not want it, and he was resolved to prevent the Assembly from adopting it. He expressed his opinion in all sincerity. The French Army was based on a law going back to 1832 which he himself had helped draft early in his career. And he still considered it the best of all possible laws. In matters of military organization, he would say, there is only one true principle, and that is the principle of the law of 1832. It stipulated that soldiers serve under the colors for seven years: that was the minimum, asserted Thiers; eight years would have been better. The parliamentary commission that studied the new bill wanted to limit military service to three years. They had sadly miscalculated, according to Thiers. Finally, a compromise was reached by settling on five years.

There were further struggles in the Assembly, which was dissatisfied with the compromise and, like the commission, wanted three years of service instead of five. Thiers protested: he would agree only to a minimum of five years. Four years was suggested, but he remained obstinate: in less than five years they would have no more soldiers, no more cadres, and no more army! Some people pointed out to him that, as he had to admit, it was the well-armed German nation that had defeated the French army. Thiers denied it. It was the German government, he insisted, that had defeated the French government; it was a good policy that had defeated a good army. An army of 800,000 men, organized according to the law of 1832, would be invincible, and it was precisely that kind of tool, or one like it, that should be forged . . .

Thiers's obstinacy was matched by that of the Assembly. The five-year law did not fulfill the need for the compulsory and universal military service which everyone from the Right to the Left strongly considered a moral, perhaps even more than a technical, necessity.* In fact, it would have been impossible to keep all of French youth confined to barracks for five years: the Army would have been too large and the cost too great. If soldiers were kept in service for five years, it would have been necessary to divide the recruits into two groups, one of which would have remained at home, while the other would have constituted an army cut off from the country—a professional army. Thiers was thus shocking people's deep feelings, which he neither respected nor understood. He was being offensive; it seemed that he took pleasure in it. Reacting to an amendment which did not seem essential, he burst out in rage and threatened to smash everything: "If the law is not voted according to my wishes, I shall not accept the responsibility of office." It was the third time in a year that he had made such a threat. The Assembly's hand was forced; it yielded. Thiers obtained 477 votes; 60 deputies from the Right voted against him; the Left shrewdly abstained. "The narrow views of the President," wrote *Le Rappel*, "are better than the bad schemes of the majority."

Thiers had nevertheless skillfully survived the storm and had managed to give Germany some semblance of satisfaction. "I was forced to struggle with the utmost vigor in order to have the essence of the system rejected," he wrote to one of the agents through whom he corresponded with Bismarck, "and I have succeeded." Yet the law that had been adopted was a good one, since it paved the way for subsequent transformations of the Army without seriously impairing the existing forces, and well-informed critics believe that no better solution could have

---

* Actually, many technical experts—chief among them, Trochu—advocated the three-year system.

been found. When in the spring of 1875 it became necessary to contemplate a new war, it was reassuring, at the early stages, to be able to rely on the old contingents that had been kept under the colors by this law of 1872.

But such diplomatic schemes and technical considerations were beyond the grasp of the country and meant little to the Assembly. Thiers's opposition to national service had been greeted with surprise, disappointment, and irritation. He had constrained, by his veto, the full play of a generous feeling, and everyone held it against him. Once again he had made the country feel that "great chill" which had saddened people like George Sand. Here is what About, the brilliant journalist, had to say:

> While our seven hundred and fifty honorable gentlemen are having a good time at their innocent revels, France is gradually losing interest in parliamentary foolishness. She realizes that the Right, the Left, and the Centers will not save her by playing prisoner's base on the green lawn of Versailles. Undermined by the perpetual conspiracy of Socialist demagoguery aimed at by the Prussians, who dream of renewing the offensive and of a second dismemberment, the nation can no longer lend her ear to the hubbub of all those long, useless debates. She is listening, as it were, to the silence observed by two or three uncommunicative men—reserved and thoughtful men— who are perhaps men of action, or so she would like to think until further notice. The first of them to break that impressive silence, the first who dares to tell the nation: Here I am! and to tell the chattering members of the Chamber: Be quiet! is almost certain to be acclaimed a savior and a master.

Who was About thinking of? Rouher,[7] the former minister of the Empire? Ducrot,[8] the monarchist soldier? The duc d'Aumale, the soldier-prince? Until recently a Bonapartist, now a wavering republican, About looked back to the recent past and had no conception of the future. Rouher, Ducrot, and the duc d'Aumale were indeed keeping quiet, but their silence was no promise of action. France was listening to another man who was far from reserved. How was it that About did not understand? I suspect that this brilliant journalist, who never succeeded in anything, was sick with jealousy, with envy.

CHAPTER 7

Gambetta

THAT man whose voice could now be heard everywhere, youthful and dazzling enough to drown out the concert of shrill and obsolete voices from Versailles and the Paris *salons*—that man was Gambetta. He has hardly been mentioned so far for the very good reason that he had hardly appeared on the scene. But here he is now, going from town to town, showing no trace of the discredit which was thought to cling to his name. Everywhere he went, he was heard and acclaimed. Whatever one may think of his policy, it must be admitted that he had a certain luminous quality, a self-confident and contagious strength which had been one of the ancient glories of France, had tarnished with the sad passage of time, and was now alive in him alone. Turning to Gambetta as a guide, I shall retrace the whole sweep of my story and look at it from a different standpoint.

Half-Gascon and half-Ligurian, descended from a wandering race of sea-faring men and merchants who, as chance would have it, had settled in the Garonne valley, Gambetta had a marvelous gift for human adventure and for getting along with his fellowmen. As a poor and merry boy of twenty, having left Cahors to seek his fortune in Paris, he had struck up a friendship with a stranger on the train before even reaching the capital, so that the moment he set foot on its pavements, he had someone to count on, he had a friend. And he was to have many more. A student in the Latin Quarter, he immediately became the prince of youth. He spoke so much, so generously, so kindly, so well! As if drawn to him by some law of nature, everyone gathered round him. Witty and lively, an extrovert who gave himself to everyone, he had soon made his way and won his place in the boulevard cafés, in the wings of the Gymnase, and at the Théâtre des Variétés. Wherever he went, he attracted an audience. His first speaking assignment at the Law School was a dull topic which he had handled so fervently that his friends not only cheered but raised him triumphantly on their shoulders. All hands were outstretched to him, and as he shook them all, he said, "Thank you! Thank you!"

A lad of this sort was cut out for public life. For quite a long time he thought perhaps of joining one of the Liberal parties, but he was not instinctively attracted to any of them. Serving the Empire was out of the question. Not that he had loathed the regime: since, deep down, he was an amiable skeptic, loathing was alien to him. But the authoritarian Empire had no need of orators, and a twenty-year-old champion of popular rights could have no career under that regime. For a time, the Orleanists interested him: he paid their leader, Thiers, a visit and was tempted. But that party lacked warmth and a popular base; it was so doctrinaire, moderate, and coldly bleak. Gambetta could not survive in an atmosphere of that type. He was asked to stand for Belleville,[1] where he was acclaimed and persuaded to run. Radical democracy was flourishing up there; he did not balk at the program that was dictated to him; he endorsed everything anyone wanted him to. So Belleville elected him to the *Corps législatif*,[2] where even his opponents were won over by his charm. Then came the war—Sedan, the 4th of September: he was thirty-five, and his turn had come to be a leader.

Gambetta

Trapped in Paris by the siege, the government of National Defense needed a representative in the provinces: Gambetta was chosen, left Montmartre in a balloon, landed in the countryside, then settled in Tours, where he soon demonstrated his burning theatrical genius and turned his delegation into a dictatorship. For four months he inspired men to action, raising and leading armies, driving them into one defeat after another, but constantly driving them, constantly inducing them to obey and to sacrifice. What flame was consuming him? Was it patriotism or his belief in democratic principles? His longing to be an histrionic orator, impassioned by the unexpected, by the grandeur of a great role? It is always difficult, if not impossible, to know what is in men's hearts. In January 1871, having taken refuge in Bordeaux, Gambetta had trained and mustered the last militias, and urging them on from the balcony, he was still able to provoke shouts of enthusiasm. To silence him and deprive him of his authority, it was almost necessary to resort to violence.

Defeat came down upon him like a bitter awakening from a wild and lovely dream: instead of the victories he had promised and proclaimed—that catastrophic downfall! Heartbroken because of the disaster and his sudden unpopularity, he withdrew from the Assembly and even left France to retire to San Sebastián, where he had ample time to dream and to catch his breath. Paris rose in revolt: he said not a word. Thiers besieged, recaptured, and carried out bloody massacres in Paris: he still kept silent. From the rostrum of the Assembly, Thiers called him unequivocally "a raging madman": still no reply. Was he discouraged, as has been alleged? It is quite possible: he, with his excitable nature, was not hardened enough for all tribulations. Once the call for immediate action had passed and the excitement of the fray had subsided, Gambetta was apt to become dejected. Did he think of abandoning politics and, following the example of his entire family—the Gambettas of Genoa, of Nice, and of Cahors—take up some kind of trade? Perhaps that capricious a thought may have crossed his mind, but it was merely a caprice. He had too much youthful vigor to yield to defeat. A great gambler who knew that circumstances change by their very nature, a great orator who knew from personal experience that words are ephemeral, he paid no mind to all the insults, he paid no attention to, and quite simply forgot, all those things which, relegated to a dead past, never bother a man of action. Besides, who knows? Thiers had perhaps insulted him only to amuse the gallery: one keen observer was of the opinion that the incident marked the beginnings of an agreement between Thiers and Gambetta.*

In June, were the French still thinking of Gambetta? An observer might well have doubted it. On July 2 the French were to vote. Would Gambetta appear as a candidate anywhere? It was not known for a long while. Yet he had given serious thought to that day on which fifty departments would elect more than a hundred deputies. For him it had major importance. Having been elected in nine constituencies in February 1871, he was now due to be replaced in eight of them.** On June 20 his candidacy had not been announced anywhere; on June 23 it was announced in Paris and Marseilles; on June 25 he appeared to speak in Bordeaux.

It was an astonishing speech. Stretched out on the sunny beaches of San Sebastián, seemingly overcome by nostalgia, yet secretly alert to all that concerned France, Gambetta had sensed, foreseen, and grasped the situation better than anyone else.

It was, indeed, an astonishing and subtle speech: without naming Thiers Gambetta was addressing him and

---

* Hector Pessard, *Mes Petits Papiers*, 2ième série, p. 137. This is an excellent book.

** He had lost his seat as deputy of the Bas-Rhin, just as his constituents had ceased to be French citizens, once the department was annexed.

calmly offered to join him. "The future belongs to the most prudent of men," Thiers had once remarked. And Gambetta: "In that case, we must be the most prudent of men; it will cost us nothing." He dwelled on the point: "To the most prudent? Precisely: it is a wager that we must take up." He was a born gambler; he liked wagers. For him to wager on being prudent at that particular juncture seemed a great risk which few would have dared to take. But why not? Gambetta wasn't mistaken; as he had so aptly remarked, it would cost him nothing to be prudent. What did that involve? Assuming a new role; and just as Gambetta liked all kinds of games, he also liked all kinds of roles. Doubtless even the role of a prudent man suited him. He had a kindly disposition and derived no pleasure from smashing everything and spreading fear. In October 1869 he had written to a friend: "The Left must give the reassuring impression of being altogether prepared to represent a tangible future, replacing what now exists and is now ending." He had thus revealed his true thoughts and could revert to them easily.

To return to his speech. Underlying all those boastful words there still quivered the same lively intelligence that was never confounded. France at the time seemed irremediably split between the large republican cities and the reactionary provincial rural areas. The future has shown that it was all on the surface. Gambetta realized that at the time. He denied that there was any profound division or that it would shape the future. "For my part," he declared, "I believe in the republican future of the provinces and the rural areas. It is a matter of a short period of time and more extensive education." His emphasis was on education; educating the masses was what the republicans wanted first of all. What Gambetta proclaimed, then, was a sober and provincial Republic, trained and disciplined by educational institutions. From that evening on—the evening which marked his return to politics—he perceived, and explained in words, the long course of future events.

His speech was commented upon everywhere. In Paris it was his prompt conversion and his bold tactics so masterfully carried out that were admired. Thiers's paper, *Le Bien Public*, combined a few reproaches with strong praise. "The speech which established the Empire was made in Bordeaux, and Bordeaux had hailed it. Now Bordeaux has hailed Gambetta." [3] Quite clearly, the implication was that by hailing Gambetta, Bordeaux had just established the Republic.

Bordeaux had been only a stopover, and the speech, a mere phrase uttered on the way to Paris. Gambetta arrived there without delay, and, as an improvised candidate, began to organize his campaign. On the morning of July 2 the Parisian electors were informed by a poster: "Adding Gambetta's name to all the ballots—Gambetta, who belongs to no electoral lists—means establishing the Republic through conciliation; it means creating governmental stability by providing the Republic with two leaders, one representing the Whig faction, the other the Tory faction. GAMBETTA AND THIERS: with them, all doors will be closed to the monarchist plotters."

He was elected by more than 60,000 votes—an astonishing comeback. Here again, *Le Bien Public* makes for curious reading. "We wish to know where he is heading, what he wants, what he is," wrote the anonymous editor who had probably listened to Thiers the night before. "We sense that he has boundless ambition, a talent for altogether neglecting in practice the principles he advocates in theory, and a positive determination to succeed in spite of that fact. We wish to be enlightened. At a time when France can no longer afford to make mistakes without running the risk of perishing, personalities of this sort are terrifying." *A talent for altogether neglecting in practice the principles he advocates in theory:* there can be no doubt that those words were

Thiers's, and drawing on his rich store of experience, it was a great compliment that Talleyrand's disciple—that old Ulysses from Marseilles—paid his junior. All the rest of the article is extremely kind. "Gambetta has been really something, and he will always be somebody." On the whole, wrote Hector Pessard, the article was interpreted as a visiting card left by Thiers at Gambetta's. .

What would Gambetta do in the Assembly? He made his first appearance there like a formidable wild beast. Piled into the boxes that served as a spectators' gallery (in Versailles the Assembly was held in a theater), the fashionable women, staring through their opera glasses, awaited him and thought about him with curious excitement. And suddenly there he was, the one-eyed champion of people's rights, casually dressed and walking with a vigorous stride. "It's not a man," said a lady spectator, "it's a wild beast." To which, Juliette Adam,[4] sitting beside her, replied, "What will you say, madam, when he begins to roar?" But he didn't roar much. He was despised by the Right and feared by the Center. With everyone on the watch for him, interrupted after every sentence, and upset by the general ill-will, good old Gambetta (who only gave the appearance of being a wild beast) lost all his oratorical zest.

He soon consoled himself, however: the National Assembly, the Assembly of Versailles, all the dukes and marquesses, the prelates and stiff-necked bourgeois, socialites such as Mme. de Troubetzkoy and the duchesse de Galliera—that whole group can hardly be said to have represented France. Gathered round him were his friends —his newspaper colleagues and his café companions—people like Ranc and Spuller, Allain-Targé and Challemel-Lacour, Adam and his young wife, the beautiful and enthusiastic Juliette. It would be well to pause and examine this new group, to see how it lived, to listen to the lawyers Spuller and Allain-Targé, and to the *normalien* Challemel-

Lacour, that bitter and ambitious intellectual in search of power and glory outside the world of letters and the university. Adrien Hébrard, later to become editor of *Le Temps* for such a long while, could not be far away, but a man of his great intelligence had both the good taste and the talent for being invisible and present at the same time. That team stood for the whole Third Republic. Spuller represented Protestantism, although his good-natured manner, typical of Baden, was not, in fact, quite suitable to his position. Indeed, undiluted Calvinism was never to have direct access to Gambetta.*

Before the war, during the Empire, those men would have been overheard exchanging radical, almost revolutionary ideas, but they had now forgotten them and would never express them again, for they promptly forsook old ideas. Did they even recall that in a true Republic the civil servants, judges, and elected officials should everywhere replace the *préfets* and *sous-préfets*, the magistrates and career officials of the old monarchies? No, they had tasted power, were eager to get it back as soon as possible, and relegated the Belleville program[5] to a past which they had neither the wish, nor indeed the time, to think about very much.

What concerned them was the future. They sensed the birth of a new France—by no means a working-class France (they knew and understood almost nothing about the rising forces of big industry and the people involved in it), but rather a hard-working and popular France, in the eighteenth-century sense of those words—a country of small workshops and small pieces of landed property,**

---

* Lacking here was the Jewish element, which was soon to be introduced by Joseph Reinach. But Judaism does not seem to have played a very active part in the early years of the republican regime. The Jewish republicans, such as Crémieux, Millaud, and Naquet (the latter's cousin), were Jews from Provence. The 60,000 Parisian Jews, who were of foreign extraction, had been absolutely pampered by the July Monarchy and the Second Empire, so that both the stock market and big business were either Orleanist, as in the case of the Rothschilds, or Bonapartist, as in the case of the Péreires. The idea of a Republic that moneyed interests might find acceptable had not yet emerged.

** An excellent observer, M. Salvador de Madaraga, has drawn attention to how the word *petit* is used by the French. "Mon petit" is a term of friendship;

liberated at last from the tinsel of courts and churches, from such trimmings as miters and stoles. Perhaps their task would be difficult, but they were united in their resolution to undertake it and confident that the country would not let them down. They knew they could count on aid and encouragement from many quarters. Universal suffrage did not strike them as that dreadful force which had terrified Renan, Taine, and Flaubert, nor as the still enigmatic and troubling force which Thiers thought he was capable of controlling. They saw it as something altogether different—a force they had observed at very close range and had dealt with—and they now began to realize that there were means by which they could tame, handle, and maneuver it. Universal suffrage would not be abolished, it would be conjured away, said Ernest Picard. That phrase, which had offended Taine's puritanism, would have been understood by Gambetta, and he would have greeted it with a chuckle. The war had provided him and his friends with a rewarding experience. It had led them to the provinces, which had hitherto been neglected. Spuller and Ranc accompanied Gambetta to Tours, where Ranc ran the national police for him—a job that molds a man. Challemel-Lacour served as the *préfet* of Lyons. And he must be singled out from the rest of the team, for although its spokesman was Gambetta, Challemel-Lacour would seem to have been its principal adviser.* As *préfet* of that troublesome city of Lyons, he managed to remain at his post despite five months of turbulence and riots. The revolutionaries controlled city hall: shrewdly resisting and scheming, he somehow or other managed to govern under the Red flag, ensuring order and providing for the

"le petit soldat" is a flattering expression. And shrewd businessmen gave such titles as *Le Petit Journal* and *Le Petit Parisien* to the most widely read newspapers of the Third Republic. Those who under the Old Regime were condescendingly called "les petites gens [the little people or the little man]" no longer blush when they are described as such. The word apparently lost its pejorative sense when that class rose to power.

* See Appendix II.

needs of the Army. If he had remained in Paris, he would never have learned many of the things he had been taught by Lyons. There he encountered a breed of men that had no counterpart in Paris—opinionated but staunch, stubborn, and diligently active on committees, bound to their party by those ties, ambitions, and also clearly-defined hatreds which develop in small, closely-knit groups and give even the most mediocre people the kind of strength that proves useful.

Here, then, are those noncommissioned officers of the republican army that were to transform France. They emerged, after eighteen years under the Empire, as mature and disciplined men. Directly following the 4th of September, they came out in the open everywhere, setting up Committees of National Defense which, immediately after the war, were so easily and promptly transformed into electoral committees that their initial and concealed purpose stood revealed. What were the origins of those men who were capable of acting in concert throughout the entire country? The unanimity and confidence of their actions tempts one to think that they had been backed by some previously existing organization, and the only one that comes to mind is Freemasonry, which had been tolerated by the Second Empire and was destined, as we know, to play a considerable role in the future. That view was put forward by Barante before the Assembly: the municipal commissions controlling the great cities in September 1871 had grown out of secret societies. Behind Gambetta and his friends, one can sense the presence of Freemasonry, and since, after all, every regime must have a ruling class, it was Freemasonry that was preparing to furnish the Republic, which it established and consolidated, with its cadres, its direction, its caution, and its spirit.*

---

* On Freemasonry, see a curious article by About reprinted in his *Causeries* (2:363), which is a protest against its recent excommunication by Rome. About, who was himself a Freemason, had been briefed, and probably

Therefore, even if the gentry in Versailles managed to curb Gambetta's eloquence, what did it matter? Their power was undermined and their angry protests lacked any real force—of that, Gambetta and his friends were certain. They could operate outside the Assembly, bringing together the scattered republicans and educating them from afar. They believed it was indispensable to have a newspaper of their own. *Le Temps*, until recently an Orleanist paper, rejected them; *Le Rappel*, edited by Victor Hugo's friend Vacquerie, still had a Romantic tone and tradition that they were anxious to avoid;* and *Le Siècle* was controlled by its own secret editorial staff, which appears to have been strictly Masonic. Gambetta and his friends needed their own home. They found no lack of support: overtures were made to Thiers, who discreetly let it be known that he favored the enterprise, and money was soon forthcoming. Scheurer-Kestner[6] secured a substantial amount from the republican and Protestant industrial

commissioned to write the article, by the Secretariat of the Grand Orient. In it he pleads the innocence, kindliness, and benevolence of the most inoffensive of all fraternal societies. "The Masonic lodge," wrote About, *"which is very useful in provincial towns, consists of a small group of men who represent a variety of political and religious views and who gather together in the spirit of '89."* Note the reference to the provinces: it is included in almost every document relating to the origins of the Third Republic. "How could Freemasonry be seditious?" asked About; "the Emperor himself appoints its Grand Master!" But what About is careful not to point out is that apart from the Grand Master imposed from above, the executive council, an elected body, is meant to protect the secret liberties of the lodges. Toward the end of the Second Empire, a great number of them were won over to atheism. (On this subject, see Gaston Martin, *Manuel d'histoire de la franc-maçonnerie française*, p. 207.) The lodges in Lyons ran the atheist campaign. Here again, it was Lyons that spearheaded the entire movement in the provinces.

Edmond About himself would be interesting to study in this context. A Bonapartist under the Empire, he was to be seen at the Princesse Mathilde's and in the entourage of the Prince Napoleon: he was thus a Bonapartist and anticlerical. After the collapse of the Empire, he began drifting over to republican circles, and around 1880 he was one of the writers for the Opportunist party. Many average Freemasons appear to have followed the same pattern, remaining consistently anticlerical, but nonetheless consistently alive to the shiftings of power.

* Actually, Thiers suspended *Le Rappel* for a long time on the grounds that it was too favorably disposed toward the defeated Commune, so that there was a void to be filled and a readership to be won over.

families of Mulhouse. As early as October, the first issues of *La République Française* began to appear.

The first issues clearly foreshadowed much that was to come. Everything was immediately visible—both ideas and people. As for the people—those who wrote and those who read—there they were, just as we might have expected. The first editorial (it was anonymous, but we know it was written by Challemel-Lacour) was addressed directly to the provincial militants, to the members of those societies that had defended first the nation, then the Republic. "It is to those societies," wrote Challemel-Lacour, "that we largely owe the victories of the municipal elections of April, the legislative elections of July, the departmental elections of October . . ." Could it have been aimed, in a veiled way, at Freemasonry, which was never mentioned? Perhaps. Who belonged to those societies? "They brought together the *petite bourgeoisie*, the artisans, and the workers." Here, then, were the masters of the future, listed as always according to a time-honored hierarchy. It was an accurate description, repeatedly confirmed by subsequent events. At the same time as *La République Française* first came out, the elections of October 8 for the *Conseils Généraux* confirmed the power of popular groups in many areas. Gambetta's comment was as follows: "In many cantons universal suffrage has rejected the former officials of all parties—officials worn out either morally or intellectually—and has favored their replacement by new men. From day to day, the people— the *petite bourgeoisie*, the workers and peasants—see more clearly that politics are closely related to their interests; they want representation that reflects those interests; and soon they will represent themselves. It's a revolution." Gambetta was right: it was indeed a revolution, was already turning into a self-conscious revolution, and was expressing itself through the provincial press, which, although neglected at the time, was destined to play such a great part in the future. "It is the provincial press which deserves most of the credit for the work that has been accomplished," according to that anonymous writer whom we have identified as Gambetta speaking through Challemel-Lacour.

> The Republican newspapers in the provinces have, alone, seized and kept a firm hold on the drifting reins of public opinion . . . Behind each of those newspapers, we can catch a glimpse of the men who are backing them . . . Our thoughts are with those dedicated groups, and we should like to encourage them—encourage that unknown France, democracy's hope and strength . . . We make no secret of the fact: it is with that section of the press that we are most especially anxious to establish close and permanent relations.

This is a remarkable example of people instinctively knowing where strength lies. Gambetta and his friends had placed their trust wisely: they had reached down to the bed-rock that was to bear the future. The legitimists looked back to the France of 1820, stubbornly believing that it still existed; the Orleanists looked back just as stubbornly to the France of 1845; Thiers was undecided, but when all is said and done, he still had his mind on the French masses of 1850. Gambetta and his friends were not undecided: as early as 1871, they were discerning and perceiving the France of 1880 or of 1904; they anticipated Lyons' newspaper *Le Progrès* and Toulouse's *La Dépêche*; they deeply inhaled the air coming to them from the rue Cadet, where the Second Empire had indulgently set up the Freemasons—the very air of the era that was then beginning.

Ideas were becoming perceptible as well. There, in the background, were two ideologies: the first bequeathed by the Revolution of 1848, the second by that other revolution that had been brewing in France in 1869, but which had been suppressed for a few months by the war.

1848 had left, as a legacy, the great dogmas—equality and fraternity for all, universal peace and progress; 1869 had left, as a legacy, a simplistic form of rationalism, scientism, and humanism, which, without undermining the great dogmas, had reformulated them in new language that was crude and badly structured. But no matter! Myths have a stubborn resilience, and once they have been assimilated by the masses, they take root and flourish in their imagination, which has no use for the laws of logic or the invalidation of facts.

But all that scientism and the idealism remained in the background, scarcely affecting the men who were determined to act. Their objective was to consolidate the Republic, to win over the masses, who were still not only intimidated but easy to intimidate. Thus their first concern was not to frighten the masses. If we try to define their program, we are struck favorably by its very simplicity: there was no reference to fiscal reform, no reference to social reform: since, on two occasions, Socialism had threatened the very existence of the Republic, it had to be rigidly quarantined; there was not a word about the Communards, who were being led to landing stages on the river and shot: having sealed their fate by making a deal with Thiers, the republicans were not to go back on a deal that useful. Last was the struggle against the Church: the party turned all its energies to it. For the republicans, whatever they were—lower-class, bourgeois, or intellectual —the Church was the institution that had to be crushed. It could be attacked without alarming those interests which, out of caution, had to be treated tactfully and, what was most important, without unduly impeding the maneuvers of old Thiers. "With the exception of anticlericalism," wisely noted the political commentator of *Le Correspondent*, "the Republic is lacking in raw materials." What the republicans used as a weapon in their struggle against the Church was the principle of popular education, to be carried out by passing a law establishing free, compulsory, and secular schooling in France. The experience of the war introduced new arguments to reinforce the old: on the grounds that it was not the Prussian officer but the Prussian schoolmaster who had won the war, the instrument of a French restoration was to be the secular schoolmaster. The republicans failed to note that the Prussian schoolmaster was a cog in an altogether Conservative administration which granted the churches their rightful place, and also that the revolutionary school of their dreams would have difficulty surviving as a national institution. They failed to note that fact, and in any case, whether they realized it or not, their chief concern lay elsewhere. They were in love with universal principles, not with the country. *Free, compulsory, and secular schooling:* for ten years those words were to resound like a trinity, a magic charm. Secular education was their goal: to prevent the child from evading it, it had to be compulsory, and to make compulsory education efficient, it had to be free.

La *République Française* was a solemn newspaper, so solemn that it would not be tolerated in our times. Even today's *Le Temps* publishes columns that try to be amusing, but *La République Française* was never amused. France had been gay under the Empire, and *La République Française* condemned everything that had been viewed with favor under that guilty regime. People were witty under the Second Empire; so *La République Française* would not be. People were skeptical under the Second Empire; so *La République Française* would be dogmatic. Every issue contained some very long feature-articles devoted to literature, history, and science, all of them doctrinaire in tone and ponderously logical. Enthusiasm was strongly suspect: the Romantics had overdone it, and their errors were now being repudiated. They had used the exclamation mark liberally: it was now prohibited. And anonymous articles were the rule: the Second Empire had encouraged sparkling individualism: *La République Française* stifled it. The principles were sound, but cold and uninspiring, and would have made no impact on the public. The heavy-handed conductor directing the entire orchestra was Challemel-Lacour, the university man, the power behind the throne, "the oracle who uttered conclusive words," as Juliette Adam described him.

But beside Challemel-Lacour stood Gambetta.

Gambetta didn't like to write. He had a lazy hand, and the printed word bored him. His genius lay entirely in the spoken word. Since it was stifled in the Assembly, it had to ring out elsewhere. Would he be allowed to harangue the crowds? With half of France under a state of siege, Thiers's authority was in fact discretionary. He had the right to grant or withhold permission; no one would have questioned any of his decisions. There is no doubt that he was consulted on the matter. And, actually, he had no objection to Gambetta's being heard out. Gambetta could go right ahead and take wing. But not in the direction of Paris or Lyons: no one was to hear him there. Thiers probably didn't want him to arouse and excite the two capital cities. But as for the rest of the country, he was free. And it was the warmth of his words spoken throughout the land that was to decide the struggle and bring victory.

On November 16 Gambetta was in Saint-Quentin. One year earlier, the city had bravely defended itself against the Germans, and Gambetta had been invited there to celebrate its powers of resistance. The anniversary celebration, however, was only a pretext. With a shrewd phrase which preceded and foreshadowed another well-known phrase, Gambetta was able to divert his audience. "Let us never mention the foreigners," he said, "but let it be understood that they are not forgotten." And launching out immediately into a political speech, he picked up the themes of his Bordeaux speech, but even more boldly. He dared to add a few sharp innuendos aimed at the Assembly and the Church. The latter, he said, should be separated not only from the State but also from the schools, and the religious orders should no longer teach the young. "If you entrust them with education, you will discover that, when the time comes to call upon the energy of men brought up by such teachers, when you want to incite all the people to action and remind them of their duties as citizens, when you want to arouse their spirit of sacrifice and of devotion to the nation, you will find yourself faced with a weakened and debilitated species of human being, resigned to submitting to every misfortune as if it were ordained by Providence." At this point, the published account of his speech includes the words: "created a sensation." Gambetta, with that passionate oratory he exploited so masterfully, had surely provoked a sensation. So faith had a debilitating effect on people! He had indeed created *such* a sensation that prompt, vigorous approval was given—even by outsiders, in fact by all the party newspapers. Mgr. Dupanloup wanted to reply to the charge. Gambetta had said that schools should be separated from the Church. And Catholic schools had been created by the old bishop; they were his pride and joy: he had come to their rescue in 1850, and was prepared to do so again. Mgr. Dupanloup was not an ultramontane; Veuillot had always been his enemy. He had no desire to see the Church control the State, but he wanted it to continue guiding the minds and souls of men and wished the State to recognize its supremacy in that domain. His reply appeared in the newspaper *Le Français.* To what metaphysical experience, asked the Bishop, would you dare subject the children? What ethics, what universal learning, would you presume to teach them? You will destroy peoples' souls, you will destroy France . . .

But in this bitter exchange of hurtful truths, the Bishop had met his match and received a harsh reply. The rebuttal was probably written by Challemel-Lacour, not Gambetta: "If France needs to be regenerated, who, then, corrupted her? Could it, by any chance, have been secular education, which is still nonexistent? . . . Your rule will destroy us altogether, and your Catholicism in the process, unless we soon have an independent Assembly and statesmen who are resolute enough to free us from it" (November 30).

Both that first speech and the debate which followed gave Gambetta a beautiful start. In January he was in Marseilles, among those people of Provence who loved him and in a region he himself loved as a warmer and more personal fatherland. The *préfet* Kératry managed to forbid him to speak, and the crowd gathering outside his windows had to be dispersed by the cavalry. In Toulon he spoke, and as a southerner addressing fellow southerners, he expressed himself forcefully. "Republican democracy *is* France," he said. "The Assembly must therefore be dissolved: this unexpectedly created body is oblivious not only to clear warnings but to all the evidences of popular sovereignty." In April he was in Angers and, as calmly as possible, in order to win over the calm Angevins, he continued to attack the Assembly, but his speech combined glowing praise for the peasant landowners and the new army that would reunite France's divided sons, as well as emphatic praise for Thiers. Ten days later, speaking in Le Havre, and won over to Norman caution, he uttered the celebrated words: "Believe me, there is no social remedy because there is no social issue. Some progress should be made every day, but there is no question of an immediate solution."

How prudent Belleville's champion of the people's rights had become, and how well he was abiding by the terms of his wager! Perhaps too well; perhaps he was showing too much good will. There were times when Thiers thought so. "Be prudent," he would tell his friends the Adams, "but not too prudent, or you will give the impression of adopting my policy and I yours, so that the monarchists would be even more exasperated." In fact, it was becoming difficult to distinguish between the two leaders' policies, as one of them became increasingly moderate, while the other grew more spirited. Having united to fight the Assembly, what was the extent of their alliance? Thiers and Gambetta: when, in June, Gambetta had dared to link his name with Thiers's, it had surprised everyone. Some seven or eight months later, no one was any longer surprised. In the spring of 1872 the whole of France linked the two names and gradually began to identify one with the other.

In Le Havre and Angers, as well as in Toulon, Gambetta went on repeating his battle cry against the Assembly, calling for its dissolution. What that consummate gambler wanted first of all was to create a breach in order to overthrow the Assembly, which ignored him, and to open wide the gates to the future.

◆§ CHAPTER 8 §◆

Radicals Victorious
in Rural Areas

In June the Radicals won a victory. There were three
electoral contests, in the Nord, the Somme, and the
Yonne, in which the radical republicans had entered their
candidates against the monarchists and liberal Conservatives. It soon became evident that the liberal Conservatives, squeezed in between the two extremist parties,
would be beaten, and that if one were to vote usefully, the
choice was narrowed down to those two parties. It also
soon became evident that Thiers had made his choice: he
would support the Radicals. They won all three seats.

This caused a great sensation. The July elections had
taken place too early and under the pressure of so many
events, under the strain of such growing anxiety, that there
had been no time either to be moved by them or to
understand them. Besides, they were confusing in themselves and their significance had remained obscure. The
same was true for the January elections: the nature of
them was not clear. The country had voted for the
government and for M. Thiers's Republic, neither of
which had yet become the sort of thing that would alarm
the Conservatives. The South and the large cities had
voted Red: that had been expected. But the June elections
were a different matter. Not only had Gambetta won a

clear-cut victory, but he had won it in an area north of the Loire—in the valley of the Yonne and in the provinces of Picardy and Flanders. The peasants, then, followed the lead of the workers, and the North followed the South— an event of double significance to which Thiers had clearly contributed.

It was the peasants' defection which was particularly striking, and that it was a cause for astonishment is a bit surprising. In point of fact, the peasantry had a great revolutionary past; if that had properly been recalled, it would have served as a warning. In 1789, roused by the entire country, the peasants had broken into their masters' châteaux and burned the manorial rolls, which had been the object of their hatred for ages; they had broken free from the crushing feudal ties that were keeping them from owning their land, and their countless, recurring insurrections, constantly erupting everywhere, had been one of the secret strengths of the Revolution, contributing to its triumph, for the *bourgeoisie* would have had a hard time conquering the cities. Yet for years the peasantry had appeared satisfied with its gains, and when around 1830 the industrial workers had started another revolution, the peasantry's reaction was first indifference, then hostility. The workers' revolution was a Socialist phenomenon about which the peasants, who were strongly attached to their rights and their newly acquired property, understood absolutely nothing. In 1848 the peasantry had united with the *bourgeoisie* and the nobility to defend their patrimony—a pleasant memory to Conservatives, who relied on it. But was the alliance of 1848 really as strong as was alleged? Hardly. As early as 1849, after the alarm caused by February and June had subsided, and even more so in 1850, the Radicals (who in those days were called "the Reds") had managed to make themselves heard in rural areas. As a new blaze began to smolder and flare up, fear gripped the châteaux. After the blaze had been smothered by the Bonapartist *coup d'état*, people began to breathe more easily and forgot. What happened then? No one clearly understood, for they did not quite realize to what extent the Second Empire, a regime created by peasant democracy, had remained loyal to the peasantry, favoring and strengthening it. The badly extinguished fire had left ashes and embers. The statesmen of the Second Empire were careful: they paid attention to the needs of the peasant. He was the first to profit from the wide distribution of accumulated and liberally dispensed material assets that marked the years 1850–1860. He was provided with roads, numerous railway stations, the telegraph, and postage at twenty centimes. His thatched roof was now covered with tile and slate, and on his table, white bread took the place of dark buckwheat bread or thick chestnut porridge. The improvement in his material lot was matched by moral progress. He was entitled to the vote; he had made one emperor, and perhaps the day would come when he would be asked to endorse his successor. In those days the peasant constituted the French masses; he expressed himself by means of the plebiscite. The *préfet*, therefore, had to please him and used all his ingenuity to that effect, granting his drafted son one- or two-month furloughs, which were far more generous than the leaves granted by the July Monarchy. The general councillor and the deputy listened to his requests and intervened on his behalf. They heard all his grievances: the tax collector had been too demanding; the road engineer had been overscrupulous; the *gendarme* had filed too harsh a report about some café squabble . . . The Bonapartist deputy was familiar with all those petty problems, and his duty was to make sure that State authority was not too hard on the little man. "Finally, the voice of authority spoke to him more politely," wrote J.-J. Weiss, whose two remarkable pages I have just summarized, sometimes quoting Weiss's own words.[1] "Gentlemen no longer addressed him as 'Hey, my good man!' The French peasant is proud, sensitive,

and shrewd. He fully understood those shades of meaning."

All that, which took place in little-known social areas,
either went unnoticed or was too quickly forgotten, and
the deputies elected in 1871, who had resumed their old
ways once again and in many places, started saying, "Hey,
my good man!" Whether they were nobles or Notables,
they neglected their duties to the people or performed
them very inadequately. The peasants had thereupon
taken offense, and as republican propaganda fanned the
glowing ashes and embers of former revolutions, they had
begun to wonder whether perhaps the time had not come
to consolidate their gains and seek some new ones. They
were no longer alarmed by Socialism, which concerned the
workers, who in any case had been crushed by Thiers in
Paris. Why go on fearing them, thereby playing into the
hands of the masters? Conditions in the villages did not
necessarily conform to the desires of the masses. Had their
ancestors, who had fought for land and liberty, really freed
the land and the population? Had they been altogether
victorious? The sharecroppers of central and southwestern
France wearily kept track of the obligations and *corvées*
listed in their leases, which grew more complex and
burdensome with every renewal. Those obligations and
corvées often reminded the old-timers of former feudal
obligations painstakingly revived by their masters and their
bailiffs, the lawyers. Could nothing be done to improve
that situation? The small landowners also had their
grievances. Both share-croppers and small landowners were
weary of being constantly reduced to the status of a
humiliated lower class and constantly forced to labor, pay
their dues, and salute their betters. As the newspaper and
the small republican book that were read aloud in the
wineshop stirred up their grievances, the peasants felt
rising and swelling within them the old yearning to resist
the nobles or Notables who owned the estates by bullying

them or refusing them. The simplest way of bullying them was to reject their candidates and to vote for the most radical ones. Later on, they would see what they could ask for and obtain.

Gambetta had called it a revolution; and indeed, it was a revolution, still the old one, the great revolution, now resumed in a new form and advancing at a new pace—the slow pace of the peasantry. This time, there were no novelists, no poets, no heroic leaders in search of danger. Even in Gambetta's speeches, what caution and what shrewd politics were mixed in with the romantic glitter! Take, for example, the case of Blanqui,[2] who had been condemned to prison on Mont-Saint-Michel. What crime had he committed? In July 1870, a week after the declaration of war, Blanqui, along with a few of his friends, had rashly tried to launch the same republican revolution that Gambetta and his friends were to carry out successfully in September. In November, in a besieged Paris which, according to him, was inadequately protected, he had once again attempted his *coup*. What had he done that the others hadn't? But to speak in his defense would have been compromising. Gambetta carefully refrained from doing so. He ignored Blanqui, just as he had ignored the Paris Commune and his Belleville constituents, who were being massacred and exiled. Where were the crowds, the banners, the parades? The idea now was not to demonstrate but to vote—to cast one's ballot, which had been drawn up by the committee, and to vote in accordance with the advice of the local republicans—the veterinarian, the wine merchant. In addition to Freemasonry, which had always been a secret society, there was now also the "Ligue de l'Enseignement." The League had been founded in 1866 by Jean Macé with the humble assistance of Jules Larmier, a Parisian police constable; Antoine Mamy, head conductor on the railway line from Lyons to Nogent-sur-Marne; and Jean Petit, a stone-cutter from the Ternes district in Paris.* But Jean Macé was a Mason, and Freemasonry rapidly gained control of the newly created League, spread its ideology, and, peripherally, broadened its cadres.**

The electoral masses had definitely changed: they no longer constituted that bewildered mob which had at times voted for the Empire, at times for the Republic, and at times for the Church; they now formed a regiment that obeyed orders and marched toward a fixed goal beyond which lay other goals that were yet unannounced. The French people were changing hands and were perhaps also undergoing a change in spirit. What would be their new face, their new fate, their new fortune? Surely the first signs of the changing era, which we were seeking earlier, are now not only visible but clearly multiple.

Oddly enough, it would seem that contemporaries gauged the importance of the phenomenon. They studied it, commented upon it, and defined the problems it entailed. The *Débats* of October 28, 1872, published a remarkable article on the subject. "Everyone is amazed," it said, "at the enormous changes that have taken place since the Restoration and at the underlying recurrent forces which brought them about." The anonymous writer went back over the whole story: 1830 marked the fall of the aristocracy; 1848, the fall of the *bourgeoisie*. At the

---

* Jean Macé, *La Ligue de l'enseignement à Blebenheim* (Paris, 1870). ·

** See a report from the Freemasons of Gray in the *Bulletin du Grand Orient* (1871), p. 333. "In May 1870," they wrote, "we spontaneously launched a Teachers' Confederation club known as the 'Cercle Graylois.'" Although it was disbanded during the war, the club resumed its activities immediately afterward. "The lodge does not act in its own name, but has created a peripheral association that is free and self-directing, and to which it belongs. Moreover, the lodge stimulates, helps, and supports it, and provides it with means for taking action by contributing the energetic and capable men it needs to carry on its work." The report goes on to point out that the Cercle Graylois asked the inhabitants of rural communes to their meetings at the county seat, and that it was looking into the possibilities for setting up evening reading clubs and village libraries. Indeed, the report provides us with a very complete sketch of the way in which the countryside was permeated with the principles of Freemasonry.

time, it had seemed that the future belonged to the workers, but that class misused its strength and discredited itself by its rebellion in June '48 and its capitulation in December '51; and when, in March '71, it reappeared in the foreground, it was only to directly discredit itself again by another rebellion. That left the peasantry as the only class almost entirely innocent of that "political guilt" which, as Littré noted sadly but forcefully, colored the whole history of France, so that power fell into its hands. Now it was a fact; its power was established. How would the peasants use it? asked the *Débats*:

Will they assert their separate identity by reforming their rural communes, excluding all alien elements and governing to their own advantage and to the detriment of the big landowners? Will they introduce their own brand of decentralization which would cause the State and national unity to be supplanted by a vast number of communes?* Instead of fretting, like the urban workers, and organizing labor, will they, like sensible men, reform taxation by shifting the burden from the poor to the wealthy, or from property to the public welfare? In short, will we have a selfish and miserly "rurocracy," or will France find security within a framework shaped by its lowest class? Will we finally achieve a social order combining both change and security and in which rural interests would be the goals of democracy? Who knows? And it is painful not to know, since it is our future which is at stake.

Many people were disturbed about that unknown future. Would it consist of bleak years filled with bloodshed or merely years of mediocrity? Or would they be happy and healthy years? Renan was one of the first to perceive and to predict the power of the peasantry. As a

---

* Such fears, which today would seem incredible, were provoked by the Communalist rebellion in Paris, nurtured by a federalist ideology that had proved to have some influence in the southern departments during the war, and was to prove to have great influence on the federalist revolution that was destroying and tearing apart republican Spain at that time.

candidate for the *Corps législatif* in 1869, he had had
dealings with it and had clearly discerned the strength and
importance of the peasant voter, a newcomer in French
history. "A commonplace government, of no great stature," he wrote at the time, "a frank desire for liberty, a
great thirst for equality, a firm resolve to make no
sacrifices for anything but tangible interests—such, to my
mind, is the peasant's view in those regions of France
where the peasantry is, as they say, most progressive."
Renan's diagnosis, as expressed here, was very restrained
and not in the least alarming. But in 1869 universal
suffrage had been controlled by a strong government.
What could one predict in that year of 1872, when the
popular vote was challenging a crippled State? Would the
frank desire for liberty perceived by Renan remain frank?
Would the peasantry be able to resist the pressures and
promptings of demagogues? There were some reassuring
answers to that question. Louis Latrade, a deputy from
Corrèze who corresponded with Thiers and was a very
moderate observer, refused to be worried. It was at the end
of an electoral campaign that he wrote to the President.
He had seen things at close range—the Notables being
jostled, the peasants challenging them with their own
candidates—and he was not alarmed. "This election," he
wrote, "shows that the people in our rural areas are firmly
resolved not to be influenced by those who had led them
and so often deceived them, and will obey only their own
promptings. They have understood the value of their vote
and, in this respect, are beginning to long for political
liberty—a feeling in which they had been totally lacking in
the past." Then, commenting on the election, he asked:

> Does it have dangerous implications for the future? No,
> Mr. President. The inhabitants of our rural areas are
> almost all landowners, and their overriding concern is to
> extend their property. By nature, they are all conservatives
> *par excellence*, and thus each one is anxious to enjoy the

fruits of his labor, and to share them with his children. No government can have a more solid foundation than the one which is based on their trust, and it is up to you to provide the republican government with that foundation.*

Here was a guarantee of stability: what a blessing and what a reassuring hope! Nothing could have been more welcome at the time, even if it meant paying the price of some mediocrity. France would stop being a war-like nation? So be it; what harm could it do? It meant an end to victories; it also meant an end to disasters! France would stop being an elegant nation? So be it; many people were resigned to that. France's elegance had often masked a most dangerous frivolity. Its disappearance might prove to be a blessing. The eighteenth century had been elegant, as had the Second Empire, and both had been disastrous; France had paid a high price for her elegance in terms of ruination and bloodshed. Whatever glamour France would have lost might perhaps be compensated by other advantages. What she would lose in sophistication, she would gain in working-class and intellectual power, and her people, the humiliated and suffering masses, would gain in dignity, wisdom, and culture. In liberal bourgeois circles, great hopes were raised by the prospect.

Thus, from the standpoint of the *Débats* and *Le Temps*, it would seem that the election was greeted more with concern than with any real anxiety. Everyone realized that the word *radical* was after all no more than a word, three resounding syllables that no longer startled the peasant voter, who associated them with a new political sentiment, very different from the high-flown radicalism of the 1848 clubs or the harsh and negative radicalism of the 1869 clubs. Amidst Gambetta's entourage in the Assembly, wasn't there already talk about "a governmental radicalism"? If the Radicals were transforming the peasantry, then the peasantry was paying them back in kind,

---

* Cf. Daniel Halévy, *Le Courrier de M. Thiers*, p. 492.

and Thiers and his friends quite rightly caught a glimpse of some vague possibilities along those lines.

The Right had precisely the opposite reaction. From one end to the other—from the *Chevau-légers* to the very enlightened Right Center—the outlook was utterly bleak. To members of those parties, which were basically structured by the rural Notables, the peasantry's defection was enough to make their heads swim. The three June elections confirmed their long-standing and growing fears. Almost everywhere, the Conservatives were losing the town halls, and in many areas the salute—that traditional form of polite greeting, respectfully given and directly acknowledged—was becoming a thing of the past. With the peasantry lost, it seemed as if the very ground had crumbled under their feet. Since that half-intimate, half-patriarchal atmosphere with which they were long familiar had disappeared, they saw nothing but chasms ahead of them, and since they identified their own threatening future with their country's, they saw nothing but chasms ahead of France as well. The legitimists and the *Chevau-légers*—the comte de Chambord's young musketeers—could not conceive of any society which was not hierarchical, which was not organized and held together by a network of loyalties, the loyalty of the servant to his master, of the master to his leader, of the leader to the king, and of the whole country to God. According to them, radicalism—which professed that all men are equal, and that man's goal is man alone—could lead only to ruin. The results of the three elections in the Nord, the Somme, and the Yonne confirmed their fears: the collapse of the great royal tree, disrupting the native soil as it was torn up by its roots, laid open the deep and wholesome layers of society to the temptations of envy and hatred.

Their neighbors of the Moderate Right and the Center Right were far less committed to notions of caste and dynasty, but they were all Catholics. Bound to their faith by religious practice or respect, they found it hard to believe that a permanent order deprived of the hopes and fears inspired by an immanent God and churchly discipline could be created among men. What terrified them about the republican party was less the principle of the Republic itself than the absence of a religion that clearly vitalized it. French radicalism was increasingly proclaiming its atheism. Adding negation after negation, it denied the existence of any suzerainty whatever, refusing to pay homage to any master, any father, any king, or God. "Neither God nor master," had said Blanqui, the prisoner on Mont-Saint-Michel; "God means evil," Proudhon had said, and not only were those "enfants terribles" of the Republic truly its children, but Proudhon himself was its revered philosopher. The violent statements formulated by both men had gained currency and even reached the attention of the people. Nowhere else in the world, in no other century, among no other peoples, had there been such a detachment from religious concerns, such a reversal of spiritual views. Even today, sixty years later, France stands alone among nations in that respect, oblivious not only to prayer and worship but even to the name of God; it is thus not surprising that, from the very start, this singular situation was contemplated by believers with anguish and horror. Both the Gascon nobleman Belcastel, an ultramontane who was a votary of the Sacred Heart, and the Norman duc de Broglie, who was a Gallican, interpreted France's denial of God as tantamount to moral suicide. "Evil is at the root of it," wrote Laprade, a deputy from Lyons who was also a competent poet in the tradition of Lamartine. "The people," he went on, in a personal letter, "have altogether abandoned Christianity and will not be reconverted. No nation has ever survived its religion." What would the Reds substitute for God? Justice. But in a world that was a prey to brute force and at the mercy of a thoroughly materialistic system, what was the meaning of that lifeless virtue, that pale reflection of dead gods? It was now no more than a word, a mask that concealed hatred and envy, an instrument of destruction. Was France caught up in an increasingly vicious cycle of ever more disruptive and fracturing crises? Was she on the verge of a fatal conflict? Many people were convinced of it. As royalists and Catholics who had nevertheless been marked and inflamed by a century of revolution, they believed in the collapse of the traditional order, just as their opponents believed in the apotheosis of the revolutionary order; like the latter, but for opposite reasons, they believed that the great retributive social upheaval had come. Mgr. Dupanloup shared that belief. In a celebrated letter which he had written on the occasion of a free-thinkers' convention, he had just previously predicted the convulsive Commune. Now that his prophecy had been confirmed, he predicted that there would soon be an even more widespread and destructive convulsion. Falloux, that cautious and sensible Falloux, was of the same opinion. One day, reproaching Thiers in the course of a conversation, he had predicted some impending disasters—the wine and liquor merchants corrupting the country people, the international agitators causing turmoil in the working-class suburbs. Sixty years later, some of the horrors he had vaguely discerned were borne out. Yet to him, nothing he foresaw was either vague or remote; he visualized it all in precise detail and anticipated the immediate future—the family hearth soon to be threatened by fire and bloodshed. And Veuillot described the vision in awesome terms: "O, you desecrators of the Cross!" he exclaimed, "deserting all that glory, all that pride, all that honor . . . If enough is left of your France to stand your bad breath, may you scrape each other up and copulate! You might produce the vilest thing the world has ever seen, but there will still be some remnants of another France that you will have to murder!" [3]

What would the Catholics in the Assembly do to avoid all those chasms and such disgrace? And would the liberal Conservatives, who were seriously worried about the rapid and unexpected propagation of radicalism, perhaps react in the same way and at the same time? There could be no doubt that the call for the Assembly's dissolution was beginning to echo throughout the country. Mentioned just casually one year earlier, it was now reverberating and becoming a powerful force. It was also raising a very serious question and perhaps cracking open the chasm itself. Popular vote had created the Assembly and had granted it unlimited sovereignty, with no restrictions and no time limit. It was agreed by general consent that it should remain in power until the war indemnity had been paid and the German occupation brought to an end. But those two events now seemed close at hand. By 1874 (perhaps even earlier), it was hoped that the two goals would be achieved and France would be free. But would France have a Chamber, a Senate, a leader, and a constitution? The Assembly would go, leaving behind a country which, although free, would still be disabled. And if there were such a deficiency in power, would the country be faced with the uncertainties of a new election? What would be the outcome of that election? Thus entrusted with the most serious problem of all, how would the voters react? Would they be able to resist radical propaganda? One man, one vote; deputies charged with specific duties and subject to recall by their constituents; a single Chamber elected for a limited term—the mere simplistic nature of such a doctrine produced among the simpleminded great expectations for wielding power and great temptations. Would France fall under the yoke of a new Convention?

Finally, what did Thiers think about all those problems? Had he tolerated and encouraged Gambetta's campaign for dissolution? Had he secretly endorsed it? The question was pressing. Thiers presided over the state, and the Assembly, through its vote of August 31, 1871, had seemed to have taken away its own right to remove him from office. It had raised him, as it were, above itself. Did Thiers take that opportunity to plot against it? The man was unreliable: after fifty years of bitter experience, the royalists knew that. Would Thiers, the incorrigible gambler, resume the tactics he had been so successful with in 1830 and 1848? Did that feller of kings want to fell a sovereign Assembly? Did he belatedly sense that there was a chance for one last fling? A conversation he had had with the Italian poet Manzoni, directly after the revolution of 1830, was joyfully recalled by the deputies of the Right. "Everything is going marvelously well," Thiers had told him. "Take my word for it—unless we are struck by lightning . . ." To which Manzoni had replied: "My dear M. Thiers, if there is any risk of lightning, one should not fiddle about in the clouds." Was Thiers once again tempted to fiddle about in the clouds? As a young man he had been almost a revolutionary. Perhaps he was becoming one again; old age is known for such recurrences. What ingredient would he introduce into that restoration of French institutions which fate had placed in his hands? Was he seeking—was all the praise from leftist parties giving him a taste for—new popularity, however dangerous or unexpected? Meditating in his Anjou house, Falloux wrote: "Who can tell just how far a great intellect can be led astray by great personal ambition?"

CHAPTER 9

Broglie versus Thiers

"With the Assembly destroyed, France herself is lost, and if she can still be saved, you have no time to lose." (Falloux, July 1872)

T HE Assembly was soon to stop hesitating: one man— the duc de Broglie—had resumed his seat, and in him the Assembly found a leader. Since all the campaign plans and decisions were to be made by him, it is imperative that we know him.

Duc Albert de Broglie, in the full vigor of his fifties, was in total command of energies which he had not yet put to use. He belonged to a renowned race and had a rich and complex personality. Mingled in his veins was the blood of both the Broglies and the Neckers, which combined to produce great stamina, the aggressive fervor of eighteenth-century marshals, as well as the subtle mind and vast intellectual powers of his grandmother, Germaine de Staël, and his mother, Duchesse Albertine. We must also not overlook his apprehensive and nervous disposition, which can be traced to Benjamin Constant, who had fathered Germaine de Staël's daughter, Albertine—the wife of Duc Victor and mother of Duc Albert.

Those natural talents and family traditions marked

him out for service to the state. As a monarchist and an
Orleanist, he had chosen not to serve the Second Empire,
even in the special area of diplomacy, where he had begun
his career. Remaining active in his retirement, he had been
one of the most prominent members of the group of *Le
Correspondent*, which, with the help of the Cochins, the
Foyssets, the Lacombes, the de Meaux, and the Dupanloups, had so admirably kept alive the Catholic and liberal
tradition promulgated around 1830 by Lacordaire, Montalembert, and Ozanam. Deeply religious in spirit, the
collaborators on *Le Correspondent* found it impossible to
imagine that a society deprived of altars and church
services could survive; in fact, fully aware of the prevailing
climate of opinion, they did not expect that the Church
could exert any influence on the age without understanding it and without reasonably satisfying its need for
knowledge, free discussion, and social justice. From their
elders, they had inherited a painful experience inflicted
entirely by the collapse of successive regimes— empires,
various types of monarchies, and republics—and colored
entirely by the spectacle of such utter destruction. Yet
they were not discouraged. Closely united—perhaps too
closely, too cut off from the masses by reason of the
solemn charm and intimacy of their group, and not at all
uncomfortable at being cut off from them—they took
comfort in their group itself and in a lofty sense of the
traditions of which they were the self-proclaimed guardians. That self-assurance, somewhat arrogant at times, gave
them the patience to await what they believed would be
the inevitable day when they would regain control of a
country their fathers had governed. They regarded the
Empire as one of the faces of the Revolution: like so many
other faces that had been destroyed by the century, it
could not but soon be destroyed itself in some disaster. At
that point, no doubt, a repentant France would again seek
the support of that strength which is never disappointing
and which did and always will sustain society—a strength

that stems from the eminent, propertied, and religious families.

That was the school of ideas that had trained the duc de Broglie, and his aim in public life was to find some use in State affairs for his friends' traditions.* As far back as the Restoration, Thiers and the Broglies (first the father, then the son) had had good and permanent, but never trustful, relations with each other. To the Broglies, who were apt to be contemptuous, Thiers remained that bustling little southerner, that clever journalist, who, around 1824, had boldly achieved success. Duc Albert never forgot his father's warning: "Beware of Thiers," he had advised; "sometimes he is truly good, but he often changes and takes on a *nasty look.*" Duc Albert was quick to recognize those recurring "nasty looks" on the ever-changing mask of his elder. As for Thiers, he too, who knew the young Duke both in depth and from afar, and had had long experience with his kind, carefully observed him and kept a sharp eye on him. He realized that he was fervent, ambitious, and—under his aristocratic mask—somewhat restless and troubled. "Look at those hands; look how they constantly move," he once told young Dufeuille, sitting next to him in the Assembly. "They are Constant's hands; they're Constant all over." With one of them watching faces and the other watching hands, the two men were bound to come into conflict.

Although Broglie had reluctantly accepted the English embassy to which Thiers had appointed him, he felt

---

* From 1856 to 1863, Broglie published the six volumes of his *Histoire de l'Eglise et de l'Empire au quatrième siècle*, a remarkable study which belonged to that fine corpus of works devoted to religious history produced around the middle of the nineteenth century in France and which was overshadowed by the publications of Renan. The political intent of Broglie's work is clear. In the fourth century the Church moved in the direction of the pagan world and managed to convert it without disrupting its cultural and intellectual framework. In the nineteenth century, would the Church prove capable of moving in the direction of the modern world after having been temporarily thrust aside by the Revolution, and of reconverting it to Christianity without destroying the liberal constitutions it had acquired? That is the question underlying Broglie's study.

that his place was in the Assembly—and Thiers was well aware of it. For a year Broglie had observed, from his London post, the situation in France, returning occasionally to make a point of his presence in Versailles. What was Thiers doing? Obviously he was pursuing a republican policy; this did not offend Broglie, who had foreseen and accepted it. "I believe neither in the Republic nor in the Monarchy," he had written Thiers in May 1871. "I must confess to being skeptical on that score . . . I believe in any regime at all, provided that it is entrusted to honorable men." This corresponded to the view frequently expressed in Liberal circles during the last years of the Second Empire. It had been brilliantly stated by Prévost-Paradol in his greatly admired and widely read book *La France nouvelle*, and had been endorsed by Duc Victor de Broglie—Duc Albert's father—in his *Vues sur le gouvernement de la France*. The name of the political regime was of secondary importance; what mattered were institutions. In a country marked by unstable regimes, it was necessary to concentrate on strengthening conservative institutions that were capable of being adapted to a monarchy, a republic, or an empire. "Politics first," a monarchist politician was to say forty years later;[1] "institutions first" was what Broglie and his friends, the liberal Catholics of *Le Français*, proclaimed, so that they were neither surprised nor even worried by the first experiments of a Republic governed by M. Thiers and controlled by a Conservative majority. But now Thiers being cheered daily by the Left, Thiers flanked by the Left, Thiers being humored and backed by Gambetta, was something else again, and Broglie was alarmed. It became imperative that Thiers be carefully observed and restrained and that his own policy, which was tending toward the Left, be opposed by another policy based on the Right Center and grouping both of the Centers, so that Broglie felt it his duty to defend a vulnerable tradition.

He was gauging the dangers that might result from

the intellectual confusion in which his Versailles friends were floundering. A man of solid intellectual breeding, he knew how to examine problems analytically; a man of traditional military breeding, he had a taste for courageous and resolute action. What was it all about? That was a military question which Broglie tackled as a soldier. Was it a question of a royalist restoration? No, since that had been attempted recently and had proved to be impossible because of the reaction of the prince himself. As Broglie realized, the monarchist position was virtually hopeless and could only be revived after the comte de Chambord's death. How many years did he have left? And then would there be time? Nobody knew. Politics is, to a large extent, the art of seizing opportunities: one opportunity had been missed, leaving a void in France's destiny that had to be filled at once; indeed, an informed answer had to be given at once. It was painful to forsake the princes: Broglie knew that better than anyone else. Deep down in his heart, his hereditary opinions, as he himself put it, rebelled against the various ideas suggested by his own observations and thoughts. But what was to be done? The Orleans had acquiesced to Bourbon discipline, and the Bourbon pretender had missed his chance; the Orleans had committed themselves and could do nothing further. In order not to forsake them, was it necessary to forsake France and, out of allegiance to them, repeat the mistake recently committed by the *émigrés* of subordinating true honor to a point of personal honor? For it was precisely a domestic emigration that the Bourbons had forced upon their followers for the past forty years. Would the Orleans, having rallied to the Bourbons, impose the same fate on their friends, condemning them to curtail their lives to the detriment of France herself? Duc Albert's grandfather, when he was almost under the knife of the guillotine, had said to Duc Victor: "Don't emigrate." Duc Victor had not emigrated and had served Napoleon I. Duc Albert, recalling every bit of his family's experience, had not forgotten his ancestor's advice. England confirmed it by setting a convincing example of rational and practical compromise. Because of that, and not without painful, heartfelt hesitation, he decided to place France above the royalist cause, even if it meant coming to terms with that popular and blood-stained word *Republic*. He thus resolved the cruel dilemma which for the past century had constantly confronted aristocratic families and which had been constantly discussed by the people around him.

Broglie could bring himself to accept a Republic duly entrusted to honorable men and duly preserved for them. Since he was no doubt still a royalist, his feelings were necessarily divided. But staunch royalist that he was, Broglie was perhaps even more an aristocrat and a Christian. Scratch a Christian aristocrat and one will often find a republican. Broglie often proved to be that kind of republican. At bottom, he believed that what really mattered in a society, even more than the king himself, was the nobleman. The king was the guardian of society, a useful protector and its prime defender. But society existed independently and prior to the king; it existed and went on existing by reason of its homes and its altars, which were preserved in their purest and most perfect forms in all countries by the aristocracy.

It was important, according to *Le Français* of July 5, 1871, "not to identify the interests of the Conservative party with the narrower and perfectly separate interests of a royalist restoration." Broglie—at that moment in his difficult career, at any rate—subscribed to the words "perfectly separate." * What had to be protected above all were the interests of the Conservative party. A difficult task: the born aristocrats in France had lost the high positions they still held everywhere else, and the plight of

---

* So did Buffet, who was such a staunch monarchist later on. According to the duc de Broglie, "M. Buffet was not at that time (1871) the resolute monarchist we knew at the end of his life. His thinking evolved in a direction opposite to that of many others."

Catholicism, which had been defeated throughout Europe, was at its worst in France. Yet a ruling elite had survived, a hard-working, well-educated elite, capable of doing good and worthy of support; and part of France was still Christian, with a devotedly diligent clergy and charitable orders which served the people well and were appreciated. Indeed, it was worth fighting for those families, that clergy, and those religious orders. They were what was left of Conservative strength in France, and duty required complete dedication to them.

Watching regretfully from afar, the duc de Broglie shuddered as he contemplated daily the confusion of his friends. Separated from them and having learned a great deal from solitude and distance, he could see just how clumsy they were being. How were they countering Thiers? With complaints, reproaches, and conspiracies plotted in *salons*—all childish and vain. Broglie, on the other hand, was working out in his mind a practical plan of campaign. It was necessary, he thought, to ignore the Extreme Right and to reunite the Centers, the Right and the Left. Thus, with the support of those 400 votes, and operating within the framework of the existing Republic, they might create a higher Chamber that would replace the Assembly itself, while preserving its spirit, and protect France and the Conservatives from the risks of future elections. That could be done, and aside from that, was there any alternative?

The principle of an Upper House, be it a Senate or a Great Council, which would have served as a bulwark for the ruling classes, had once been the liberal and aristocratic dream of the nobility—the family dream, for some hundred years, of the Broglies and the Neckers. Germaine Necker[2] had lent it brilliance by her eloquence; it had been fulfilled under the Restoration with the establishment of a Chamber of Peers to which Duc Victor had belonged by right of birth and on the sole basis of his race. There, he had freely shown his independence by taking some notable stands: he alone, for example, voted for Ney's acquittal. And in the wake of July 1830 he had been distressed when that noble Chamber, which had not been responsible for the King's errors, was drastically reformed, abased, and turned into an instrument to be used at the discretion of Louis Philippe and his ministers. As he had written in his memoirs, "The gem in our royal casket is lost." To restore a viable aristocratic institution in France that would have been even more useful in a republic than in a monarchy was Duc Albert's dearest ambition, even if it meant sacrificing the princes themselves. Carried away by Gambetta's words, France was heading toward a Jacobin Republic, a single sovereign Chamber, and a dictatorial presidency. This had to be blocked. Broglie was eager to leave London. Now that the most critical postwar months were over, he felt he had done his duty and in May 1872 handed in his resignation.

Broglie returned to the Assembly at a critical juncture. All the parties of the Right—the Extreme, the Moderate, and the Center—had been badly hit by the victory of the Radicals and were confusedly groping for a way to parry the blow and retaliate. Their first idea was to approach Thiers. Since he owed them his election, he could not refuse to listen and adopt a policy that would suit them. They therefore decided to send him their leaders in a delegation so that during the intersession they would firmly but discreetly present their conditions. Although Broglie approved, he pointed out that it was necessary to act cautiously, to state the question explicitly, presenting it as a choice between a Conservative and a Radical Republic, and to avoid raising the question of the Monarchy, which always came up when personal traditions and passions were involved, and which, at the time, was insoluble. Thiers, on the other hand, wanted to bring up that question; he wanted to talk about the Monarchy and the Republic. That was a tactic which had to be thwarted.

The End of the Notables

To avoid any ambiguity, Broglie and his friends asked that the initiative be taken not by the Rights alone but by a coalition of the Rights and the Center Left.

Broglie's advice was taken, and the leaders of the Center Left were immediately approached and asked whether they would take part in the Rights' initiative. The Casimir-Périers and the Chanzys[3] did not reject the offer without having weighed all its implications. They had rallied to Thiers, but by no means to Gambetta, and they fully realized the seriousness of the Radicals threatening them in their own constituencies. They were therefore prepared to cooperate with the Center Right, but on one condition—that the agreement be sealed by a joint statement in favor of the Republic. Deep down, Broglie and several others realized that such a statement was justified. But when the moment came to endorse it, they were unable to: they could not overcome all their memories, their honor, their loyalty. They accepted the fact of the Republic, yes. But accepting a fact is not the same thing as professing one's loyalty, which is what the Center Left demanded of them. "I pledge to serve the Republic," had written Casimir-Périer in September 1871 in a public letter announcing that he rallied to the Republic. Such a pledge was unequivocal. Did the Center Right monarchists want to, and could they—by what amounted to an oath committing themselves to a new regime—become involved in this third attempt at a Republic that was still so weak and deny themselves and their princes what still seemed great opportunities for the future? It would appear that Broglie, isolated in England, had not accurately gauged the very personal problems that stood in the way of uniting the two Centers. Influenced once again by his group's advice and the atmosphere of Versailles, Broglie drew back. He found it too painful to make the statement; the Center Right rejected it; and the Center Left ruled out the proposed alliance.

Thus left to themselves, the Rights had to act on their

own, and their initiative took on the appearance of a monarchist protest—to their great embarrassment. It suited Thiers, however, for he was able to seize this convenient opportunity to easily outmaneuver them. No doubt he owed them his election; but his vast personal authority made him independent and he well knew that they wouldn't dare—that they couldn't—overthrow him. He agreed to meet the right-wing delegation on a specific day, at a specific time. General Changarnier,[4] the ducs de la Rochefoucauld and de Broglie, together with some lesser nobles and a few bourgeois—nine in all—arrived punctually. Thiers, who was busy, kept them waiting at first, but finally received them amiably and affectionately: "I'm so very pleased to see you . . ." Then, addressing Changarnier: "My dear general, my renowned friend, do sit next to me and talk; I'm listening." The octagenerian General sat near the President, who was in his seventies— two mummies shaking hands, one of them tall and swaying; the other, short but steady, looking up with a glint in his eye. "Order?" exclaimed Thiers. "Who could possibly defend it better than myself? I understand you would like a monarchy. Can I establish one? Why you yourselves . . ." "No," protested Changarnier, "that's not the point. It is precisely order and the threat of radicalism that worry us, and we ask you . . ." Thiers heard them out, but wanted to dodge the issue and persisted in defending the Republic, which his visitors were not challenging. Stronger, more experienced, and quicker than the rest of them, and a more skillful fencer, he managed to send them away feeling sheepish. "Sorry," he said as he saw them to the door, "the Republic is one of those things that we have inherited from the Empire." Then, delighted to have fired that parting shot, he turned his back to them.

The leaders of the majority, disappointed and anxious to make it known, expressed their displeasure the very next day in the form of an official communiqué. The communiqué was greeted with joy, for those high dignitaries, who were so conspicuously important, had been flouted and admitted it; they had been taken in by the amusing old trickster from Marseilles. People laughed as they thought back to 1848, when similar attempts had been made by other equally important dignitaries such as Molé, Dupin, and Montalembert, all of them the seniors or deceased friends of the men Thiers had just flouted. They had been given comic nicknames—"old fossils" or "bearskins." It was the latter that the Parisian Liberals of 1872 remembered, and the "bearskins" of Versailles became a figure of fun. The Changarniers, the La Rochefoucaulds, and the Broglies belonged to the past and were not spared the ridicule of failing to realize it. Their stiff manners, reminiscent of the court and the Church, were out of tune with a France which during the lively Second Empire, with its gay and vulgar style and its free, easy-going court, had lost touch with the aristocratic tone—a France which daily seemed to become even more republican than it was thought to be and more detached from the old and different ways of ancient France.

Holding the trump card, Thiers pressed his advantage and announced a forthcoming loan issue which would finally free the land. The leaders of the majority repeated their warnings: the first condition for a successful loan was the trust of property-owners; what chances would a loan have now that the election of the Radicals had destroyed that trust? Thiers paid no attention. He had taken the necessary steps to guarantee success. The high interest rate, with its very special and burdensome conditions (if one includes the cost of issue, interest came to over 6 per cent), appealed to all the European banks, which, having been approached and given fair warning, unanimously joined forces to underwrite the transaction. The cashiers' desks were opened on July 28 and closed on the 29th: three billion had been asked for and forty-one were subscribed, including twenty from abroad. Forty-one billion—in other words, taking into account the subsequent devaluation of the franc, it would make some two hundred billion francs today, even more. Obviously, the subscriptions were a sham, and the creditors had anticipated substantial discounts. But no matter: it was such a great triumph that the opposition was silenced. There was now proof that Europe as well as France gave credit to the government, to Thiers's Republic.

Yet Thiers had not achieved victory; far from it. Between the French Assembly and the European courts, he still found maneuvering difficult. In France he had joined forces with Gambetta; but outside France, in the chancelleries and courts, Gambetta was still a bogy, and the obvious bargain he had made with Thiers created something of a scandal. Saint-Petersburg gave Thiers advice. Be careful, he was told, not to jeopardize useful sympathies. Berlin, where Gambetta was still identified with war and revolution, had the same reaction. The Emperors of Germany, Russia, and Austria had met in Gastein, and although little was known about their conversation, it was suspected that they had discussed Gambetta. Bismarck undoubtedly had his own strongly independent views on the subject: he refused to do Gambetta the honor of fearing him; he predicted a mediocre future for French democracy; he realized quite rightly that it had lost the contagious power it had once wielded, and wished that slow, pernicious disease on France. But he had to take into account the aversions and fears that prevailed around him. Thiers, who was beginning to negotiate for the German evacuation of the occupied departments, sensed the growing resistance to it. Since the occupation was a guarantee against French anarchy, the Prussian general staff could use any victory of the Radicals as a pretext to keep a foothold in the conquered territories. For France, and even for Thiers, evacuation was more than important: it was crucial. Thiers expected that its successful completion would increase his prestige and his sovereign authority. He therefore had to scheme, and in order to succeed abroad, he had to conceal the true nature of his domestic alliances and postpone the adoption of a policy altogether favorable to the parties of the Left.

Although the warning signals from the Assembly were of a different nature, they also urged him to be cautious. As the Center Left deputies became increasingly fearful of the Radical threat, Thiers found it difficult to reassure his friends. He suspected that they were being shrewdly and strongly manipulated, probably under the direction of Broglie. For Broglie was plotting with his Liberal friends—Jean Casimir-Périer, for example—and urging them to consider a close coalition between the two Centers which alone would succeed in detaching Thiers from the dangers of an alliance with the Radicals. We agree to a Republic, said Broglie, but don't ask us to pledge our faith to it, for it is not ours to pledge; we shall consent to providing it with institutions that will make it permanent, but on one condition: that it be done by you and by us, by a coalition of the two Centers, and not by you and the Left against us—a bad alliance that you yourselves would soon have cause to regret. It was in effect that conception of a Republic without republicans which Thiers had skillfully proposed and which he was even more skillfully undermining in practice. As he listened to the rumors, Thiers was obliged to contemplate taking measures which might perhaps change the Assembly's mood. Up to then, he had been able to tell the Right: "It is your fault if we cannot come to an agreement; every time I wanted your support, I was greeted, not with support, but with conspiracy." Would Broglie together with Casimir-Périer call a halt to the conspiracy and offer their support? Would Thiers trust those noblemen and *grand bourgeois* who, seemingly on his side, were stealthily closing in on him? Having tasted the new fruits of popularity, he was hardly inclined to. "You represent unpopularity," he told Lacombe, one of the plotters, "whereas I stand for popularity"—a considerable advantage, which he had no intention of losing. But it was important not to precipitate matters. He therefore behaved somewhat differently. In July, as the session drew to a close, he finally came out with some reassuring words. He rejected in vigorous terms any solidarity with those who were campaigning for dissolution. "I owe everything to the Assembly," he said in substance. "If I had anything to do with its opponents, I would consider myself to be plotting against the sovereign authority." As Broglie listened to those words and thought back to 1830 and 1848, he probably thought: "And this would not be the first time . . ." In any case, the conciliatory words had been spoken; the Conservatives welcomed them; and parting on what appeared to be fairly good terms, the Assembly and its irascible leader adjourned for the recess.

Thiers went one step further: he somewhat modified his relations with the Left. Gambetta was becoming a major liability: ignoring the lazy summer holidays, he was preparing to resume his blustering oratorical forays in the provinces. Thiers was anxious to avoid those eloquent outbursts. Would he be able to, either by negotiations or by force? He had Gambetta warned that henceforth he would be denied the right of holding public meetings. That official notification, however, contained some conciliatory words. "Barthélémy-Saint-Hilaire," wrote Thiers, "will explain the rest in person." Barthélémy-Saint-Hilaire, Thiers's private secretary, was an impassioned republican on whom he frequently relied to grant the Left some favor or concession, either verbally or in writing, without committing himself personally. In fact, Barthélémy-Saint-Hilaire's conversation made things considerably easier. Gambetta was permitted to speak freely at private meetings, and by sending out numerous invitations, it was possible for him to make private meetings as well attended and effective as public meetings.

Gambetta considered that prohibition—however toned down—a bad sign. It was obvious that Thiers, whether acting freely or under duress, was yielding to the very persistent negotiators of the Center parties. The republicans were thus faced with the following problem: In relation to Thiers, who was now shifting to the Right, how ought they behave?

Gambetta and his friends hesitated at first. Several of them were of the opinion that Thiers, who at bottom was still firmly on their side, had to be carefully handled and that it would be wise to ease up on the polemics that hindered him in his negotiations with Germany. Barthé-lémy-Saint-Hilaire had probably let it be understood that some caution was advisable because of outside pressure, but only so long as the pressure lasted. *La République Française* announced that the campaign against the Assembly would be called off, and it was said that Gambetta himself had promised Thiers he would watch his words. Given his speeches, that would seem doubtful; it is more likely that, from the very beginning, he preferred using strong measures to manipulate Thiers.

In answer to an invitation he went to the Rhône valley. Whether the meetings were private or public, the effect was virtually the same: he spoke, he was cheered, and his printed speeches were distributed everywhere. And yet again, in each of his speeches, he strongly hammered away at the Assembly, calling for its dissolution. As for Thiers, Gambetta did not make a single reference to him. He no longer pronounced his name, no longer used it to provoke cheers from the audience, and sometimes even quoted Thiers's arguments, only to turn them against him. Thiers had just let it be known that, in agreement with the Assembly, he was prepared to establish a Conservative Republic. Gambetta refused to combine those two words. "There are not two Republics," he said at Firminy. "The country is all the less likely to make any distinction between a so-called Conservative Republic and a so-called

Radical Republic since it knows that those words are ephemeral." At Chambéry he was greeted by delegations of mayors, councillors, and republican party workers from nearby towns and villages. But there was one false move: since the republican press had made the mistake of announcing the private meeting, the *préfet* thus considered it public and forbade its being held. This did not embarrass Gambetta, who received separate groups of his audience in his hotel, and instead of one private meeting, he held thirty. Receiving one delegation after another, he welcomed each of them with a friendly word. He was admirably suited for that type of gathering, always ready with an outstretched hand and an appropriate comment.*
And always interspersed with the polite greetings was the persistent and constantly repeated battle cry, "The Republic must be established by a new constituent assembly." To others he said: "We shan't have to wait much longer . . . This Chamber has reached the height of unpopularity, impotency, sterility, and incompetence." To everyone he said: "Dissolution!"

Finally, he arrived in Grenoble. What was the mood communicated to him by the audience, what breeze was sweeping across the Dauphiné from the Red South? Was Gambetta acting on impulse or by design? By that time, at

---

* Veuillot wrote a lively passage describing Gambetta as speaker at a public meeting: "M. Gambetta dances about all alone just as though he were performing at La Chaumière, without ever watching where he kicks his feet. His treading-on-eggs dance consists in breaking the eggs, and his omelet is most especially delectable because of the egg-shells he beats into it with his heels. The more one listens to him, the more one realizes that the speaker who best holds the attention of the mob is the one who relies enough on the intelligence of his audience not to blush at the silly things he is about to say, or one who is so silly himself that he doesn't notice how silly the things he says are. He gets as much applause for his vocalizing as would a tenor singing Scribe . . . Tenors get that kind of applause from an entire audience. M. Gambetta's curious talent lies in getting applause for words without music—as he performs by mere candlelight—from 150 Allobroges, a few of whom are officials and a few others of whom once had good sense. But there is that wind blowing down from the mountains, as well as the effect of that good little wine from Savoy and the prospect of reaching the top of that greasy pole . . ." In fairness to Gambetta, it should be noted that he spoke better before the National Assembly. But, then, he always had that talent for mimicry which put him in tune with his audience.

the end of September, the tactics of the Right Center seemed very close to succeeding. The details are still unclear and will not be known until the Broglies, the Decazes, the Casimir-Périers, and the Pasquiers open their archives to the public. But judging from the diary of a man like Lacombe, their activities were clearly energetic. Lacombe noted down the rumors that reached him and passed them on to Falloux, who, although a legitimist by birth and conviction, listened without any indignation. How could Falloux forget that, throughout his long life, the only times he had been able to serve his Church and his country were during the republican years of 1848, 1849, 1850, and 1851? Those memories remained with him and kept him alert to the possibility of a Republic—of yet another Republic! "If we should fail to get the monarchy," Lacombe had written, "we must frankly consider the possibility of improving present conditions and, rather than rejecting them, of using them to our advantage, provided that a strict policy of order is adopted." Then, quoting a phrase of Berryer's[5] and giving it a republican meaning, he added: "What we must do is safeguard the legacy—safeguard it for our heirs, for future generations— and safeguard France's moral foundation, that whole body of principles, beliefs, and freedoms which once shaped her and will enable her to survive." Falloux was willing to listen to that and agreed to come to terms with republican institutions. "A quasi-monarchial constitution," he said, "has the advantage of bringing the country closer to reality, reviving not a taste for it, which the country has never lost, but the habit of it; and an upper Chamber has the advantage of bringing us closer to that realistic policy." "But all of that," added Falloux, "would mean little unless it were accompanied by a good electoral law." He was categorical on that point: universal suffrage was the source of all our evils. "If I were given a choice between the most monarchical monarchy in the world, with unlimited direct universal suffrage, and a Republic based on universal suffrage which is restricted and controlled by the natural forces of any civilized country, I would take the Republic, for order would be in safer hands under it than under a monarchy." *

As the Right Center shifted to the left, the Left Center seemed to veer toward the right. This provoked a quarrel between the *Journal des Débats* and *La République Française* as to whether it marked the beginning of a new policy. It was said that Broglie had offered Thiers the presidency for life under the Republic and that Thiers had perhaps not been insensitive to that rather obvious bait. Until then, he had vigorously turned down any proposal for constitutional revision on the grounds that his personal authority provided France with a perfect constitution. But he allowed this to be discussed by his entourage and in the press, and he even referred to it himself.

The Grenoble speech was meant to make Thiers feel the full blast of the anger that Gambetta was about to unleash. Reacting to the threat of a Republic which might be founded and which would not be his own, Gambetta exclaimed:

> Yes, it is likely that, when Parliament meets in Versailles, it will say that there is really no time to waste before establishing a Republic—but what does that mean?
>
> It means that appearances notwithstanding, people feel that dissolution no longer needs to be preached or even demonstrated, but that dissolution has already taken place. For unless they were not personally convinced that dissolution was standing right there, like a gravedigger, about to throw a handful of earth on the corpse of the Versailles Assembly (*this created a sensation*), unless they did not feel the pangs of death, you may be sure that there would be no talk of getting married to the Republic *in extremis.*

* Falloux, who was full of ideas, expressed his views on the organization of universal suffrage: it was the representation of interest groups, which many people recommend today, that the solitary old man favored. See his letter of September 4, 1872, in Lacombe, *loc. cit.*, 1:123.

The End of the Notables

(General laughter.—Repeated applause.—Shouts of "Long live the Republic!")

Gambetta scorned that idea of marriage "to the Republic *in extremis*"—of the Right rallying to it—and he disparaged the motives for it, dismissing it as a disgraceful farce. His veto against the very principle of rallying was to carry weight for the next half century:

> I should like to suggest the rejection of all those who, for the sake of politics, and in the most recent party intrigues, were the professed leaders of royalist schemes and conspiracies—all those who, by serving the pretenders, have unpatriotically contributed to national disorder: I should like them all to be expelled from our republican party lists. I should then like a distinction to be made between such leaders and their followers, since the latter might be of good faith and perhaps were merely led astray. They are assuredly few in number; and in any case, we would only accept, from among them, those who had not compromised themselves by taking a stand against their country and in opposition to universal suffrage.

Thus the monarchists—whether legitimists, Orleanists, or Bonapartists—were all blamed at once and stood condemned together in spite of their differences. They were blamed for not having realized soon enough that their loyalty was barren, and for not having rallied to the Republic soon enough, either actually or emotionally. They were condemned in the sense that they were denied the right of rallying, or at any rate allowed to do so on terms that were so stringent as to dissuade them. Pardon was granted only to a handful of those who had gone astray and whose numbers had been limited beforehand; and even they were warned by Gambetta of the humiliating price they would have to pay before they could expect forgiveness. They would have to "justify their behavior by acts of unimpeachable repentance and contrition." This

constituted a sweeping ban, debarring virtually all aristocratic families and the vast majority of bourgeois families,
all those who, under the Old Regime, had been described
by the (still applicable) term *Notables*, and whose descendants, serving in the army, the courts, and the civil
service, upheld the ancient traditions of the French State
and society. If they were excluded, who would take their
place? Gambetta, in his speech, also proclaimed their
successors. "Today we must delve down into the strata,
into the deep ranks of society," he exclaimed. And here is
the rest of that well-known speech:

> Have we not seen emerging on the whole surface of the
> country—and I want very much to bring this out—a new
> generation of democracy, a new political and electoral
> personnel born of universal suffrage? Have we not seen the
> workers of our cities and our countryside—that world of
> labor to which the future belongs—entering the political
> arena? Isn't this a characteristic sign that the country, after
> having tried out so many forms of government, is now
> finally ready to turn to another social stratum in order to
> test a republican regime? Yes, I sense, I feel, I proclaim the
> political emergence of a new social stratum which has been
> active in public affairs for some eighteen months now and
> which is assuredly far from being inferior to its predeces-
> sors.

The first warning to reach Paris was a telegram which,
because of its brevity, made the meaning of Gambetta's
words seem even more momentous: he was alleged to have
said that it was necessary to replace the existing political
personnel by a new one, drawn largely from the working
class. A revolutionary newspaper, *Le Corsair*, was the first
to publish the full text of his speech. *La République
Française* kept silent, which probably indicated hesitation
and an attempt to soften the blow; finally, *La République
Française* published and thus confirmed *Le Corsair's* text.
"Gambetta has thrown out the Conservative republicans,"

wrote Lacombe in his diary; and the *Débats* was indignant:
"If the Radical party intends to proceed by excluding and
outlawing all classes and citizens who refuse to pass
through its Caudine Forks, then we shall resume the
battle," wrote John Lemoinne, a monarchist of long
standing, but who had recently rallied, with Thiers, to the
Republic.

While Gambetta had been clear about who was to be
debarred, he was less clear about who would benefit. What
were those "deep ranks," those "new social strata," which
Gambetta had claimed would rule? Was he thinking of
the working-class masses? Was he referring to the anonymous and still enigmatic rebellious mobs of June 1848? Or
to the sixty unknown figures who had governed Paris
under the Commune? This was the time when the rigid
form of German Socialism advocating class warfare and
defining revolution in terms of the total destruction of the
propertied classes had started to spread in France. Young
Guesde[6] had begun to propagate that doctrine; the
Communard Cluserot wrote that "the *bourgeoisie* as a
class must be annihilated"; and according to *Le Corsair*,
the paper that had been the first to print the Grenoble
speech: "The goal is to replace the five hundred thousand
families of the ruling class with twenty million peasants,
workers, wage-earners, artisans, manufacturers, and shop-
keepers." Was Gambetta looking for allies among those
elements? He was later to deny it. "I said 'new strata,' " he
explained in 1874, "not classes. *Class* is a bad word which I
never use . . . It is impossible to tell where this French
bourgeoisie, to which the country owes so much, begins or
ends." But would he have given that clear an explanation
in 1873? Was it true that he had then avoided using the
word *class*, which the *bourgeoisie* found so distasteful,
because, still used in the full sense of the term, it showed
the utter futility of the social accomplishments of the
Revolution of 1789? "Despite the law, despite what is said
about it," he had declared at Saint-Quentin in November

1871, "there are still classes." Had Gambetta wished, in Grenoble, to proclaim and provoke a new social war? Certainly not, for beneath his conveniently imprecise and vaguely threatening words, which had been deliberately meant to evoke all kinds of reaction, one must look for a far more moderate tone, much closer to the realities of the future. But few people had any conception of that future, and the past alone—that deadly past which continued to serve as an example—perplexed educated minds which were still haunted by too many memories.

Thus the enigmatic speech was interpreted by everyone as a statement of a confused and unpleasant truth, a blinding ray of light.

Gambetta had fanned the flames of a badly extinguished fire. At the same time as he was delivering his powerful speech in Grenoble, pilgrims returning from Lourdes were jeered at as they left the Nantes railway station. They had returned in three trainloads. At the first exit, they were greeted with whistling and catcalls of "Boo! You *lourdauds*." [7] The crowds became increasingly excited at the second and third exits, and there were brawls during which the sick, the crippled, and women were beaten up. Since Nantes was a republican city, the local police took no vigorous action, which created a stir. Flaubert referred to the incident in a letter to George Sand: "What do you think of those who go to Lourdes and of those who jeer at them?" He considered both groups equally foolish. But the country, which was troubled in every direction, did not react with the same detachment. Where was it all leading?

CHAPTER 10

Six Stormy Months

"Four months from now, I shall give all those people a good kick in the behind." (Thiers, as quoted by Hector Pessard)

D URING the holidays the Assembly was represented by a standing committee which met once every fortnight. As a rule, its meetings were vacuous and dull. Now at last it was to serve some useful purpose: Gambetta's words called for a reply; Broglie roused the committee to action. Thiers was in Trouville, very busy inspecting the English navy and ordering artillery maneuvers for himself alone. (He claimed to be an authority on all sorts of matters, considering himself an expert on artillery, chemistry, and mathematics, as well as a statesman, an historian, an art critic, and a philosopher.) Asked to appear before the committee, he arrived in Versailles in a rather foul mood. None of the implications of the Grenoble speech had escaped his attention, and perhaps none had surprised him. Gambetta had condemned the Right Center's strategy, and by deliberately refraining from mentioning Thiers or his services to the nation, Thiers himself had been threatened.* Would he react to the threat by an act of

---

* Only once during his campaign did Gambetta refer to Thiers by name, and it was not in a speech, but in reply to a toast to Thiers's health as well as to

retaliation? Certainly not; that would have meant surrendering to the parties of the Right, which is precisely what he didn't want. Would he listen to Gambetta, yield to him, and renew their former bargain? It was unlikely, for that would have meant breaking off with the parties of the Right, which he couldn't do. He was unable to for the two reasons mentioned earlier, which the turn of events had made him re-examine, and which we shall re-examine here: first, there were the events of domestic policy, which compelled him not to offend the Conservatives, who were powerful in the Assembly; secondly, there were the events of foreign policy, which compelled him just as strongly to refrain from hurting the feelings of the European courts. Saint-Petersburg was advising him to act cautiously, and every time Gambetta's star was in the ascendant, Germany would again show reserve and resistance.

Gambetta's calling upon new social strata had resounded throughout Europe, and nowhere had it pleased the ruling classes. Thiers had to take that into consideration. After all, as he made his way to Versailles, where he had been asked to appear, he realized that none of the views expressed in a closed session of the committee meeting would ever make any direct impact on the world outside. It was a good place and perhaps a fine opportunity to persuade the Conservatives of his good intentions. He decided to take that opportunity. In answer to a question on the Grenoble speech, he burst out saying: "It was a bad speech, very bad indeed. I know nothing about new social strata; I reject any distinction between classes . . . Whoever makes that distinction in order to champion the interests of a single class is guilty of sedition." The man had a splendid gift for improvisation and vehemence. Dazzled, the members of the Committee listened. Here again was the great Conservative of 1848,

his own. He obliged and played the game, but very cautiously, dropping the hint that Thiers ought not "pay too much attention to the voice heard in the department of the Seine-et-Oise."

who had never been forgotten by the *bourgeoisie* he had reassured; they all admired him. There's no doubt of it, they thought, Thiers is with us. And Broglie himself perhaps shared that illusion for a moment. In a few words, speaking on behalf of the others, he expressed his satisfaction.

The parliamentary Notables returned to their estates and their hunting, while Thiers returned to Trouville for a few more days. What, in fact, were their innermost thoughts? The seeds of distrust had been sown and could no longer be rooted up. Yet given the uncertainty of history, there is always room for expectation and certain modest hopes. The fusion of the two Centers was still considered a likely possibility and the only hope that an enlightened Conservative could latch on to. The talks in Versailles strengthened it.

By the end of October, the French, having safely garnered and stocked the fruits of their harvest in their lofts and cellars, could confidently confront the rigors of winter closed up in their houses. But what about their State? They were worried about it. The State was their communal household, and the masses were astonished that the regime was allowed to remain without a name and without any absolute statute. Soon the Assembly was to meet at Versailles, and everyone hoped that its members would decide and, in deference to public opinion, promptly come to grips with the constitutional issue.

Broglie, well aware of the situation, took one step further in the direction of the Republic by declaring in an open letter to the press that he personally had "no objections to the Republic of M. Thiers, as our peasants put it." He had done his best, which was not much. And he had cause to rue his words. Naïve and unpremeditated, they bore the overly conspicuous stamp of a ducal pronouncement. "*Our* peasants?" retorted *La République Française.* "What does that mean? That the duc de

Broglie has peasants of his own? And that serfdom still exists in Normandy? The noble duke is behind the times . . ."

On October 20, elections were held in five departments. Broglie and his friends tried their luck, but they ran into trouble. Everything was simple for the legitimists, the Bonapartists, and the Radicals: they stated their positions and they were believed. But no one believed the candidates of the Center, for they called themselves Conservative republicans. They were asked to pronounce a single word, but they pronounced two—which was one too many. The republican newspapers listed the legitimist and Bonapartist candidates under their proper party labels. But they added a question mark after the names of the Conservative republicans. The masses like to know where they stand; they like plain speaking, and that question mark, those republicans' sly tactics, aroused their suspicions. Yet the Conservative republicans persisted and repeated their complicated party label. No one questioned their being Conservatives; they had always been considered as such. But republicans into the bargain? Who could be sure of it? They professed their willingness to accept republican institutions. But accepting was not enough. They were expected to proclaim their allegiance to republican principles, which was quite a different matter from accepting them. Rather than talking so much about "republican institutions," they were expected quite simply to proclaim "the Republic." How difficult they found that! They had never been able to pronounce the word correctly. And try as they would, the fact of having been debarred in the Grenoble speech worked against them.

What, in the end, was everyone demanding of them? Saint-Marc-Giradin, in an open letter addressed to the *Débats,* expressed his view with forcible indignation:

> It is quite hopeless to try to persuade these new inquisitors of the faith that the Assembly is doing more than pledging

its allegiance to the republican creed; its members are putting it into practice and accepting its procedures. But the inquisitors want more than that. They want everyone suspected of harboring hopes for a monarchy to repent publicly in order to do credit to those who consider themselves the exclusive guardians of republican orthodoxy.

That was precisely the case: the Conservatives were expected to confess their sins and—as Gambetta had demanded in Grenoble—make their penitence public. They were to embrace the Republic as an act of faith and acknowledge it not merely as the legitimate regime but as the only legitimate regime for ever more—for ever more in a country which for the past century had undergone a change of regime every eighteen years! Did the republicans wish to restore the loyalty oath which the Empire, to the disgust of the republicans, had required of all civil servants and elected officials? Yet another oath, which so often was a lie! Broglie and his friends refused to lie, so they were accused of being hypocrites.

There was no limit to the disavowals demanded by the new inquisitors. In addition to, and by way of, the faithful monarchists, they hunted out the faithful Catholics. Indeed, it was primarily the Catholic faith that they wanted to strike out against. This was clearly perceived by Littré in one of his invariably honest and almost invariably lucid studies. "The clericals," he wrote (perhaps "the Catholics" would have been more appropriate), "do not regard the republican faith with blind hatred and invincible prejudice, but our side identifies the Republic with the absolute principle of the secular State, and that unpardonable offense directly provokes their aversion." To state it somewhat differently, Littré might have said: "The Catholics do not regard the republican State with blind hatred and invincible prejudice, but our side identifies it with a revolutionary faith diametrically opposed to Christian

faith, and that antithesis directly provokes their aversion."
The converse was equally true, for the Catholic faith, that
unpardonable offense, directly provoked the republicans'
aversion. And the legitimists' traditional aversion, which
was unrestrained from the very beginning, succeeded in
making life difficult for those who rallied to the Center
Right. As a scoffer from the Extreme Right put it,
"Tartuffe would nowadays be known as 'a Conservative
republican.' "

Is it possible to discover how much truth there was in
those charges? When men like Broglie, Pasquier, and—
somewhat later—Decazes[1] declared that they accepted the
Republic, they must be believed. But how is one to define
their acceptance of it? Total, active—not passive—acceptance implies a will to make the Republic last. And neither
Broglie, nor Pasquier, nor Decazes ever showed any will to
do so. Besides, they were honorable men, they spoke their
minds, and they never claimed any such intentions. As the
duc Pasquier put it: "If you don't ask us to betray our past
or to believe in the definitive future of the present regime,
then you may rest assured that we shall support the *status
quo* with determination and loyalty." It was precisely that
reluctance to commit themselves to the future which
spoiled matters. They were constantly anticipating a
change of regime, whereas France was craving for something quite simple—surely not the Monarchy and, among
the rural masses, still not the Republic (many, at heart,
looked back to the Empire with nostalgia), but rather a
more simple and elementary blessing: a permanent regime,
whatever its name. Those who rallied to the Center Right,
given the nature of their overrational and oversubtle
acceptance of the *status quo*—accepting it in fact, but not
as a lasting regime—thus set themselves apart from the
people.

Being held in suspicion, attacked, and insulted, they
were clearly heading for defeat. It was obvious that even
Thiers was against them: his newspaper, *Le Bien Public*,

supported the same candidates as *La République Française*, one of whom was a man like Méline[2] who denied
that the National Assembly had any constituent power.
Out of the five October elections they gained only one
seat, as against one monarchist victory in Brittany and
three leftist victories. In proclaiming their triumph, *La
République Française* took the opportunity of thanking
the audacious leader who was responsible for it:

> If, as is possible, the Grenoble speech has contributed to
> overthrowing M. de Broglie, M. Saint-Marc-Girardin, and
> all the leaders of the Right and the Center Right who were
> prepared to rally to the Republic and even to proclaim it in
> order to establish it according to their own principles upon
> their return to Versailles next month; if the Grenoble
> speech has prevented the so-called "fusion of the Centers,"
> has nipped in the bud that dreadful conspiracy—then the
> Grenoble speech was a master stroke.*

The newspaper, addressing Thiers, added: "France
has once again declared herself, and she is still against the
Assembly. Would you hesitate to choose between France
and the Assembly?"

Thiers had made his choice long since, and what he
had said to the Versailles committee were only words. His
goal remained the same—to establish the Republic. His
means of achieving that goal were still the same: the
support of the republican masses. Thiers wished to comply
with the warning and threat contained in the speech at
Grenoble. He was more and more anxious to stand apart
from the *grande bourgeoisie*, from whom he no longer
hoped for power and glory; he was more and more
attracted by the temptation of a popular dictatorship, to
which all French leaders are traditionally drawn. He
identified France and the Republic with himself in a wild
surge of ambition and pride. Fifty years of activity, power,

---

* The style of this garbled sentence would seem to be Gambetta's rather
than Challemel-Lacour's. Gambetta wrote many articles just the way he spoke.

and study had made him come to think of himself as the
very embodiment of the nation—a view that was not his
alone. He accepted no one but himself. He dismissed the
Versailles Assembly as a group of troublesome dissenters.
"By my reckoning," he would say, "it is made up of four
hundred and fifty cowards and three hundred madmen,"
the cowards belonging to the Center, and the madmen to
the two extreme wings. The strategy he planned consisted
of coercing the cowards, defeating the madmen, or
deceiving the whole lot of them. After having first
maneuvered and outwitted the Rights insofar as was
necessary to bring the occupation to an end, he would
then, supported by popular acclaim, exploit his personal
triumph by imposing himself and the Republic, his
Republic, on the Assembly, or else dissolve it and appeal
to the people to overwhelmingly endorse his action. Like
Proteus, Thiers—that very petty but often great creature
—was something of a rogue but also something of an
artist. He had a keen and lively sense of the noble event,
the thrilling crisis, the crux of a situation, and the
denouement. As he himself expressed it in his history of
the Consulate: "The life of a people is made up only of
unique moments"—the words of a somewhat histrionic
poet, not a statesman. One unique moment: the night of
August 4th; another: that Sunday in the year 1801 when all
the church bells of France rang in the Concordat; another
(this one conceived and carried out by him): the return of
Napoleon's ashes; another and unforgettable moment,
due entirely to his genius and which was altogether to his
advantage: that day, which now was surely imminent,
when Germany, after having been paid so rapidly and with
such astonishing ease, would finally withdraw from France,
leaving the country free and inviolate. What glory, and
what strength he would derive from it! He was already
savoring the former and gauging the latter. What precisely
was in his mind? What tactics was he devising? Even his
most intimate friends never knew. According to Pessard,

Thiers sometimes spoke of a plebiscite. As a southerner and a man of letters, he imagined and hoped for that sort of triumph, or, as people were then saying—and as he, above all, liked to put it—"that fine chapter in our history."

But if that October election-day had thus merely strengthened certain of his own convictions, it had had a disruptive effect on those members of the two Center parties who, with no training and no real faith, began to form a coalition. What good would it do to go over to the Left Center, murmured the hesitant followers of Broglie, who himself was essentially confused; the friends we are diverging from insult us, they said, and we have fought with those we are drawn to, just as if we had been loyal to our old true colors. And many of the deputies of the Center Left wondered: What good would it do to go over to the Center Right if those tactics mean being even more surely dragged down to defeat with them?

At the same time, the split that had profoundly divided the French *haute bourgeoisie* in the past was once again apparent. Although they were almost totally Conservative in spirit, they were by no means altogether in favor of Catholicism; some striking examples mentioned earlier have shown that to be true. So that a resultant difficulty was revived which disrupted the unstable coalition between the two recent allies, who still bitterly resented their defeat. France was at that time stirred up by pilgrimages to Lourdes organized by the Assumptionist monks, as well as pilgrimages to La Salette or Paray-le-Monial promoted by other religious orders. The pilgrims paraded down city streets, the most fervent of them tying white handkerchiefs onto their walking sticks, which seemed like so many white flags. Such puerile antics were bound to lead to noisy brawls and scuffles. But it was more especially the festive crowds at Lourdes who made the greatest sensation, for it was at this time that Lourdes had begun to acquire its world-wide reputation, and the intellectuals, who had long scorned such provincial thaumaturgy, recognized it as a force that had to be reckoned with—not only a religious but a political force, for the symbolism of the white banners and the fleurs-de-lis was proof enough that Henri V's accession to the throne was one of those miracles the Virgin was being asked to bring about. The whole new wave of devotion provoked a flow of indignant protests in the press: Schérer expressed his indignation in *Le Temps*, while *Le Journal des Débats* published a forceful article denouncing both the recent examples of devotion and the pilgrimages. The article was anonymous, and it would be interesting to know who wrote it.* "God," said the anonymous author, "has been made into a political figure who, in the Assembly, sits on the Right. It cannot be denied that his opponents have been provided with many grounds for complaint, and that it was not at all necessary to add to them by organizing the parades and pilgrimages of La Salette and Lourdes. Because of those tactics, all the benefits from the slaughter of the Commune hostages have been lost; the martyrs' blood is now of no use; and democracy, that powerful wave of the future, has been antagonized."

Such polemics served to undermine the Center coalition at its most vulnerable spot and to wound it willfully. *La République Française* pounced on the article as a godsend, and to fan the embers, reprinted it in its entirety. The editors of *Le Français* did not belong to those groups

---

* I wonder if it may not have been written by Bersot, who, three days earlier, had had a letter published in the *Débats* dealing with the same question: "The devotional cult associated with Lourdes has as little to do with that advocated by Bossuet as the smug, ingratiating manner of M. Louis Veuillot has to do with that of Fénelon." It is possible that after the letter was published, he was asked to write the article, which altogether corresponded to his way of thinking and to his style. The letter appeared on the 17th, the article on the 20th. Bersot had, justifiably, great moral authority. Veuillot, in l'*Univers*, conjectured that the anonymous author was either Bersier or Pressensé, both of whom were Protestant ministers. But, then again, Veuillot was quick to attack Protestant ministers.

within the Catholic fold that were responsible for promoting the pilgrimages and increasing the devotional cults. They belonged to an altogether different tradition which was Gallican in inspiration. They were accustomed to reason and found such Lourdian practices, which excited the mobs and promised miracles, little to their taste. Indeed, the anonymous attack launched by the *Débats* was in no way directed against them, but rather against Veuillot and his ilk—the ultramontane bishops and their wild, fanatical congregations. But since subtleties tend to be forgotten in the heat of battle, the attack hit at all believers, and the fact that it had been printed in the *Débats* was a significant factor: *Le Français* published a spirited reply, thus widening the breach even further.

Around November 10 the deputies were back in Paris, broken up into their own circles, or in the Versailles palace corridors, or in the wings of the theater where they held their meetings, or in the crowded railway carriages between Paris and Versailles, where they exchanged views.

On the 13th the Assembly was due to reconvene, and there was much speculation about the speech that Thiers was to deliver on that day.

Both sides were stirred up. Broglie, Lacombe, and their friends were dismayed to discover that their very private deliberations of the previous summer had received little publicity. The Conservative deputies, who were gathered together, were steaming with passion and instinctively alarmed. To them, the Republic was still repellent, and the Monarchy was still the magic key to everything they hoped for. Falloux, who only shortly before had, in private, seemed amenable to making a deal, had recently written a harsh article on Thiers's skepticism which killed any possibility of negotiations. "I find everyone in a state of great agitation," wrote Lacombe. "The men whom I believed had been converted to ideas of conciliation speak of nothing but fighting any plan regarding M. Thiers's

authority and of taking up a monarchist position." Yet in
the course of a private meeting that included deputies
from the Right and the Center Right, Lacombe won a
hearing when he spoke up in favor of making a deal. Since
we do not have the power to provide the country with a
better government, he said, we have no right to turn down
any proposal that might improve the *status quo*. The duc
Pasquier, the duc de Broglie, Witt (Guizot's son-in-law),
and Chabrol (a friend from the *Correspondent*) supported
his position: Decazes challenged it; Ernoul raised strong
objections; and the surge of the arguments was such that
everything remained obscure and nothing was settled.
Nothing much was lost, actually, and Thiers's words had
every chance of deciding the issue. What would he have to
say?

He began with a clear and detailed account of the
recent peace negotiations: the government loan and its
success, the German evacuation and what might be hoped
for regarding it, and a restrained and proud summary of
what had been accomplished. Then, after a short pause,
Thiers, in a typically sharp and provocative tone, explained his policy: "The Republic exists; it is the lawful
government of our country; to contemplate any other kind
of regime would mean a new revolution—the most deadly
of them all . . ." The parties of the Right trembled: they
well knew that kind of language; it was the language of
republican propagandists. Thiers pointed to the trouble-
makers: they were at the right. At the right sat those who
would be responsible for the revolution—the most deadly
revolution of them all. With one stroke, Thiers had meted
out both blame and praise: blame to the parties of the
Right, praise to their opponents. The parties of the Left
were the champions of order! "The Republic was proclaimed by storm," wrote Lacombe. The Left, over-
whelmed, burst out into cheers, while the Right—from the
Center all the way to the Extreme Right—reacted with
deep and painful sighs of despair. But they kept on

listening. Would Thiers at least speak of the reform of universal suffrage and of controlling the number of voters, which they were still dreaming of and which he himself had suggested in private? Would he propose creating an Upper House, which would earn him the backing of the Center Right and antagonize the Left? No, neither of those two points were mentioned by Thiers. But, then, would he condemn the bold revival of radicalism? Nothing of the kind; rather, he hailed the Revolution for having laid the foundations of social justice, and his fervent tirade seemed deliberately calculated to rejoice the Left and to mortify the numerous aristocrats in the Assembly whose families had been decimated by the Terror, who had been raised on tales about banishment, and who were still haunted by memories of the bloody guillotine. Gambetta would not have spoken any differently. No doubt Thiers uttered some soothing words here and there. The Republic, he stated, should be Conservative . . . But to the Right they were only words, mere blossoms skillfully tossed about with treacherous intent. "None of the oratorical precautions I had suggested to facilitate the transition to a republican form of government had been taken," wrote the duc de Broglie in his *Memoirs*, "but not an effort was spared to make the medicine even more bitter . . . I felt every one of those words fall, drop by drop, next to me, like boiling oil on an open wound. A muffled shudder could be heard from the seats on the Right, whereas the applause of the Left gave the whole scene a truly revolutionary character." *La République Française* had the same impression and pointed it up in a single word: *Dissolution.* "Behind each pause in the speech lurked the threatening specter of *dissolution.*" Was Thiers paving the way for that gravedigger evoked by Gambetta in Grenoble, was he announcing the Assembly's dissolution? Was Thiers himself not the gravedigger? He finished his speech. The deputies of the Left rose and applauded for a long while. Those of the Right, who were staggered, rose and gathered round their leaders, muttering: publicly and insolently, Thiers, who owed them not only his election but everything, and to whom they had remained loyal despite all his insolence and evident treachery, was forsaking them, was rejecting their alliance; he was deliberately insulting them.

"A restoration of the Monarchy would mean a revolution—the most deadly of them all . . ." It was those words, more than all the others, which were bitter. Since presidential addresses were then posted on the walls of every commune, they would be read throughout the country; they would be discussed even in the remote countryside; they would stigmatize all those who had remained faithful to the old cause. Thiers knew it well: he had used cutting words; he had meted out the poison. His speech called for an answer. Audren de Kerdrel followed him to the rostrum and, speaking for everyone, demanded that Thiers's address be referred to a committee. Thiers gave his consent, but made a significant reservation. "I refuse to make any distinction between the majority of the Chamber and *the majority of the country,*" he said. "Speaking as I did, I meant to express the views of the *true* majority . . . I want my address to be examined publicly *in view of the whole country.*" Speaking cryptically but intelligibly, he told the Assembly precisely what any Assembly hates to hear, and what this threatened Assembly hated more than any other: that its last day had come, and that it was to be judged by the country.

The Assembly was in too much of a turmoil to await the committee's report. It simply had to blaze out and resume the struggle. On November 18 the veteran African general, Changarnier, climbed up to the rostrum and asked Thiers whether or not he wished to repudiate in public, as he had previously done in private, the declaration of war against the *bourgeoisie,* that excommunication which Gambetta had proclaimed in Grenoble. Changarnier spoke badly and addressed himself too personally to

Thiers, whom he accused of being "senile and ambitious." That spoiled everything. Then Broglie intervened. The fact that he went over to the Republic had provoked and precipitated Thiers's disastrous address; he had had some responsibility for it, and many of his friends blamed him for it in no uncertain terms, and also for having led them to that dreadful impasse. Broglie, wanting to clear up any misunderstanding as to his thoughts and actions, followed Changarnier up to the rostrum and asked expressly that Thiers confirm, before the entire Assembly, the statement he had made a month before to the standing committee— his categorical repudiation of radicalism, which had satisfied Broglie and the permanent committee. Once and for all, would he or would he not break with the Left and disavow Gambetta as well as the secret alliance he had made with him?

For the first time, Broglie took the floor on an important issue—and challenging the greatest living orator of the day at the peak of his career was no small feat. His manner of speaking was shrill, rather disagreeable, and somewhat lisping. Moreover, his general bearing as an orator made an unfavorable first impression. Yet although the *Figaro* compared him to a cavalry officer flinging his arms about as a peacock spreads its tail, his high-toned manner and energy, which derived from both strength and arrogance, had a caustic effect that commanded respect. He confronted Thiers with quite a ticklish request. It has been said that the ducal tone in which it was stated made it appear impertinent and more like an order. But that is most unlikely, and neither the Center Right nor the Right itself had got the impression that Broglie had shown any hostility to Thiers. In fact, they were so sure that Thiers would respond favorably to his demands that they applauded him enthusiastically when he made his way back to the rostrum.

But they were bitterly disappointed. Thiers had interpreted, or chosen to interpret, Broglie's question as an impertinent insult and countered him with a fit of temper—his one and only reply. Since he had an excitable nature and was a born actor, he excelled in such tactics. "This time it was the last straw," wrote the republican historian Zévort. "The *petit bourgeois* rose to his full height and for half an hour lashed out at the trembling majority with virulent reproaches." The *petit bourgeois* was Thiers, who had once derived pleasure from aping the great, growing in stature as he mingled with them, but now, changing his policy, he rejoined the little people. And lurking behind his typically shrewd and calculated reproaches lay the threat of what *La République Française* called "the specter of dissolution." The sharp peroration of the old man's tirade deserves to be quoted: "You realize that it is unparliamentary to want to hang on to power against the express will of one's country . . . If that is what you want, then I shall accept the country's verdict." Then, following a brief interruption, he added: "*I do not refuse it. I insist upon it.*" Without mentioning the word itself, Thiers was perfectly clear; he was insisting upon dissolution.

Thiers had gone to an extreme. Many of his faithful friends of the Center Left would have liked him to make the public statement demanded by Broglie. Since Gambetta frightened them, they were coming to terms with the Right and working against him. The majority of the Assembly evaded the issue and grumbled among themselves, so that Broglie sensed the possibility of achieving total victory. He was prepared to seize the opportunity, to thoroughly exploit it, to replace Thiers with MacMahon, to assume power himself. Emboldened by his own words, he wanted to complete his triumph. But the time was not yet ripe. Thiers was backed by powerful interest groups. High finance, which was extremely influential, was altogether committed to government loans, hoping for a lull on the political scene, and, at least temporarily, supporting

The End of the Notables

Thiers.[3] Many members of the Right, aware of the
problem and susceptible to influence, reacted against their
own triumph and wanted to restrain Broglie from acting
too rashly.* Thiers himself, who had decided that, given
the outburst, caution was the best policy, drew back and
left Dufaure, his Keeper of the Seals, to try to wind up the
operation and save the day. Acting evasively, Dufaure
agreed to an order of the day which stated both "the
majority's confidence in the government's vigorous action
and its condemnation of the doctrines proclaimed at the
Grenoble banquet." This conciliatory motion was adopted
by 263 votes from the Center parties as against 116 from
the two Extremes, with 277 abstentions. But it was not
much of a victory and amounted to no more than a truce.

At last Batbie submitted the committee's reply to
Thiers's address. It was also—and perhaps more especially
—a reply to the Grenoble speech. Gambetta had outlawed
the ruling classes, and Batbie, speaking in their name,
demanded that radicalism be outlawed. He defined it as
he understood it and as it was conceived by all contemporary Conservatives, from a legitimist such as Francœur to a
Liberal like Casimir-Périer:

> Our wretched country is challenged today by forces of
> disorder which are more numerous and more powerful than
> in any other country . . . The soldiers in those forces
> called themselves Socialists in 1848, Communalists in 1871,
> and today they are generally known as Radicals—a label
> which has recently been adopted to describe the league of
> destruction. Their goal is to destroy all that exists, without
> saying what they would set up in its place. They attack
> what we defend, destroy what we wish to preserve, and
> insult what we respect. Their hopes give us grounds for fear
> . . . It would seem that their objective is to stifle the great

* Cf. Ludovic Halévy, *Trois Dîners avec Gambetta*. Alphonse de Roth-
schild claimed that he had played no part in bringing about Thiers's downfall.
He said, on the contrary, that by using all the influence he could muster in
Parliament, he had kept him in power for six months. Thiers fell on May 24. Six
months before—November—marked the crisis provoked by his address.

voice of religion—the only voice that somewhat vigorously struggles against the strident proclamations of demagogues who seek to provoke the passion for individual rights.

"That force," Batbie noted, "is heading for a constitutional victory—an evil for which there is no cure and which is far worse than the ephemeral victory achieved by insurrection." Batbie demanded that the government refrain from blatantly favoring such a course of events, and that—having been invested with power by the majority of the Assembly—it refrain from directing its own power against that majority. Moreover, in order to resist the possibility of a Radical victory, he—and the Committee he represented—thought of creating a "war cabinet" consisting of a coalition of all the Conservative forces in order to enlighten public opinion as to the schemes of their Socialist opponents. "In our country more than in any other," said Batbie, "the government is the last bulwark for preserving order, and its withdrawal from this struggle might well lead the people astray."

Batbie's idea of a "war cabinet" corresponded precisely to a profound craving that had been in the air for long years. Why should the *grands bourgeois*, the Notables who controlled the Assembly, be the only ones who were denied the right of exploiting the power of the State, which had always been so great in France? Under the Second Empire the *préfets* had controlled the masses; from September 1870 to February 1871 the *préfets* appointed by Gambetta had boldly followed their example. Why should the majority of the National Assembly allow themselves to be excluded by a head of State and by *préfets* whose devious schemes were turning France against them?

Batbie concluded:

> The majority is of the opinion that the root of the trouble lies in the personal intervention of the head of the

executive power in our parliamentary debates. Although the constitutional authority of the President of the Republic does not exceed the rights of a delegation, it in fact is, in itself, exalted, and the confidence it enjoys in this country endows it with a power that cannot be disregarded. The fact of it does not leave us totally and morally free, for there is nothing to prevent the head of the executive power from constantly intervening in favor of ministers who are called to account, and from turning a cabinet issue into a governmental issue.

It was therefore necessary to revert to proper parliamentary procedure: to define and limit the President's authority and to subordinate his cabinet to parliamentary control, by adopting, *"as soon as possible, a law establishing ministerial responsibility."*

In other words, through Batbie, the Assembly made its wishes clear to Thiers: it demanded that he rule the Republic as would a constitutional king; and it conceded the principle of presidential stability provided it did not involve ministerial stability, and that the cabinet of ministers serving under an irresponsible president be at all times responsible and govern under the control of the Assembly. In short, the Assembly challenged Thiers with the very same doctrine which he himself had invoked against Louis Philippe and Napoleon III; it demanded from him, but this time to his own detriment, one of those "essential liberties" he had previously defined and demanded.

But by now Thiers cared precious little about those "essential liberties." We can tell from the rough drafts he used for outlining his rough plans that he was contemplating a political and philosophical treatise on "the essential truths." And there is no doubt that those truths were merely judgments formulated by him and to his own satisfaction. But he found resistance to his ideas difficult. While giving ground, he clashed swords, and clashed swords like a master. Since he was under personal attack, he thought it best to identify himself with a greater cause and asked that the committee elected to draft a law on ministerial responsibility also be entrusted with studying, as a whole, the problem of constitutional laws, of the electoral law, and of an Upper House. The royalists were perturbed. Thiers, by way of a clever maneuver, used the committee to lure them into a republican trap. You want to reduce my power, he told them. Fine! But replace it with something reliable. Several members of the committee—and not least among them, the Orleanists—would have agreed. "I don't see how we can refuse," said the duc Pasquier. But the majority, including Batbie, Broglie, and Ernoul, stuck to the original plan: first attack Thiers. Only then would they investigate the constitutional laws, but on condition that they had complete freedom from a President who exploited his position by constantly blackmailing them with threats of resignation. The Assembly had to choose between them and Thiers, and Thiers carried the day with the backing of all the parties of the Left, but just barely. Gambetta, who had saved him, henceforth had an advantage over him. A Committee of Thirty was elected, and it was that same Committee of Thirty which, after two years of hesitant and rigidly intricate procedures, was to produce the Third Republic. The majority of the Committee consisted of Conservatives whose first objective was to conduct a campaign of harassment directed against Thiers under the leadership of Broglie.

Harassed as he was, Thiers held his own. His formidable responsibilities fully satisfied his instinctive craving for hard work and scheming, as well as his high hopes. Since his unchanging objective was to win the country's support, beyond and against the Assembly, the profound national desire to hasten the end of the German occupation was admirably suited to his purpose. The Versailles debate was merely a quarrel, so that whatever reverses he suffered from it were of minor importance. His main goal was the liberation of the fatherland, and he devoted himself to it completely, with all the complex fervor of a patriot, an artist, and a believer.

To pay off the Prussians as quickly as possible, to get rid of them, to see the last peaked helmet leave the country—that was the passionate hope and task of all France. She was enflamed and regarded it as a matter of national honor, whereas it would perhaps have been wiser and more cautious to quench her ardor. The example of Germany fifty years later was to show her conqueror that in such a case the most expedient policy is to plead poverty and use delaying tactics. But the French in 1872 were far from thinking in such terms. Thus freeing themselves by filling the German treasury with gold, by inadvisedly and perhaps naïvely feeding and fattening their enemy, was a point of coquettish honor to the French, and to Thiers as well, for he took coquettish pride in being a man of action—an old man hankering for glory and prestige.

The negotiations were far from easy. Although Germany was ready to receive her due, she was less inclined to reciprocate by returning the occupied departments and the remaining forts—Belfort, Toul, and Verdun (especially Belfort).

The military, who were so powerful in Berlin, constantly sought to hold on to what they still possessed, using as a pretext the specter of revolution and of Gambetta, its embodiment. "The cloud on the horizon," wrote the comte de Saint-Vallier, one of Thiers's diplomats, "is still M. Gambetta; his very name inspires a loathing that recurs with growing strength . . . M. de Redern, who is on intimate terms with the Emperor, is reported to have said: 'As far as we are concerned, this man's rise to power is tantamount to the coming of revolution, which we shall never allow.'" All the more reason, then, for Thiers not to break with the Assembly.

By December and January he was negotiating on two fronts: on the one hand, with Germany; on the other, with the Assembly. In Versailles he found himself on slippery ground. The Committee of Thirty gave him a rough time, being firmly resolved to stick to its original plan to restrict his power and to stifle that voice of an old friend who had gone over to the enemy, and who, through experience, had become too skillful in sharpening and aiming his arrows. Although he vainly tried to persuade it to tackle the constitutional issue as a whole, the Committee, bearing a personal grudge against him, claimed that the first order of business would be to define the limits of his own authority. It no longer wanted to hear his obtrusive voice. What king had ever had that right to march up to the rostrum of an Assembly and to throw all the weight of his authority into the issues of debate? Not one of them. Thiers, therefore, should not have had that right, and his prerogatives had to be restricted. If he wanted to talk, he had first to ask permission. The Assembly was to adjourn, was to set an appropriate date for him, and at a specific time, would listen to him, and then, having heard him out . . . At that point Thiers protested and amused the country with a graphic reply: "All that is rather complicated. Allow me to say that we are behaving like the Chinese, who bow courteously on solemn occasions. As they take their leave, one bows in turn. Then they come back and bow courteously again. It is all, actually, rather futile. In financial discussions five or six days of debate would thus be required to clarify matters which could be settled in a matter of minutes."

Broglie held his own, reminding Thiers that the disagreement between them had to do, not with Chinese etiquette, but with the very nature of his executive power, which once and for all had to be clearly separated from the legislature. Whereupon Thiers again protested, even more graphically and more vividly. What did they want to make him into? he asked. "A warrior with his sword nailed to his behind? A political puppet, a fattened pig in the Versailles prefecture?" Then, adding a touch of impertinent humor, he hastened to tell the noblemen who were banded together against him: "*If I belonged to those noble races* who have done so much for the country, I could comply and accept the role of a constitutional monarch. But since I am a *petit bourgeois* who, as a result of hard work and study, have managed to become what I am, I can only repeat that it would be truly humiliating for me to accept the position you suggest." "The *petit bourgeois*," "the noble races"—none of those words fell on deaf ears. In no time, they spread throughout the country, from the towns to the villages and from the country fairs to all the thatched cottages.

It looked as if the chances for reaching an agreement were a long way off. But there was Berlin; Berlin hoped and, indeed, demanded—before finally ratifying the treaty—that Thiers and the Assembly come to terms.

Gontaut-Biron, the French Ambassador to Germany, wrote constantly to that effect, and to everyone. To Thiers he wrote: the German Emperor dreads Gambetta and wants you to come to terms with the Assembly's Conservatives; if you both come to terms, everything will be made easier . . . To his Conservative friends he wrote: only Thiers has Bismarck's trust and sympathy; come to terms with him; unless you do, we shall find it difficult to overcome the remaining obstacles that stand in the way of evacuation . . . A settlement was reached; Thiers accepted the restrictions imposed; and the Committee, in turn, agreed to examine the question of a constitution as well as the creation of a second Chamber. Broglie drafted and submitted to the Assembly the terms of the settlement. His policy had finally prevailed.

It amounted to a conspiracy, in which Gambetta did his part, which was very difficult for him and did him credit: he said not a word either in the Assembly or outside it. He was seen spending an entire day at the

Sorbonne, probably better behaved and more attentive than he had ever been in his student days, listening to the young Fouillée defend, in opposition to his elders, his ideas on liberty.

January came, then February. "There is no longer any need to form a great Conservative majority," exclaimed the duc Pasquier. "It is formed!" He was crying victory a little too soon: the sense of calm was merely a lull which the Pasquiers, the Broglies, the Dupanloups, the Ernouls, and the de Meaux tried to turn to their own advantage. The fusion of the Center parties, a shaky coalition, was insecure and rather stormy. Even among those who had agreed to it, there was no mutual trust. Thiers invited the Conservatives to his dinners, the atmosphere of which was described by the vicomte de Meaux. He tells how he met a few friends at them who seemed somewhat surprised at having been asked. They had found the company questionable and the food mediocre (it was traditional that Thiers never served decent meals). They were consoled, however, by an inoffensive epigram to the effect that the menu was no better than the new majority.

Yet the coalition was not altogether unproductive, although its fruits were not flourishing; from the very beginning, they were tainted by a Conservative policy which another leader might perhaps have put to better use. We would do well to examine those fruits and to get just a taste of their late autumn flavor.

The Assembly first passed two laws which, in Batbie's phrase, were "fighting laws." One was directed against Lyons, which, from then on, was to be divided, like Paris, into *arrondissements*, six of them, each with its own mayor, and with a *préfet* assuming duties which, elsewhere, were the responsibility of the central city hall. The second law was directed against the International Workingmens' Association, which was held responsible for the Paris Commune as well as for disseminating revolutionary propaganda in the mines and factories of the cities' working-class suburbs. The Conservatives were terrified by the secret feelings of the masses, who were always ready to rise against them, and the International was the body on which they based their fears; once they had stamped it out, they felt reassured. But, in fact, they had stamped out little more than a ghost and a bugbear, since the International had very little power, and what power it had sprang from depths on which fear had no effect: the International was prohibited by law.

Finally, the Assembly adopted four constructive laws which give us some idea of what a lasting Conservative policy could have achieved in the France of 1873. One regulated women and child labor in factories by cutting down their working hours. Another regulated the sale of wine and the repression of drunkenness. Yet another reformed the Higher Council of Public Education, which, by virtue of the law of 1850, and in collaboration with faculty members who had been elected by their peers, had brought in representatives of the so-called "social interests"; this had transformed the Council into a body "of free and true representatives of all the social elements with a mutual interest in shaping the minds of future generations," and the Council was designed "to play the role of a father deciding what lessons to give his son rather than that of a teacher who instructs." * The Empire, legislating in an entirely different spirit, had transformed the Council into an altogether bureaucratic body; the law of 1873 re-established the law of 1850, adding delegates from commerce, industry, and agriculture to a body hitherto restricted to State representatives. And the fourth law implemented Mgr. Dupanloup's desire to have the clergy represented in State charitable organizations.

Two bills were finally studied and reported on. One, dealing with freedom in higher education, was to be

---

* A report made by the duc de Broglie, June 27, 1871.

adopted in 1875 and remains advantageous to Catholic universities. The other was neither adopted nor discussed, and it never was to have its day: it concerned a subject of major importance—primary education, which was universally regarded as the most crucial question of all. The die-hard republicans insisted that elementary education be free, compulsory, and secular, and their watchword indissolubly linked the three terms. Since compulsory education necessarily implied free education, would the State agree to pay? Who would, if not the State? It followed that the State would assume the responsibility for education, and the schools, like the State, would be secular; therefore secularism would become compulsory. The Conservatives rebelled against the trinitarian conception, and in rejecting the last principle instinctively and out of self-defense, they had also to dismiss the first two. As early as 1871, seeing Jules Simon set up as Minister of Education, they were troubled and had questioned Thiers about the situation. Wasn't Jules Simon, on the rue de Grenelle, representing the enemies of the Church?* Thiers had reassured them he would never yield on that particular question. Did they suspect him of repudiating his struggle of 1849 against the schoolmaster-politician, "the frightful little teacher who was the enemy of the priest"?[4] Thiers was shocked by the implication.

And yet in 1872 he had signed into law the bill by

---

* One should not forget the speech he had given shortly before—on March 14, 1869—to a Masonic lodge in Paris: "It is often said quite rightly that the Revolution is not over. We want it to be. How can one end it? By setting up schools everywhere, by emancipating people's minds everywhere." Cf. Adrien Leroux, *La Franc-maçonnerie sous la Troisième République d'après les discours maçonniques prononcés dans les loges*, 2:165. Cf. also a curious passage on Jules Simon in Mme. Adam, *Nos Angoisses*: "He gives secret but tremendous backing to anticlericalism . . . He has taken over *Le Journal des Instituteurs*, which today is entirely controlled by the Minister of National Education.

"The other evening, at a party given by some of our friends, Macé told him, 'My dear Simon, give the Right everything it may ask. Satisfy it, deputy by deputy. If necessary, sacrifice us, but give us a France which will be free of clerical obscurantism.'" The Macé referred to here was the founder of the "Ligue de l'Enseignement."

which Jules Simon laid down the first two principles, Compulsory and Free education. The third, secularism, was implied. The Conservatives had reacted straightaway, and Ernoul, with the assistance of Mgr. Dupanloup, had drawn up a counterproposal whose provisions were, and still are, highly interesting: communes were to have the right to decide, by a two-thirds majority, between secular and religious teachers. As for free tuition, the question was covered by a most ingenious and liberal clause whereby the child of parents who could not afford to pay school fees would receive a voucher that corresponded to an educational grant; that voucher could be used for any school, public or private. Such a scheme would have paved the way for a proportional school system which a good many people are still concerned with today and even still hope for. Although Ernoul's plan made no provision for compulsory education, *compulsory* is no more than a word which can easily be evaded, and the financial aid to all schools provided by Ernoul's bill, as well as the competitive spirit among them it might have provoked, would have achieved far more for the education of the people than our centralized and cumbersome system of national education which has offended so many and, after fifty years, has allowed so many illiterates to exist.

A way had thus been opened; Jules Simon promptly and diligently closed it. Realizing the dangers that would arise if the bill reached the Assembly, he tabled Ernoul's report, even his bill, and indeed the entire question. The overriding goal as far as his party was concerned was not that the French people be educated but that they be educated in a certain way.*

---

* M. Seignobos, in the seventh volume of *L'Histoire de la France contemporaine*, edited by Ernest Lavisse, wrote the following lines on the subject: "It was suggested that free tuition be granted to needy families and that elementary schools be entrusted to autonomous 'Associations' (in other words, to the religious communities). Since a proposal so revised no longer interested Jules Simon, he did not call for a debate on it, and primary education was not reformed." Ernoul's bill indeed called for only limited free tuition, but so did

The tabling of this particular bill seems less regrettable when one considers the fate of all the other legislation proposed at the time. Because of an active lobbying group's power of the veto, not one law, except that regulating women and child labor in factories, was to last: Lyons was to regain its mayor; the International Workingmens' Association was to spring up again in the Socialist party, which was to be organized publicly in Paris sixteen years later; the law regulating charitable organizations was to be altered; the republican *préfets*, responding to the pressure of the wine merchant—a privileged voter under the nascent Republic—were never to enforce the law repressing drunkenness; the free universities were to lose their very fair and very useful privilege of awarding their own degrees; and finally, since the representatives of the "social interests" left the Higher Council of National Education, it was once again to become a government agency consisting of faculty representatives, either appointed by the Minister or elected by their own colleagues, as a first try at administrative trade-unionism.

Thiers had failed to show the slightest interest in the passage of all this abortive legislation.

Since the Assembly reproached him for intervening in its debates, he decided that the best course was to abstain from attending its sessions. Dufaure, Keeper of Seals, who alone represented him, thereby set a precedent for the position which today has fallen to the President of the Council of Ministers. The Assembly was only too happy to follow the leadership of an old Gallican like Dufaure, who was a bit too republican for its taste, but who at least did

---

Jules Simon's, for what were then pressing financial reasons. M. Seignobos would seem to know nothing about the freedom given to the communes, and he makes no reference to the school vouchers. His concluding words are significant and probably reflect his turn of mind, which was so typical of the underlying spirit of the Third Republic: "a proposal so revised no longer interested him." M. Charles Seignobos, a Calvinist from the Cévennes, is traditionally radical and anti-Catholic; he often expresses himself with invaluable clarity.

not insult or betray the Assembly. One evening in January he held a reception at the Ministry of Justice, which was jammed full of members of the majority. Thiers did not attend; he was at the Luxembourg,[5] where his republican friend Calmon was holding a reception in honor of the republicans. Also present was Gambetta, extremely well-behaved and listening to the President, who was in great form as he held forth on the arts. "Mr. President," said Gambetta, "your Republic is really an Athenian Republic." "Not in the least," replied Thiers; "it is Florentine!" His hero was Lorenzo de Medici, and since he wanted to emulate him in France, he had probably set the stage for it by decorating the walls of his study with watercolor reproductions of Michelangelo's Sistine Chapel frescoes. So what did all those Conservatives' schemes in the Assembly matter to him? As he confided to his friends: "Four months from now, I shall give all those people a good kick in the behind . . ." He withdrew only that he might concentrate all his efforts elsewhere, in order to prepare more carefully for France's liberation and his own triumph.

That was no easy task: the powerful Prussian general staff, including Moltke himself, was reluctant to abandon the occupied fortresses—more especially, Belfort, the key to Southern Alsace. Until almost the very last moment Thiers was apprehensive. Around February he was still receiving reports to the effect that the German government was seeking ways to evade its commitments. In matters of that sort, when one seeks, one finds. England, in similar circumstances, had once found a way to hold onto Malta[6]—a historical precedent which was being studied by the staff of the Wilhelmstrasse. But the Emperor was an honest soul and hoped that Germany would abide by the treaty. Bismarck, whose motives had little to do with honesty, and in agreement with his sovereign, dissociated himself from the military. Germany, he thought, had conquered enough territory, and it was well to take France's money and to take it as quickly as possible. Besides, Bismarck did not share the views of those reactionaries who wanted the Parisian republicans to dance to their tune. On the contrary, he favored a democratic semi-anarchy (what he called "a disintegrating Republic") for his defeated adversaries, and part of his policy was to grant the republican Thiers a kind of success. As he jestingly reminded Gontaut-Biron: The man you need is Adolph I; take him and resign yourself to him . . .

In March of 1873 both of Thiers's negotiations—with the Committee of Thirty and with Germany—were on the verge of being simultaneously concluded. On the 13th Broglie read his report, and on the 15th the peace treaty was signed in Berlin.

That parliamentary session during which Thiers and the Assembly finally came to terms was truly curious. Although the Center Right was victorious and the Left yielded, the Assembly, with Broglie as its spokesman, had taken a new step in the direction of the Republic. It abolished the semidictatorship that Thiers had set up under the pressure of events; and it gave the presidency the detached, passive, and ceremonial nature it still has today. The President no longer appeared before the Assembly except under certain specific circumstances; he no longer addressed the Assembly until he had first obtained its consent, and only during an extraordinary session, which was held for him and was adjourned once his business had been attended to. The agreement also stipulated that the Assembly would not dissolve before having enacted a law regarding the organization and transmission of its legislative and executive powers, as well as the means of creating a second Chamber, or before the passage of an electoral law. Substantially, it amounted to a commitment to organize a Republic. Broglie, who was chairman of the committee, never put that into words, but probably admitted it to himself. A dedicated parliamentarian, he was not at all distressed. Although the Moderate

Right monarchists followed his lead, they were troubled: they realized how very strange it was to have been destined to become the founding fathers and unwilling members of a regime that threatened their own interests and which their loyalty to the Crown condemned. As for the Extreme Right, it was fulminating, and against Broglie in particular. "M. de Broglie," wrote Veuillot, "is a half-breed, a blend of France and Geneva, of Catholic and Protestant, of yes and no." The agreement in its totality was adopted by 400 votes as against 200 from the two extreme parties.

The peace treaty concerned the entire country. On March 17 Rémusat, the Foreign Minister, informed the Assembly that by September 5 of that same year, 1873, France would pay the balance of its debt, and Germany would thereupon evacuate Verdun, the last remaining city under occupation. He added that Belfort would be returned by July.[7] The Assembly responded to the news with prolonged cheers. "Long live France!" shouted the Right; "Long live the Republic!" shouted the Left; and the two shouts mingled into a general uproar which was all that could be heard at first. The country was freed; everyone was overjoyed. But would the Assembly's initial and spontaneous outburst, its shouts of joy, subside? Wasn't a written text, some kind of resolution, needed to formalize it and make it lasting? It was also felt that something should be said to acknowledge the fact that the country had worked hard and that the country had been well served. Christophle, the deputy who was president of the Center Left, climbed up to the rostrum, read a text, and proposed that his colleagues adopt it as a resolution: "The National Assembly proclaims that the President of the Republic has deserved well of his fatherland." And not a word more.

That day's session provoked some virulence among the parties. Needless to say, everyone was thankful to Thiers. But what subtle implications did that expression of thanks imply? Not one escaped the attention of the alert parliamentarians. Thiers's name resounded, throbbed, and was constantly repeated during all the clamor and the cheers from the Left. Still Thiers. The parties of the Right sensed the implications and remained silent. Christophle's motion insinuated something. Didn't anyone guess what it was? There was general agreement throughout the country that the National Assembly would have completed its task the day it had paid its debt to Germany and had brought the occupation to an end. Even the Conservatives were at one on that point. Then, dissolution! That, indeed, was the idea of the Left and, because of Thiers and the Left, was assumed by the Center Left. The reader will perhaps recall that it was Christophle himself who had repeatedly recommended in January 1872, after Thiers's resignation, that the Constitution of 1848 be restored—in other words, that the Head of State be elected by universal suffrage—a plebiscite, in fact; an appeal to the people: it was shocking that only two years after the collapse of the Empire, the threat loom large again and that it derive from Thiers's own supporters.

Thus the Center Left's motion corresponded to what nowadays would be called an electoral gambit (an expression not then in use). This was clearly borne out by the exultation of all the parties of the Left. *La République Française* remarked soon afterward: "Let us think about what will happen after the Prussian evacuation. The Republic now has the right to address France and to demand that she repay the debt of national gratitude she owes it." Thiers, who was triumphant and sanctioned by the Assembly, was going to appeal to the people, Parliament's acclamation preceded and was preparing for the acclamation of the people. No doubt the time was soon to come for Thiers to "give all those people a good kick in the behind . . ." And it was from those very people—that is to say, the Assembly—that the sly politician asked for the power and the glory that he planned to turn against them. The Conservatives sensed that there was double-dealing in the air—a trap. They realized that behind the tribute they were asked for lurked a specific policy and, into the bargain, a flagrant injustice. Indeed, was it fair to grant one man the glory that several deserved? What a curiously divided Assembly yet again: the republicans were unanimous in demanding an immediate vote on Christophle's motion; contrary to their own principles, they were seeking to glorify one man, and at the expense of the Assembly. The Conservatives—monarchists of every opinion, and even Bonapartists—sought, on the contrary, to discourage any personal tribute so that the Assembly might receive its rightful share of honor. They were in an extremely difficult position: if they fought the motion, they would run the risk of being, or seeming to be, ungrateful, and of thus getting an odious reputation; whereas if they yielded, they were dupes.

A decision had to be made. The Orleanist Saint-Marc-Girardin, a university professor and member of the French Academy, climbed up to the rostrum. With no tact whatever, in a situation that demanded a great deal of it, he proposed the following: "The Assembly . . . pleased that it has carried out the main part of its task, expresses its gratitude as well as the country's to M. Thiers, President of the Republic, and to his government." Whereupon the Left began muttering and laughing: the Assembly congratulating itself—a real brainstorm! Surely it is more gracious to congratulate others. This was followed by a tumultuous debate on Saint-Marc-Girardin's proposal, amid constant cheering for Thiers. Someone shouted: "Three-quarters of an hour of deification is quite enough!"

Since the shout had come from the Right, the Left shouted that the Assembly was guilty of ingratitude and disgraceful behavior, which provoked an uproar. The Assembly's leaders—Grévy, Rémusat, Broglie, and Dufaure—realized, with great concern, that the splendid occasion was deteriorating into a bitter wrangle. Fortunately, Andren de Kerdrel succeeded in putting an end to the confusion by introducing an element of fairness, moral elegance, and patriotism which had often earned him the respect of the Assembly in the past:

> Someone said that the Assembly should be able to bear the burden of gratitude. But gratitude is not burdensome; it is the most exquisite of human emotions, and since it is an exquisite emotion, its scope should be skillfully gauged.
>
> SCHEURER-KESTNER: Let's vote! We've talked enough already.
>
> KERDREL: In order that this emotion be expressed fairly and fittingly, it must include all those who have deserved it and no one must be omitted . . . If the government has performed a great act—the greatest in its history—it was indeed thanks to its patriotism, but it was also thanks to the peace that has reigned in the nation, for which much of the credit belongs to this noble Assembly.
>
> PELLETAN: You tried to overthrow M. Thiers.
>
> KERDREL: But now, to go on, and to pay our debt of gratitude to all those to whom we are beholden, I look farther afield, and I see the poorest and most humble people in the country sacrificing themselves to liberate the fatherland, so that I am unable to omit the country, which is represented by this Assembly.
>
> Therefore, let us pay unreserved tribute, with no ulterior motive, to the President of the Republic and to his government! Also a tribute to this Assembly! And a tribute to the noble country of France!

Thanks to Kerdrel, a compromise resolution was accepted and unanimously adopted. Grévy, who was president of the Assembly, suggested that the entire body leave the Chamber and present Thiers with the motion that had been carried. The parties of the Right balked and delegated their executive committee. It was all conducted without the slightest propriety: the parties of the Left rushed off immediately in order to reach Thiers first, and got to him before Grévy; the Conservative deputies, who were exasperated, kept to their benches.

The acclamation of the Left echoed throughout the country, and the honest vicomte de Meaux noted mournfully: "Being traditionally inclined to put itself in the hands of one man, the country admired and was grateful to M. Thiers alone." He had been the leader; all gratitude went to him. Municipalities and *Conseils Généraux* united to thank him, and to thank only him. The French Academy sent a few of its members as a delegation both to Thiers and to his minister Rémusat (also an Academician) to express its joy. Poor Assembly.

It seemed as though France were celebrating a victory. In fact, it was a harsh victory, and the rejoicing was frankly excessive. All things considered, the Germans had merely honored the Treaty of Frankfurt. They had withdrawn, but not until they had felt like it and in return for a good sum of money, without yielding an inch or giving up a penny. Although Article 3 of the draft treaty of Versailles had provided that financial guarantees could replace territorial guarantees, the March treaty contained no such concession, and the Germans prolonged their occupation until the last cent had been paid. Meanwhile, Strasbourg, seeing the gold from its lost homeland being brought in and piling up in its banks, reacted with lamentations and some bitterness, given the shouts of joy which would not have been all that exultant were it not for the fact that one party was profiting from them. I might also repeat that it is by no means certain that France acted sensibly in settling the indemnity with such alacrity, for the prompt payment of the five billion francs made Germany regret that she had not demanded more to replenish a war treasury which many believed would soon be used again.

But France, oblivious to all that, was unanimous in her desire to give free rein to all those feelings of joy she had been deprived of for two years.

CHAPTER 11

Barodet

"Barodet is a world unto himself." (Francis Magnard)

Wɪᴛʜ the departure of the last peaked helmet, the war phase came to an end, leaving the liberated country with only one problem—its future and its rather shaky institutions. Laying the foundation for permanent institutions, establishing a Chamber, a Senate, and an electoral law, would not have sufficed. Either the word *monarchy* or the word *republic* had to be pronounced, and since a monarchy was out of the question, there was nothing for it but to say "Republic." It was perhaps merely a word, but words can shape men's minds, and France as well as the rest of Europe was anxious to hear the name of the regime under which France would resume her place in the family of nations. The Assembly had either to say it or to withdraw and cease to exist. But for the Conservative majority, still fighting shy of the issue, Thiers was the most pressing problem. Ought they continue to put their trust in the man they had originally supported and helped to keep in power, but who was now indisputably their enemy? Jules Simon had no illusions on that score: "Your task has now been accomplished," he told Thiers; "it is time for you to say your *Nunc Dimittis*." Although taken aback, Thiers was well aware of the accuracy of Simon's warning, but it was hard for him to adjust to the fact that his power could come to an end or that anyone would dare oppose him.

"They have no one," he replied.

But Jules Simon knew that Broglie was prepared to have him replaced by Marshal MacMahon, a gentleman and a soldier who was quite capable of holding an office that signified order and representation.

The parties of the Right scarcely needed to take the trouble to try and overthrow Thiers; he accomplished it all on his own. Besides, that was his style. As Veuillot had so accurately noted as early as 1871:

> He is today what he has always been—skillful, bold, stubborn on many questions, including his own words, and irresistible because of his cunning; but he has to be able to resist himself and refrain from jumping over the brink of a parapet he can *no longer straddle.* Although he has taken many serious tumbles in the past, he thrived on them because he always picked himself up again; yet he never stopped. At this point, he is rapidly heading for his final fall, which will cause him to lose everything he ever gained: his overrated reputation as a man of wit and as a sly politician.

Veuillot was quite right: Thiers was indeed rushing to the brink of a parapet—and one, as we shall see, he could "no longer straddle." Although that restless Ulysses never lacked wit, he was often imprudent.

There were thirteen seats to be filled in the Assembly, one of which belonged to Paris. Since the whole of Paris, from Belleville to Sainte-Clotilde, was to vote on one and the same day, Thiers had the idea of asking the great city to provide him with the support he felt he needed. Since the mayors of the city's twenty *arrondissements* had come to congratulate him, he received them as a group and introduced them to his Foreign Minister, Rémusat, who

175

was standing at his side. "It is easy to succeed," he said, "when one is backed as I have been." Turning the conversation in that direction, he made no secret of the fact that he would be delighted if Paris, in the forthcoming elections, would make his associate and very old friend Rémusat a deputy. If Rémusat were elected, what a triumph it would be for him! It was Thiers's first try at that dazzling plebiscite which so haunted his dreams.

Rémusat was a perfect exemplar of that very elegant and clever society which had ruled France from 1814 to 1848. He had been a friend of the young duc and duchesse de Broglie, and through them, had been introduced to Mme. de Staël, whose famous *salon* on the rue du Bac epitomized the spirit of the eighteenth century and was trying its hand at that of the early nineteenth. His name was associated with politics as well as with literature, and all he lacked were the diligence and ambition that are essential to great careers. His philosophical and historical studies, and his fine philosophical drama, *Abélard*, had been highly regarded and quite properly admired, as they still are today. He had served as a minister under Louis Philippe for three years, and had been chief commissioner of the Paris Police for another three; he had been successful in both offices, but had left them both with no regrets. Debarred from public service by the Second Empire, he had had no trouble resuming his literary career. In 1871, still a very competent, reliable old man, he had rallied to Thiers as soon as he was called, and supported him in his tragic endeavors. Thiers himself once sketched out an excellent portrait of him:

> The great-nephew of M. de Vergennes and the grandson of M. de La Fayette, a true noble in his ways, a true noble in heart and mind, perfectly at ease in life despite his modest means, a man of great and broad intelligence and phenomenal culture, subtle to the point of being profound, M. de Rémusat—somewhat skeptical due to his vast

experience, but unshakable in his high principles, invariably a Liberal, a fervent patriot, a judicious politician, a bit mocking at times, but never at all offensively—was admirably suited to persuade the aristocratic courts of Europe to accept a well-ordered Republic.

Thiers quite rightly had found him qualified to conduct foreign affairs under his direction. Whether he was qualified to represent the people of Paris was a different matter. His very virtues were to work to his disadvantage, for he was too typical a representative of that old country of France which the still-unknown country of France was in the process of destroying. In backing Rémusat as a candidate, Thiers had counted on his own prestige and popularity to assure victory; but he failed to reckon with the persistent memories of May 1871, when, on his orders, the blood of Parisians had gushed forth, and also the deep resentment of the *communards* he had defeated. In Montmartre, Mélimontant, and Belleville, in the small workshops of the Marais, among the carpenters and joiners of the Faubourg Saint-Antoine and the construction and tannery workers of the Faubourg Saint-Marceau, the masses were still armed. Even to this day, Paris has neither a street nor a monument in honor of Thiers;[1] Paris never forgave him. The Parisian working-class suburbs interpreted Rémusat's candidacy as a challenge following a flagrant offense. Rémusat was Thiers's man; he was therefore an enemy. The Radicals sensed that climate of resistance and not only interpreted it at once but expressed it, as well as their amazement at the ceremonial presentation of the candidacy. The Head of State had introduced and recommended his own candidate to the Paris mayors: Was France reviving the Empire's practice of supporting official candidacies? They personally did not accept Rémusat and counted on finding one of their own candidates to run against him. But who? They were at a loss. Victor Hugo, who had returned to his Guernsey retreat, refused to be considered. A few young hopefuls, such as Lockroy and Ranc, were willing to try their luck, but they hardly had striking reputations. As the Radicals tried to make up their minds, a Red newspaper suddenly printed the name of a dark horse: *Barodet*. Curiously enough, the name spread quickly throughout the working-class suburbs and the editorial offices, and immediately found favor.

Barodet was that mayor of Lyons whom I have already mentioned once or twice. In 1872, after the death of the old republican Hénon, the town council had recommended him to the Head of State as its choice for mayor. Taken aback, Thiers had consulted the *préfet*: Who was this Barodet? A few police reports, now in the National Archives, had informed him. One of them read: "Barodet, former schoolteacher in Louhans, fired in 1849, later an associate of Tournier, a former swindler who founded a bank in Algiers, embezzled 300,000 francs, and escaped to England. Barodet then returned to Lyons and became a traveling salesman. He lived by his wits. Leader of the Lyons freethinkers, he is the Venerable Hénon's* chief spokesman and the ghost writer of his proclamations. He belongs to the Grolée club and is an esteemed Communard party worker." Much of that report consists of police slander with a reactionary bias, which another report, submitted by the Governor of Algeria, rectified: "According to information I have been given by the attorney general, M. Barodet, presently deputy mayor of Lyons, was never directly involved, or so it would seem, in the transactions of the Tournier bank. Indeed, it would appear that no one by that name has ever been heard of in Algiers." ** In short, Barodet was a revolutionary teacher, a Red, and a militant freethinker, who was representative of a new breed of men that were beginning to claim the

---

* The Lyons republicans had called their mayor the Venerable Hénon. The nickname may have some relation to Freemasonry.
** National Archives, Rhône file, 1871–73.

public's attention. Thiers once again consulted the *préfet* of the Rhône: "Should Barodet be appointed?" "He's as good a choice as any," replied the *préfet*; "Barodet is not really a bad sort, and we should be able to handle him." So Thiers had appointed him, and indeed, Barodet hadn't been too bad a sort. The *préfet* had managed to get along with him on financial and police matters. But he remained intransigently anticlerical and had created many difficulties not only regarding schools, the keys to which he refused the teaching Brothers in defiance of the law, but also regarding Church processions, which he persistently forbade. So that those constant quarrels in Lyons were an endless source of news for the press and of indignation for the Conservatives, leading ultimately to the passage of that law of March 1873 stipulating that in Lyons, as in Paris, the *préfet* would take on the duties of the mayor. The real purpose of the law had been to exclude Barodet, and the mention of his name in Paris had only one meaning: the defeated Paris Commune was welcoming and honoring the ousted mayor of the Commune of Lyons.*

---

* Here is a sketch of Barodet from one of Magnard's articles: "Barodet no longer stands for the masses; he has always worn a frock coat and he will always wear one; he represents not the crowds of low wage-earners, whether they work in the fields or at the anvil, but rather that new ruling class which intends to supplant those who have governed us since '89.

"It is a shabby version of the Third Estate which amounts to nothing and which wants to become everything—a class which, caught between the worker and the bourgeois, has neither the expectations and freedoms of the former, nor the comfort and apathy of the latter. It is that class which took over the Republic when it was being weaned and which seeks to relegate the old Conservative party to the background. It has no program, only desires; and it fails to provide any real and serious solution for the grievances of the proletarians: it leads them by way of new words instead of the old rights of man; it makes them believe that freedom of the press and freedom of assembly— which in fact only serve to advance its own interests, because it uses those freedoms to make reputations and to handle situations—as well as secular education and the abolition of funds for religious purposes, will suffice to remedy everything and make for equality in everything. And the people—that big child, with its characteristic simple-minded meekness—take all this sham seriously; all former jailbirds and all those who are destined to become jailbirds will vote unanimously for Barodet out of conviction, since to them Barodet stands for amnesty, for freedom of thought and expression and the right to

In Paris, would Barodet be the Left's candidate? One thing was certain: Gambetta's first reaction was unfavorable. He had a taste for a kind of glitter and splendor where the State was concerned. He was, in sum, a Parisian of the Second Empire and he was not at all pleased that Barodet be set up as an opponent of Rémusat's, or that Thiers be insulted by having to rely on such a dull candidate. But he had to give in and yield, as he put it, to the pressure of a spontaneous movement of irresistible popular opinion. The word *spontaneous* recurs so frequently that it makes one wonder. "Several candidates were in the public eye," wrote *La République Française* on April 9. "One among them—backed by such an altogether spontaneous current of public opinion that even the oldest electors could not recall having ever seen anything quite like it since the beginning of universal suffrage—suddenly stood out from the rest as the most popular candidate. It was M. Barodet, mayor of Lyons." Two days later *La République Française* reproached *Le Temps* for having raised objections against Barodet: "The staff of *Le Temps* is perhaps more aware than anyone else that democratic elections are decided by an irresistible wave of public opinion . . . It is an irresistible wave of public opinion that has brought M. Barodet to the fore and that will be responsible for his victory." *Le Rappel* activated the impressive phenomenon of a spontaneous candidacy, printing on the front page of its April 10th issue two unsigned letters by Paris voters, both of whom wanted Paris to appoint Barodet. It was they who spoke for the people. Two days later, *Le Rappel* took a position: "Now that M. Barodet's candidacy has erupted of itself, now that it has sprung to the fore from every corner of the land all at once, now that it has been engendered by everyone and no one, we commend the instinct of this great population." *Le Siècle* used the same

reduce everything to stupidity, and for the end of martial law—in short, for the beginning of a new era of Socialist steaks and chops freely walking straight into the mouths of the workers." (*Le Figaro*, April 15–16, 1873.)

language: "Two candidacies sprang forth spontaneously—
M. de Rémusat's and M. Barodet's. We endorse M.
Barodet's candidacy." The word *spontaneously* yet again.
But Rémusat's candidacy had not been spontaneous.
Thiers had suggested it—indeed, almost demanded it—
from the twenty mayors of Paris, and the editor of *Le
Siècle* perhaps gave himself away by the excessive use of a
word that had been printed too often. It is easy just to say
"spontaneous." If Barodet's candidacy was indeed as
spontaneous as Rémusat's, one should like to know where
and how such a decision was reached and by whom.
Actually, *Le Siècle*'s conclusion rather intrigued truly
well-informed Parisians. The paper's largest shareholder
was Cernuschi, a financier of Italian and Jewish extraction
who tended to favor Rémusat; Henri Martin, Carnot, and
others, who also favored Rémusat, were members of its
administrative board. Yet the paper had decided to
support Barodet. Who had given the order? As M. Gabriel
Hanotaux points out in his history of the period, there
were "some underhand practices" involved, which is very
probable. But one should like to know more about some
of the threads in the plot which M. Gabriel Hanotaux
merely glides over. Weren't the Freemasons at the bottom
of it all? Possibly Barodet's name had been mentioned—in
print, at first—by some defeated Communard, and since
nothing is ever forgotten in the Parisian working-class
suburbs, which had been decimated by Thiers, Barodet's
name had been approved as a sign of revenge. But if it was
taken seriously and preferred over all the others, it was
probably due to a deliberate and well-organized conspiracy. Barodet was a Freemason; like his predecessor, the
Venerable Hénon, he belonged to one of those Lyons
lodges which had such great influence in the area,* and

* "Public opinion in Lyons was controlled by the lodges," wrote the
Freemason Lepelletier in the *Bulletin de la Grande Loge Symbolique*, 1885–
1886, quoted by Adrien Leroux in *La Franc-maçonnerie sous la Troisième
République, d'après les discours maçonniques prononcés dans les loges*, 2:433.
These two volumes, which consist entirely of extracts, are highly interesting.

which, in April 1871, had convinced Thiers to promise to come out in favor of the Republic. As Thiers's paper, *Le Bien Public*, bitterly put it: "The Radical committees give orders and everyone must obey." But the Radical committees said themselves that they took orders from above. Wasn't the anonymous writer in *Le Bien Public* really of the opinion that "the lodges give orders and everyone must obey"? *Le Bien Public* was Thiers's paper, and both he and his followers were far too cautious to expose the great organization to which many of them (including Thiers himself in his youth) had belonged, and in which they had no doubt often wielded power.

The campaign began, and was to be short: between April 12 and April 27, it was settled. And it was all the more fervent for being so short. The walls were splashed with posters; the streets were in an uproar. Flaubert, who was passing through Paris and in a rush to get out of it, described the city as totally bewitched by "Barodetian idiocy." Barodet put in an appearance and did not make an unfavorable impression. He was neither a fool nor a bombastic orator, but rather the man everyone expected— a provincial without much style but with great dignity. He proclaimed his principles: dissolution of the Assembly, a truly republican Republic, a truly Radical constitution; elected mayors, a single Chamber—the good old conventional position. Rémusat was not in that much of a hurry to explain his position. Wasn't he sufficiently well-known? Had he anything to say that everyone hadn't heard? According to his friends, he did not intend to make any declaration of principles, probably because that would more easily unite those whose votes he expected, whether moderate republicans, Conservative republicans, monarchists who had rallied to him—however temporarily—or republican sympathizers. He was Rémusat, he was a friend of Thiers's, and that was enough. *La République Française* reacted immediately: "No, Paris cannot vote for

M. de Rémusat for precisely the same reason that M. de Rémusat cannot say what his position is as a candidate." Rémusat decided to explain. But instead of writing a declaration of principles, he penned a charming letter, the tone of which can be properly understood only if one imagines it written by some elderly Parisian Notable chatting with his friends and neighbors. "I have always held," he said, "that the only stable type of government is a moderate regime that derives its strength from public confidence." He also hoped to see the Assembly adopt constitutional laws: "Such laws, in my opinion, should have no objective other than organizing the government of the Republic on the basis of legitimate institutions consistent with past experience and the integrity of universal suffrage." The republicans found the wording too weak. Rémusat spoke of "organizing the government of the Republic"—a phrase which aroused their suspicions. The Republic had to be *proclaimed*—a word that distinguished the orthodox from the others. Rémusat's name was plastered all over the walls: "Rémusat: candidate." Nothing more. But a candidate of which party? The lack of one made people laugh. The poster was therefore altered and shortened to "Rémusat." Not a word more. What did that enigmatic name mean? Shortly before, Rémusat was a candidate; since he eliminated that word, had he ceased being a candidate? The republicans reacted with glorious jeers and laugher. Then came a third change: "Rémusat: republican candidate." At last the word *Republic*, which seemed to give so many people sore throats, had been uttered! But rather late in the game. In point of fact, Rémusat was a republican, but he did not like the historical, philosophical, and mystical resonance of the word; he found it unpleasant to awaken the revolutionary echoes that so endeared it to the people of Paris. Moreover, he had to humor his supporters from the Center Right, whom he was not quite managing to please. The duc de Broglie and his friends, who were committed to him and had promised him their votes, found him too humble in the way he reacted to the republican demands and to all the mocking in the streets. Rémusat had declared that he would respect the integrity of universal suffrage, a statement which was considered a platitude among those who had not yet given up the idea of limiting the terrorizing rights of the masses by imposing restrictions based on age and residence qualifications. As for the republicans, they questioned an idea that had not been taken in all that quickly. An old and renowned leader, Louis Blanc, explained his own doubts in an open letter: "It is difficult to believe that the Orleanist in M. de Rémusat has suddenly made way for a republican." So that Charles de Rémusat, the man Thiers had chosen and singled out, was himself excluded by virtue of the ban which Gambetta had proclaimed in his Grenoble speech, and the republicans refused to accept him in the Republic. All of this struck Veuillot as most amusing. Opposed to both candidates and having decided to vote for neither one of them, he tried his hand at comparing them, and Rémusat did not come out ahead:

> I am repelled less by Barodet than by Rémusat, because Barodet is acting in character, whereas the comte de Rémusat is not. Barodet is still wearing his threadbare clothes, whereas the comte de Rémusat is ripping up his velvet suit; Barodet is trying to climb up, and Rémusat to climb down; Barodet is seemingly aspiring to higher things, whereas Rémusat is rushing headlong to the bottom. Barodet may induce one to fight, whereas Rémusat's conduct leads one to flee. I do not accuse Barodet of defection or of betraying society. He has declared war, and we are forewarned. Rémusat is opening a postern which he was protecting and is laying a bridge across a ford he should be defending.

To the writings of both candidates were added the speeches or letters of their friends. The lawyer Allou spoke for Rémusat: "We must protest against the tendency of demagogues who drag their candidates out of nothingness, as if to set the brutal tyranny of the majority against the dazzling qualities of talent and generosity of heart." "Forsooth, you gentleman of good taste!" retorted *La République Française*. Among the leaders of the republican party, many protested: Langlois, Proudhon's old friend; the historian Henri Martin; Arago, the son of Arago the astronomer and the republican of 1834; Tirard, who was later to become Premier—all came out in favor of Rémusat, as did Grévy and Littré. But they were all leaders without a following or, as in the case of Littré, philosophers who worked on their own. The latter was smartly called down by *Le Rappel*: Stay in the Academy, M. Littré; stay in the Academy!

Then, suddenly, the republican masses asserted themselves in the provinces, as the Radicals emerged victorious in many municipal elections. Avignon celebrated its victory with Bengal lights as red as the victorious Radicals, while the Provençal crowds sang in their local dialect:

> It is Marianne that we want
> And one-eyed Gambetta will be President!

The songs in Paris were less naïve and more worrisome. As the Parisians emerged from their political meetings, they could be heard humming the revolutionary tunes that everyone thought had been finally suppressed:

> Vengeance has been properly sown.
> Also well-fertilized. So see, if you will,
> How reprisal has grown
> On the graves of those who were killed.

The whole business was turning nasty, and Thiers, losing a little of his self-confidence, was worried. He found it very difficult indeed to hold his coalition together, all the way from republicans such as Littré to monarchists on the Moderate Right. One evening Broglie went to the Élysée, where he had been invited to a reception. There were a large number of republicans gathered round Thiers, who, embarrassed by the Duke's presence and afraid of appearing to be compromisingly civil, managed to make his way from one group to another and to ignore the fact that he was there. It is safe to say that Broglie made little effort to break the ice. Yet Thiers needed reactionary votes. The candidacy of Colonel Stofflet, set up at the last minute by the Bonapartists, who this time were in open alliance with the die-hard legitimists, vexed him exceedingly, for Stofflet would surely attract votes that would have gone to Rémusat. Thiers, at the Élysée palace, summoned Villemessant, the editor of *Le Figaro*,[2] a man who, since he was anxious to humor the subscribers of the Faubourg Saint-Germain, remained neutral, supporting neither Stofflet nor Rémusat. A legitimist, Villemessant gave Thiers the reasons for his apparent neutrality and explained that it did not mean he was hostile. His paper, he pointed out, was not closed to the friends of M. de Rémusat. And since Thiers answered with his usual fiery sparkle, Villemessant, shrewd editor that he was, suggested: "I shall print that as an article." "Be sure to quote me accurately," said Thiers. "Then I want it all down in writing," replied Villemessant. Thiers thought for a moment. "I'll write you a letter," he finally said. "You can be sure it will be printed," replied Villemessant. It appeared on the morning of the election; it was the last cartridge used in that battle; it was also the last article to be written by the journalist, who, in the spring of 1830, with pen in hand, had brought about the fall of the Bourbon king. The letter ended with the following words: "*Barodet* means theft, plunder, the slaughter of hostages, destruction, annihilation." And it was signed: "An old legitimist." O, that *Marseillais!*

The votes were cast: Barodet was elected by 180,000

votes, as against 136,000 for his opponents. Stofflet received 27,000. And so Paris, the romantic city which for so long had been proud of imposing its will on the provinces, treating them like mindless servants—Paris, a Paris that no one knew—had elected a provincial schoolteacher.

The decisive votes had been cast by the defeated Communards, who, until then, in fear of the police and of being belatedly prosecuted (for they were still being prosecuted), had not dared to register and, in a body, had abstained from voting. Suddenly, they had mustered enough courage to vote against Thiers's candidate, thereby providing the vital impetus for Barodet's victory.

Thiers, who had arrived from Versailles that evening, heard the news surrounded by friends and visitors in the drawing room of the Élysée palace. Although they had long been accustomed to losing, those Parisian Liberals were dumbfounded. They had clearly foreseen defeat, but not to that extent. All those votes for a man who, only yesterday, had been a dark horse! In 1849, in rather similar circumstances, the Paris Socialists had elected Eugène Sue.[3] Although the disagreeable incident had frightened the *bourgeoisie*, it had not in the least disrupted their habits. Eugène Sue was a well-known writer, a *grand bourgeois* of good breeding and elegance whom one would meet at the theater, in *salons*, in the elegant cafés; Eugène Sue, the deputy of Paris, represented nothing that would have revolutionized the habits of a Parisian of the eighteenth century or the early nineteenth (which came to much the same thing). But that Barodet have such a triumph—Barodet, that provincial from Lyons, that schoolteacher! Victor Hugo had been a candidate in Paris and had received only 80,000 votes. It seemed that the very mediocrity of Barodet—the fact that he was unknown and colorless—had charmed the majority. John Lemoinne wrote that politics in Paris were changing: "The Radical republicans declare war on the Liberal republicans; the

fourth estate claims that it wants to be the prime force in
the nation and is closing the door to the third estate. The
sectarians tell us: 'The house is ours; it's up to you to get
out.' Fine. We're being put out; we shall stay out." There
were many who felt the same way. When you're in a sad
plight, put a good face on; so they had rallied to the policy
recommended by Thiers and which Thiers had assured
them would continue to serve their own interests and not
disrupt their habits. As the young Rémusat had advised in
his charming song:

> If you want to save your reapings,
> Leave your interests in our keeping.

Had Thiers, then, been wrong, or had he done *them*
wrong? He himself, always ready with an appropriate spicy
remark, had told Broglie in the spring of 1871: "The
Republic is a little slut. She no sooner enters the house
than she puts her ass in the window and everyone flees."
This time, that delightful part of her body mentioned by
Thiers had taken on Barodet's features, and many fled.

Paris had not been alone in its choice of Barodet: the
results of seven other elections held on that same day had
been identical. Their meaning and the obvious conclusion
had been expressed on Barodet's last poster, printed in
red, completely in red, and still clearly legible on the walls
of the city. It stated concisely: "*Dissolution. — Republic.*"
Was one to go along with that *Mene, tekel, upharsin?*

CHAPTER 12

The 24th of May

T HAT cruel a blow could not remain unchallenged. When Eugène Sue had been elected in 1850, the Conservatives had retaliated by passing a reactionary law. Thiers had led the entire operation with his usual courage, standing up to the republicans and offending the masses by calling them a "vile multitude." Universal suffrage had been maimed; two million electors had been denied the vote. Nothing much had been gained: the republicans were still winning the elections, and Louis Napoleon— fighting the Assembly as an enemy of the people, and the bourgeois parliamentarians as revilers of the masses—had had no trouble bringing off his *coup d'état* and his plebiscites. Would the whole business start over again? Because of confusion, anger, fear, and the fighting instinct, the immediate reaction was to revert to those simple tactics. Too simple, obviously. Magnard, the great political observer who had just begun his long career with *Le Figaro*, was of that opinion. Universal suffrage, he wrote, was perhaps one of those slow-working poisons which could not be eliminated once it had been introduced into the organism. And what he half-heartedly hoped was that during the next elections in the provinces, strong governmental pressure would be brought to bear. But, again, it

was all too simple and meant merely reviving the procedures of the Second Empire. What Magnard and all his
readers failed to realize was that the Second Empire owed
its popularity to military prestige and to a certain Caesarian tone that appealed to the people, both of which
were altogether lacking in the defeated Notables in
Versailles.

Besides, the wheels of government were in the hands
of Thiers, and no one knew how he would react to the
affront of the Parisians. Magnard wrote that he might have
interpreted it as "a foretaste of the surprises that a new
Constituent Assembly held in store for him." Was that
how he understood the incident? No one knew. Now that
he had been cast aside by the Radicals, would he change
sides and draw closer to the Center Right? Would he tell
them: "Agree to the Republic, and together we shall
establish an Upper House; it will include representatives
of the great bodies of State, as well as commerce and
industry, and a few delegates from the National Assembly;
its elected members will be selected by a system of limited
suffrage which would be heavily weighed in favor of the
rural areas as opposed to the big cities; to the Upper
House, let us give, among other prerogatives, the right of
dissolving the popularly elected Lower House; to the
President, let us give the necessary stability by having him
serve for a long term. Thus armed and well provided for,
and making allowances for the hazards of the times, we
shall be able to let the country have its say"?

Did Thiers ever intend to make any efforts in that
direction? I shouldn't think so; he had already thrown the
dice and was gambling on another possibility. There is
some indication, however, that there had been one last
conversation between him and Broglie. Taine cites a very
indirect, hence a not altogether reliable, source as his
authority. "In private," wrote Taine, "I was given details
on a conversation between M. Thiers and M. de Broglie.
Its substance was as follows: 'Recognize the Republic, and

the next elections will give you Center-Left Chambers, the color of Christophle.' 'Even if we recognize it, the next elections will give you Red Chambers, the color of Peyrat.' After that harsh disagreement, they left, ready to fight it out." And much to Taine's regret. "If I were a deputy for the majority," he wrote, "I would immediately and loudly proclaim allegiance to the Republic, and once that was established, I would walk straight on." *Immediately and loudly*: It was easy for Taine to speak in that way—the way of a Conservative bourgeois who, at heart, was a republican; the way of a philosopher who was in no way hindered by what Broglie called "hereditary opinions," those stern protectors of one's thoughts. In order for Thiers and Broglie to come to an agreement, both parties would have needed the kind of courage neither of them had: for Thiers, the courage to give up the popular prestige that depended on republican support; for Broglie, the courage to come right out and consent to the Republic (let us not go so far as Taine and say "proclaim" it; just consent to it). For although the Republic had often haunted him, and more than once had seemed to be necessary in the interests of the State, he never managed to articulate his views distinctly and convincingly.

Yet Thiers was still supported by the republicans. He cried out in rage a few times; they bore with him and then assured him of their support in the most flattering terms: Paris did not vote against you, they said; the overwhelming results of the Paris election should be interpreted as the voters' rebellion against an Assembly that has constantly rebelled against you and is proof of their attachment to the Republic that you, by way of your declared convictions, have made your very own . . . Thiers listened. He was increasingly convinced that the people's party was the party of the future. "The strength of the demagogic party," wrote Broglie in his *Memoirs*, "and the danger involved in combatting a power that had toppled so many thrones and caused such bloodshed, was, I fear, the factor that determined the weak and wily behavior of a seventy-four-year-old man."

Fear was perhaps a factor, but so too was Thiers's feeling about the Assembly. More and more, he had come to despise it, as well as the spirit that informed it and the nobility that belonged to it—the fashionable society that took refuge in it and that used it for its own purposes. He had once admired and envied that fashionable society into which he had wormed his way, and for a long time he had delighted in the fact that he had managed to. But he had never forgotten all the disdain and irony he had endured, or the duchesse de Dino's gibes, or the insults of, for example, Balzac, or the restrictions he had had to put up with. In spite of the success he had had in that society from which he was now drawing away, he was still a stranger in its midst, and he knew it well. Having forced open the doors of the nobility's houses, he now took pleasure in walking out of them, and the commoner from Marseilles and Aix, the former Carbonaro of 1820, was only too glad that the ugly rumors of the street mobs were reaching the ears of the nobility and to sense that they were upset by the threatening masses. That was what had happened in 1830, and 1830 was a heartwarming memory that made him feel young again. Gontaut-Biron who had returned from the embassy in Berlin for a few days, reproached him one last time: "So you don't want any part of us any more?" "No," replied Thiers. Perhaps he was still embarrassed by the astonished and accusing looks of the friends he had had for some twenty to thirty years whom he met, in too great numbers, on the benches at Versailles.* He no longer wanted to see them; he had had

---

* It is significant that many of the letters addressed to Thiers by his former friends cannot be found in his papers. Where are Decazes's letters, Thiers's answers to which have been kept at La Cave? Where is the letter written by Augustin Cochin shortly before his death and which we know about from the draft he left behind? Where is the long letter written by Falloux on May 22, 1872, and which he himself cites in his *Mémoires d'un royaliste*? Anything Thiers preferred no one to know about, he concealed or destroyed.

enough of that Assembly; he was looking for something else.

There were more elections on May 11: Lyons voted and nominated two Radicals, one of whom was Gambetta's friend Ranc, who was still suspected of having been initially in favor of the Commune. (In fact, he had lingered a bit too long on the revolutionary council.) Since the gulf between the country and the Assembly grew wider every day, a choice had to be made, and both sides were running great risks: the Assembly might in the end resort to heaven knows what reactionary policy, and the country might elect a Red Constituent Assembly. Many moderate republicans were deeply concerned about the situation. "Certain general elections," wrote the Protestant Liberal Pressensé, "might have as many disastrous consequences as a *coup d'état*." Yet what was to be done? The *Journal des Débats*, after having recovered from the momentary shock of Barodet's triumph, and again in the grip of its affection for the republicans, advised against resistance. What government can go on saying "No," asked the paper, when the rest of the country continues to say "Yes"? On May 16 Gambetta gave a speech in Nantes, summing up recent events: "For the past year we have witnessed the most dramatic duel imaginable in the annals of any country. We have seen an entire nation won over to the cause of democracy and the Republic, and proceeding slowly, cautiously, peacefully, and legally to eliminate gradually a system of political government which that nation rejects and repudiates because the system represents the past." Then, addressing himself to Thiers, he shouted:

> So you mustn't hesitate. Can't you see that France is heading for disaster. We republicans are moving toward you; come with us . . . Why don't you have confidence in the country? What did the voice of the people mean, what did it recall, in its repeated and commanding decisions? It recalled, it demanded, your message of November 13. It is

that message, your greatest claim to glory, your noblest work—the message that will ultimately place you in the front rank of your contemporaries, which you should never have allowed to be criticized.

Then, after all the flattery, came the warning. Should Thiers resist the call of the people and creep over to the Right, it was no cause for despair, "because however eminent a man may be, no matter how important he is to his fellow citizens, a people does not perish because it may happen to lose one man." Those words made it abundantly clear that the republicans would not hesitate to show the same kind of criminal ingratitude for which the Conservatives had been reproached in the past.

Thiers shifted entirely to the direction in which he had been leaning for two years. Since a quarrel had arisen between two of his ministers, Goulard and Jules Simon, who, in a public speech, had made insolent remarks about the Assembly, Thiers took advantage of it to clean out his cabinet. He sacrificed Jules Simon, but dismissed the Right-Wing Goulard and in his place as Minister of the Interior appointed Jean Casimir-Périer, who had resolutely rallied to the Left. That meant not only excluding the Center Right but insulting all the factions of the Right and challenging them.

Did Thiers believe he could govern with the support of the Left? Did he think he was capable of winning all the Radical votes—and he needed them all—along with some twenty votes from the Center Right? They were necessary to constitute a majority. And what would he have done with that majority? Did he think he could induce the Extreme Left to vote for an Upper House, an institution it considered odious? Barodet's victory followed by Ranc's had encouraged the Radicals on to even greater victory and made them even more fervently wish to bring about the Assembly's dissolution. "We shall never stop demanding it," Gambetta had shouted in his speech at Nantes, "because it is the first indispensable step in organizing the Republic; then we shall refuse the royalists the right of organizing that Republic, for what kind of a Republic could be organized by monarchists? Let me repeat, fellow citizens, what I already said in Grenoble: it would be an unspeakable farce." Was Thiers hoping to persuade the Left to have any part in such an "unspeakable farce"? No, he meant dissolution to be his final effort, and he intended to submit his plan for constitutional laws not so much to the Assembly as to the country at large: it was to be his own campaign program, leading to that national plebiscite from which he expected so much glory.

Broglie realized that the strategy of the Center parties was over and done with. Since the very notion of it had been demolished by Thiers, who had openly come out against it, Broglie acted accordingly and called a halt to the fight. He immediately began all over again, however, since he was so fervent that the idea of standing down never even crossed his mind. In his view, universal suffrage, that deity worshiped by the Reds, was a false god, a hostile idol, and the louder it spoke, the more resolved he became to struggle against it, to strike it down, to stifle its despicable voice. The Bonapartist masses had forced him to waste away the best years of his life, his thirties and forties, so that he refused to submit to the acclamations of new plebiscites which, merely because they were couched in other words, were to him no less barbaric and perhaps even more so. Since the voice of the people declared against the Assembly and clearly opposed it more and more each day, it would be necessary to fight for the Assembly even more strenuously each day. It was in the same spirit, and for the same cause, that Ernoul had beseeched Thiers in December not to cut the cable which bound him to the Assembly. As Ernoul put it, "It represents our sheet anchor!" But Thiers had cut the cable, and the fight was on; the fight against him was on.

Broglie suddenly regrouped his forces. With subtle and fervent strategy, he brought in the legitimists, whom he disliked, and managed to win over the Bonapartists, whom he despised. But their votes—the votes of some thirty deputies who met in secret, though everyone suspected who they were—could provide him with the necessary margin for victory. Both the legitimists and Bonapartists acknowledged Broglie's qualities of leadership and went along with him. Supported by that Right-wing coalition, along with a few members of the Center Left who had firmly broken away from Thiers, Broglie felt confident enough to attack and submitted a motion of interpellation[1] to the Assembly: "The undersigned, convinced that the seriousness of the present situation requires that our leadership be entrusted to a cabinet strong enough to win the country's confidence, demand to interpellate the government on the recent ministerial changes, as well as on the necessity of imposing on the government a strictly Conservative policy." The motion was signed by over three hundred deputies.

Thiers saw to it that the battle was waged in such a way as to keep all the initiative on his side. The very same Committee of Thirty that had defined and limited his own authority had been entrusted with studying and recommending a plan for constitutional laws. The Committee shifted the responsibility of it to Thiers, who carried out the task without delay and decided to use his plan as a reply to the interpellators. Dufaure, vice-president of the Council, introduced it to the House; the *Journal Officiel* printed it. Yet oddly enough, the plan went almost unnoticed. Probably passions were running too high, the expectation of a great oratorical duel was too keen, and no one was particularly disposed to read a long and dry treatise on constitutional law. As the duc de Broglie noted in his *Memoirs:* "The overriding issue for some was to replace the Monarchy once and for all by a Republic; for others, it was the problem of what political direction the new regime would take. As for institutions, the subject did not seem worthy of the slightest consideration." (We should bear in mind that "Institutions come first" was the Broglies' political maxim.) And he added: "I don't believe anyone took the trouble to read the text of the constitutional laws that was presented by M. Dufaure, and actually, I think it a pity. For it would have shown how the laws were not at all adequate when it came to safeguarding Conservative interests."*

Thiers's plan was indeed highly interesting. There would seem no doubt that France was then extremely adaptable, apathetically Conservative, and Caesarian or republican in the sense in which that word is commonly understood today. Just as we discovered that the legislation adopted early in 1873 provided a framework for a Conservative regime that was still viable, if we were now to read the constitutional laws that Thiers proposed to the Assembly, we should find possibilities for a Republic very different from our own, and which, had it been tried, would have profoundly changed our perils and our fortunes. The Republic conceived by Thiers consisted of two Houses—a Chamber and a Senate. But he proposed a weak Senate which would have been established on the same principles as the Chamber. "The Senate," he wrote, "will be elected by direct universal suffrage." But what, then, would be the point of a Senate? All the political

---

* Taine, in a personal letter, wrote quite the contrary: "What swayed the majority were the laws proposed by the government for a second Chamber and an electoral system. In the latter the cult of universal suffrage, the stupid worship of sheer numbers, was more than obvious; such laws would have soon led to political suicide." Which of those two accounts are we to believe? A study of newspaper reports confirms Broglie: Thiers's constitutional proposal appears not to have been known to them. There was merely a word about it in the *Débats*, which in fact stated its reservations: "The bill could be improved . . ." It would seem that it was barely noticed, and to this day historians still make no reference to it. Yet Taine was an unimpeachable witness. Perhaps a few scholars and other informed intellectuals in his circle paid some mind to that bill which was ignored by the general public. And, indeed, they must have been surprised. But they were ingenuous enough not to perceive that they were the only ones, or almost the only ones, to have read it and to have been surprised.

theorists—who, like Victor de Broglie, Paradol, Laboulaye, and others, had reflected upon and written about the French system for the past ten years—demanded a Senate whose main purpose was that universal suffrage, represented by the Chamber, would be held in check by an institution created by another source and imbued with another spirit. Thiers's proposal merely used the term *Senate* and offered no such safeguard: it gave free rein to the pressures of the masses which the Liberals dreaded quite as much as the Conservatives, and which even Thiers, when addressing the Committee of Thirty the previous December, had admitted should be kept in check. "Such laws," wrote Taine, "meant ruin within a calculable period of time." No doubt, Thiers's plan did not give everyone a chance to belong to the Senate: there were certain age qualifications and the requirement of a certain rank in the civil service. But the choice of members was nevertheless determined by universal suffrage. To control any signs of unrest, and in keeping with his Caesarian and self-seeking tendencies, Thiers, who disdained a senatorial aristocracy, counted on quite a different form of authority—presidential authority, his own. As he wrote: "The needs and habits of France make it necessary to concentrate very extensive and very diverse powers in the hands of the President of the Republic . . . Among the French, unity of action in the government is absolutely essential for the public well-being." The precedent invoked here was the Constitution of 1848, the very same constitution which had paved the way for the Second Empire. Yet again we are faced with the specter of dictatorship which colored all of Thiers's thinking and which, then even more than today, constituted much of the political thinking in France.

Having thus stated the necessity for a leader, Thiers sought to safeguard his independence. "He cannot be the delegate of a single Chamber or even of two united assemblies, for he would thus be lowered to the rank of a subordinate authority"—an accurate statement of the shortcomings of the system that was to be adopted and which is still with us. Was the leader, then, to be elected by popular vote? Thiers would probably have been highly in favor of that arrangement: it would have meant reverting to the Constitution of 1848, which he persisted in regretting. But its disastrous results had not yet been forgotten; Louis Napoleon, the first leader to be so elected, had too easily become Emperor; the danger was too manifest, the wound too painful: it was still smarting. Thiers thus proposed an ingenious compromise between the popular and parliamentary systems: the President would be elected by an electoral college consisting of both Chambers, to which each of the *Conseils Généraux* would send an additional three delegates.* Thus Parliament would not have complete control over him. The Chambers and the President would be elected simultaneously for five years, and the President would have the right of dissolving the Chamber with the Senate's approval, as well as of addressing the Assembly under certain circumstances. What the proposal came down to was a presidential form of democracy, very similar to that of the United States then and now, which Laboulaye and others were constantly recommending as an example to be followed.

But the plan was never even looked into. From then on, the Assembly and Thiers were at war. Everything was ready for the decisive confrontation, and the man who was to replace Thiers in the presidency was chosen. Broglie, in order to put an end to the recurring feud between the Orleanists, who were eulogizing the duc d'Aumale, and the legitimists, who refused him their vote, had suggested Marshal MacMahon, an upright soldier who had honorably survived the disasters of 1870 and who, although he

---

* Similar views were put forward in an interesting book, *Vingt Mois de présidence*, which was published in the second half of 1872 by an anonymous author who, in fact, was Edmond Texier, editor of *Le Siècle*. His writings endorsed Thiers's position.

had conquered Paris in May 1871, had had the rare quality of managing to behave humanely during the civil war. No one distrusted him. All the Orleanists, legitimists, and Bonapartists had agreed to vote for him. The decision was made unbeknown to him (the same cannot be said for his wife) and had its comical side. But Broglie, by appealing to his sense of duty, undertook to obtain the Marshal's consent to the responsibility that was to be thrust upon him by the Assembly.

There was nothing for it but to fight it out. On the 19th, the Assembly rejected a motion to discuss the draft constitution; it wanted, above all, to be enlightened on the intentions of a government in which it would not participate. What was the meaning of the new cabinet? That was the first question to be answered. On May 23 Broglie spoke up and warned Thiers:

> Beware! If you carry the vote today, the haphazard majority responsible for it will include the entire staff of the Radical party, which would be a vanquishing and dominant force. The cabinet as well as the rest of the majority would be, not allies, but the wards and protégés of the Radical party.
>
> To perish for the sake of a cause with one's flag in hand, and defending a rampart, is a glorious death which will eventually honor the memory of its public figures.
>
> To perish, on the contrary, after having prepared—but having not yet suffered—the triumph of one's enemies, to perish having opened the gates of the citadel, to perish being not only miserable as a victim but ridiculous as a dupe and sorry for having unintentionally been an accomplice, is a humiliation that destroys not only the renown but the lives of statesmen.

Thiers listened in silence. Under the law of March 13 he had the right to speak only at an extraordinary session and one that had been convened for that purpose alone.

Buffet, whom the Right had elected to succeed Grévy as chairman of the Assembly, would not have tolerated the slightest violation of that law.

On May 24 Thiers replied to Broglie, and from his very first word, reversed the situation. The question, he said, the real question, concerned not social conservatism as against radicalism, but the Monarchy as against the Republic. If the country was stirred up, it was because it was denied the regime it demanded, which, in fact, was the only regime conceivable. If society was imperiled, the reason for it was the Assembly's exasperating refusal of that regime.

> I believe, gentlemen, that the true Conservative policy is that which lies between the two extremes and represents the obvious interests of the country. We are doing the most Conservative thing in the world by providing you with the laws of a Conservative Republic, saying to some of you: "Make the sacrifice of voting for a form of government which is the only practical form possible, and give it your legal stamp of approval"; and when we say to others among you: "Whatever (and excuse my wording) you think of this Assembly, which you are treating as harshly as we have been treated harshly—this Assembly in which you have no confidence—bear in mind that our purpose is not to dissolve it but to keep it functioning long enough to provide a Conservative Republic with laws."

But Thiers was asking for the impossible. How could he hope to work with the Assembly, to get it to vote for a constitution, while he was governing without the approval of the majority—that is to say, in opposition to it—and drawing his ministers from the minority, many of whom were denying the Assembly the right to frame a constitution, as Thiers wished it should do, demanding a Convention and a Radical regime? Thiers was asking for their cooperation, but he was in fact breaking with them. Although his words were conciliatory, he still managed to slip in a few useful gibes. Addressing himself to Broglie, he said: "I thank the speaker for his sympathy; he gave me the opportunity of saying that I, too, pity him. He shan't obtain a majority any more than we shall, but he, too, will be a protégé. I am going to tell him whose—the protégé of a patron whom the former duc de Broglie would have rejected with horror: he will be the protégé of the Empire!"

So Thiers knew that he did not have a majority! He was right in warning Broglie: Broglie, a liberal Catholic, would—like himself—be defeated. But he was wrong to say that he would be a "protégé of the Empire." Broglie had accepted the Bonapartists only to strengthen his majority; he would never tolerate their dictating to him. And when their group was to become a threat around June 1874, he broke away from them, allowing his friends to establish the parliamentary Republic and finally endorsing it himself. Broglie's advantage over Thiers lay in the fact that, in coming to the rescue of the Assembly, he was remaining firmly attached to what Ernoul had called "the sheet anchor," whereas Thiers, precipitating events as he had done so often throughout his career because of a desire to satisfy his own personal ambition for greater power and glory, turned the odds against himself. Luckily for the future reputation of the agitated old man, Broglie's victory concealed and suddenly put a stop to the consequences of his rash behavior, thereby earning him fame for political wisdom which was not deserved.

Had Thiers convinced the Assembly? All the manifest dangers and the perceptible disenchantment among his own followers was still counterbalanced by his continued and enormous prestige as well as his fantastic skill. His "bold and proud speech," wrote de Meaux, had made a sensation, and neither of the parties dared to believe it had won. The meeting was adjourned after he had spoken, to be resumed in his absence, according to the stipulations laid down by the law of March 13. It was at this point that

Thiers briefly rebelled. "What will you do," he asked Buffet, "if I return to the hall once you have reopened the meeting?" "I shall adjourn the meeting," replied Buffet. Thiers, knowing the man and his integrity, decided to drop the matter. So, alone and out of hearing, Thiers awaited the day's verdict.

For Broglie wanted everything settled that same day. After only one brief adjournment, which was a matter of form, the meeting was reopened. Once all the issues had been discussed, they would be voted upon in silence. Was Thiers finally to be defeated? If so, what would happen? What would become of the presidency were it taken over by a colorless man like MacMahon? Thiers's incredible vitality, which was sensed by his enemies the moment they had voted him down, was in itself a blessing. Thiers was a moving force; he was all aflame; he had never been touched by the cold bleakness that was the fatal enemy of mankind, and it seemed that, because of him, France, which had been so sorely tried, had been protected from it. Everyone feared silence and emptiness; and everyone feared—I repeat—the cold bleakness that would follow. What risky ventures and perhaps even violence would they be heading for as a result of confusion and weakness? The atmosphere was thick with dreams and apprehension—apprehension, because both the Left and the Right were haunted by ghosts, by specters. For some, they were specters of revolutions; for others, specters of *coups d'état.* Would Broglie and his victorious friends perhaps take forceful measures and arrest the republican leaders? And would Lyons, Paris, and Marseilles react to the triumph of the nobility and the Church by raising the barricades and rebelling? The anguished memories of former upheavals was like a setting sun that continued, and would long continue, to cast large twilight shadows on that France which was quietly settling down—indeed, which had, without knowing it, already quietly settled down.

The deputies voted, and due to the defection of

fourteen members of the Center Left, Thiers was defeated by 360 votes as against 344.

He was not obliged to resign. The Rivet law stipulated that he would remain in power as long as the Assembly; as long as the Assembly continued to meet, he would preside over the State. The law voted in on August 31, 1871, was responsible for that ill-matched pair. Thiers therefore had a right to prolong a hopeless conflict and to remain there stubbornly opposed to an Assembly which was itself stubbornly opposed to him. But he was too strongly defied by both custom and common sense; morally, he did not have the right to persist; and he was too well acquainted with parliamentary procedures not to be aware of it. So he handed in his resignation and, without delay, confronted the Assembly with the consequences of its own action. However, the haste with which he did so was yet another of his tactics. Thiers was too good a fighter not to fight to the end. The idea of Thiers not being there, the very idea of it, had long caused the most dauntless deputies to tremble, so that Thiers kept and cherished a glimmer of hope: perhaps they would come back to him after all. "They have no one," he had once said to Rémusat. And he still believed that once he and his followers were gone, there would be no one. Probably, he had heard the name of MacMahon mentioned. But he was still convinced that the Marshal, who owed him many favors, would not agree to be his successor and would refuse the candidacy. Indeed, MacMahon, that upright soldier without the slightest ambition, was not involved in the plot, even secretly, and had no desire to be; he was innocent and aboveboard. Broglie himself had found it more convenient that he remain in the dark and (with the help of his party, his friends, and his followers, not to mention his fervent wife) be faced with the *fait accompli*. MacMahon was a good man; once off the battlefield, he lived an honest, straightforward life and could easily be trapped. As he watched the session of May

23 from the visitors' gallery, he said to his neighbor Mme. Dufaure: "They simply must get your husband to speak. If we have *him*, everything will work out. If we have Thiers, everything will go wrong." His candor was becoming so embarrassing that a few friends, probably together with his wife, contrived that he would miss the session of the 24th. They somehow confined him to his room; they kept him home.

The whole process was over in no time. Buffet read Thiers's letter, and then, as he opened his mouth to pay him tribute, the Left burst out shouting and shrieking. Buffet had himself contributed to bringing about Thiers's downfall; he had presided over his liquidation; so that the parties of the Left refused him the right to say anything in his praise; they would not allow him to speak. Buffet persisted a bit, but was unable to make himself heard. He could have put a stop to the uproar by adjourning the meeting, but what would have happened? It was a crucial question, a cause for apprehension. Perhaps the republicans, all the republicans, would leave the palace, thus making it impossible to elect a new President. Perhaps they might even leave Versailles, rush to Paris, and try to stir up the city. It was rumored that at nighttime the boulevards were already filling with angry mobs. How pleased the parties of the Right were to be in Versailles, beyond the reach of the crowd! In Paris they would not have dared overthrow Thiers. Had the Left really worked out that type of scheme for revolution? It was a fearful possibility, and Buffet, upon reflection, decided to let the uproar die down by simply not making a move. He succeeded: the moment there was a lull, he declared the balloting open. Since all the parties of the Left abstained, MacMahon was elected by 390 votes. Thirty deputies, who had previously supported Thiers out of habit, caution, or in deference to his prestige, had at that point rallied to the Conservative majority.

The Marshal, still unaware of what had taken place, was in his house on the rue de Gravelle. Since his consent had to be obtained, Buffet decided to go and inform him of the Assembly's decision, accompanied by the vice-chairmen and the executive committee. Under his orders, the ushers grabbed some candelabra and lit the way for the parliamentarians, through dark corridors flanked by marble busts and statues, to MacMahon. His personal friends had rushed to get there first. Buffet found MacMahon in his drawing room, angrily pacing the floor and loudly protesting the unexpected verdict and impossible appointment. Thiers had been his chief; Thiers had placed him in command of the Paris army; and he had never ceased telling everyone, including Thiers, that he would under no circumstances challenge him for office; he could not and he ought not accept. Not only honor but good sense forced him to refuse: Was he a politician? No, he was a soldier, a soldier and nothing more. A burden that Thiers had borne with difficulty would crush him; he would be dishonored, he would be of no use, and he would not accept the office.

He spoke passionately and with conviction. In fact, it was later revealed that he had just been severely lectured. Shortly before, having learned that Broglie and his followers were counting on his name to carry the election, he had immediately gone to see Thiers and had asked him, most urgently and seriously, to be frank: Had he resigned and was his resignation irrevocable? The Marshal had always maintained that he would never run against him, and he had no intention of going back on his word. Yes, of course, replied Thiers, I have resigned and it is irrevocable; the Presidency is pure hell and I shall not return to office. And you yourself, he continued, with the warmth of an old and true friend, you yourself, my dear Marshal, don't touch it! You will have such hideous problems, such troubles . . . You will wear yourself out, you will kill yourself; the Presidency, I tell you, is pure hell. Stay away from it!—

The good Marshal had listened with horror to that solemn entreaty addressed him by the most vehement and persuasive of speakers, and thanked him heartily for his sound advice. Thiers, behind his back, congratulated himself, because, in fact, his little speech had been a sham; his words had been deliberately calculated to dissuade the Marshal from accepting the office offered him by his friends, and he was delighted at his success. When their man disappointed them by refusing, what would the members of the Assembly do? What a let-down, what a glaringly obvious sign of their impotency? What else could they do but come back to him, Thiers, and acknowledge him as the victor?

Yet it was all something of a joke. Thiers had deeply troubled the Marshal; he had not affected Buffet in the least. Buffet, very resolute by nature, never weakened for a second. The Marshal, who persisted in recalling that he refused to be a candidate, was informed by Buffet that he had not understood, that he was faced with the irrevocable result of having been voted in, that he had a duty to fulfill. The Assembly was a sovereign power, and its decision was tantamount to a command. Since Buffet, as its spokesman, expressed himself with authority, MacMahon was too much of a soldier not to sense the weight of his words. Yet he persisted. He maintained that he had to uphold his personal honor and that he considered himself unsuitable; politics was not his thing; he knew nothing about it. Buffet again faced him with the fact that he was duty-bound to accept. If he refused, what would the Assembly do? What would become of the State? It was at this point that a few of his legitimist friends approached him, using different terms: if Thiers was overthrown, the political picture would change; one of these days the House of France might be in need of authority and perhaps even of a sword and a devoted soldier. Would MacMahon, who had been so faithful to the country, fail the House of France? It was a curious reversal of fortune: while the Marshal listened to all the apprehensive voices and tried to avoid the eyes of his imploring friends, he remembered that less than two hundred years before—1690, 1873—another MacMahon, an Irish Catholic whom the English Protestants had driven from his lands, had come and asked Louis XIV, in that same town of Versailles, for asylum and had offered in exchange his allegiance and his sword. Louis XIV had listened and had been generous; France herself had been gracious, friendly, and generous to his ancestors and their descendants in return for services rendered. Would he refuse to repay such a debt of gratitude? Honor and those vividly recalled memories had their say: he held out his hand to Buffet; he agreed to assume the burden and fulfill his duty.

It has been said that, upon assuming the presidency, his first act was to ask for the Rules of Procedure: "Where are the Rules of Procedure? I want them brought to me immediately . . ." What a fortunate man: when one is simple, everything is simple. But what was the duc de Broglie thinking on that particular evening, now that the State had been handed over to him. What were the thoughts of that exceedingly cultivated man who, instinctively, was torn between conflicting interests? After all, it was he who had led the operation and would continue to; he had to give some direction to an indecisive country; it was up to him to act on its behalf and to exercise his influence. "When the results of the election were read to me," he wrote in his *Memoirs*, "I was deeply moved, and I was able to judge the accuracy of certain stock rhetorical metaphors which have lost much of their meaning by dint of repetition. The responsibility weighing upon me felt exactly as if the vaults of some edifice were sloping above my head and pressing down upon my shoulders." What would he do? He had wanted to conquer, and he had conquered; in order to conquer, he had joined forces with the legitimists, whom he disliked, and with the Bonapartists, whom he despised. Did he have any idea of what would happen in the future? Did he have any scheme, any plan? Only one thing was certain; only one thing do we know for sure: Broglie had saved the Assembly and had kept France from the dangers of another election for quite a long time. Beyond that, what can one say? The National Assembly was merely an instrument; it consisted of nothing more than a wretched crowd of bewildered deputies who could not cope with what had occurred. Using the Assembly, what future was Broglie preparing for France? One of his associates, someone close to him, the duc Decazes, guessed what he had in mind, made it known, and fortunately, his remarks were most preciously safeguarded. The duc Decazes, on the evening of May 24, at Versailles, sharply interpellated a Center Left deputy by the name of Pernolet:* "How could a Liberal like you, an independent man," exclaimed Decazes, "have voted against us?" "I voted for Thiers," replied Pernolet, "because Thiers is in favor of giving us a Conservative Republic." "No," retorted Decazes, "and don't ever forget this, Monsieur Pernolet: if there is any chance for a Republic, its foundation will date back to the presidency of MacMahon."

And he was right.

---

* The same Pernolet, who represented the department of the Seine, had long taken an active part in the intrigues and unrest of the century. In a letter to *La République Française* of January 19, 1873, he described himself as "perhaps older than the paper in my republican loyalties, which date back to 1830." He was the author of a *Plan de reconstruction de la patrie française sur ce qui reste de solide dans ses fondations anciennes*. He was truly a Conservative, truly a republican.

When in 1875 the Constitution was drafted under the circumstances described by Decazes, he himself recalled those words in a published letter. Decazes filled in the details of their conversation on a clipping of the letter and made a slight correction: the words "if there is any chance of a Republic" were added to rectify Pernolet's reply. (Cf. Bibliothèque Thiers, Decazes Papers, TMSS, 729, No. 144.)

On the Petitions Received
by Thiers in 1875

The Thiers papers in the manuscript collection of the Bibliothèque Nationale consist of three volumes (call numbers: Nouvelles Acquisitions Françaises 20661, 20662, 20663) made up entirely of petitions. The first two are described on the title pages as "Expressions of adherence to M. Thiers's Government, chosen freely by the National Assembly elected by universal suffrage, and protests against the Commune—Expressions of confidence in M. Thiers for the prompt restoration of order." The title page of the third volume reads:

> List of petitions contained in this volume, given by subject and in chronological order:
> (1) *Petitions requesting the proclamation of the Republic.*
> (2) Petitions requesting, *in addition to the proclamation of the Republic,* the dissolution of the Assembly and the restoration of municipal liberties.
> (3) Petitions expressing congratulations and gratitude for the defeat of the Commune and the success of the first loan.
> (4) To M. Thiers, on behalf of the grateful inhabitants of that area of the Haut-Rhin which remained French.
> (5) Petitions expressing confidence in M. Thiers and

requesting that his authority as chief executive be extended.

This classification by subject also corresponds to a chronological classification. On June 20, 1871, the municipal council of Toulouse voted in a petition denying any constituent power to the National Assembly, thereby requesting it not to proclaim the Republic but merely to extend Thiers's power for another two years "in order to protect him from any conspiracies and to prevent any threat of a *coup d'état*." This petition is of major importance. Circulated in printed form by Toulouse to all the French communes, it precipitated a truly national movement of communal opinion which is expressed in almost all the republican petitions in the third volume. Twenty-four communes scattered throughout all of France, from Bône to Remiremont and Douarnenez, used its wording as a model for their own petitions and, like Toulouse, demanded that Thiers's power be extended.

Thus the first two volumes reflect the views of the more moderate communes during the first few months of the National Assembly's rule, especially April and May. Now, it is strange that those very same communes, petitioning Thiers at a time when his republican sentiments had never been made known to the masses (quite the contrary, he was still regarded by many as a monarchist), never called for the restoration of the Monarchy and would seem not to have been aware of that word, which already belonged to a forgotten past.

The communes expressed their loyalty to Thiers and their respect for the National Assembly, which was elected by universal suffrage. Not a word regarding monarchy. The commune of Sallon (Alpes-Maritimes) concluded its petition with the words: "Long live God! Long live France! Long live the Republic!" The commune of Bétaille (Loiret) requested that the social structure be based on its natural foundations—religion, family, and property—and at the same time professed its sacred loyalty to the Republic.

In the case of four communes, we are informed on the debates within the councils. Since there was no unanimity, the dissenters wanted that fact recorded. A really rather moderate petition submitted by Garindein (Basses-Pyrénées) was signed by only four out of nine councillors. "The other five, although satisfied with the petition, wanted to await the *préfet's* instructions before signing it." This could perhaps be interpreted as a pretext invoked by monarchist dissidents. In Arbois (Jura) it was certainly a monarchist who refused to vote for the petition on the grounds, as he explained, that, politically, the town was divided in its opinion. In Saint-Omer there was a debate. One councillor pointed out that politics were not within the province of the municipalities; another said that "the process of assimilation taking place in many minds must be respected" and that "so many people still cannot decide between a Republic or a Liberal Monarchy that it is unfair to force them to choose too early on." At the request of the mayor, who openly declared that he was a republican but considered the petition both untimely and divisive, the council tabled the motion.

In these three volumes, which show the communes of France to be so exceedingly talkative, only one monarchist proved to be outspoken. This occurred in Moissac (Tarn-et-Garonne), where the republican petition was adopted, but not without protest. After M. Lagrefe stated that a municipal council had no right to meddle in politics, M. J. Tienfal—a courageous man, that one!—declared that France "must make haste to summon its legitimate king, Henri V, to the throne, for he is the last hope."

Many regarded the Republic as the only obvious choice: "The Republic is the government of the people, for the people, and by the people. —It is the natural form of government for all "(Bourg-de-Péage, Drôme). The simple people, the masses, cannot grasp the crucial difference between a plebiscitary empire and a monarchy. In vain do the publicists try and point out that France had been defeated and her frontiers cut back uniquely because of the failings of democratic and aggressive empires; to simple people, to the masses, there is no distinction between empire and monarchy as regimes: "Since our past experience of monarchies is itself proof of their disastrous consequences, and since they have led us from one frightful catastrophe to another . . ." Such is the opinion of Vercheny (Drôme). What is left? The Republic.

Challemel-Lacour

M. GRELÉE has provided us with a good two-volume work on Challemel-Lacour (published by Champion). It is a pity that the third volume has not yet come out, since the second stops at the year 1869. Nevertheless, the first two are enough to shed light on an interesting figure.

Challemel-Lacour was descended from an old and worthy family of lawyers from Lower Normandy which, at the end of the 18th century, tried to add the nobiliary particle to its name: Challemel-Lacour's great grandfather, a notary, signed his name "de la Cour." Early in the 19th century the family came to grief in the most unfortunate way: Challemel-Lacour's grandfather was condemned for forgery in 1815. His father lived courageously but unhappily under difficult circumstances. During the Restoration his republican opinions earned him a few months in prison. He tried his luck in business, but without success: in 1815 he was declared bankrupt. Challemel-Lacour was eleven at the time.

His mother, an energetic woman who had faith in her son, came to his rescue and guided him until he passed the examinations for admission to the Ecole Normale in 1847. From his professors' comments and the reminiscences of his schoolmates, it would seem that he was a fervent and very diligent adolescent, strongly marked by tribulations, humiliations, and bitter memories. In June 1848 the students at the Ecole were summoned by their Director to take up arms and to fight the Socialist insurrection. Only Challemel-Lacour refused to take up arms against the people. In February 1849 he gave a speech at a Socialist banquet, the text of which has survived: it was a revolutionary statement, denouncing all the forms of compromise that constitute the structure of bourgeois society. He ended his speech with a solemn oath: "It is to the people that I owe my leisure, my knowledge, and my life; in return for that, I owe the people the truth; I pledge to repay that debt to the best of my ability." In December 1851, as a professor in Limoges, Challemel-Lacour joined the local Republicans in armed resistance against the Bonapartist *coup d'état*. The attempt was abortive, and Challemel-Lacour left the country.

The curious story of his exile in Belgium, Germany, and Switzerland reads like a Stendhal novel. Actually, it is perhaps one of those derivative works inspired by poets and novelists of the past: the students at the Ecole Normale in 1849 were ardent admirers of Stendhal's *La Chartreuse de Parme* and *Le Rouge et le noir*, and the story of Challemel's life in exile often reflects the fictional life of Julien Sorel. While a family tutor in Belgium, Challemel-Lacour seduced his pupils' mother, who gave up everything to follow him and to share his life in exile. People asked in surprise: Who is that woman who accompanies him everywhere? My sister, said he. No one liked Challemel-Lacour: he was too haughty, too insolent, and since in no time his deceit was discovered, it caused a scandal which led him to be exiled even from the society of exiles. Challemel-Lacour adapted to that solitary existence. Perhaps it never even bothered him. Very aristocratic by nature, he had nothing but disdain for the facile ideology of the revolutionaries. As a distinguished German scholar, he discovered Schopenhauer, whom he went and talked with in Frankfurt; he also discovered Wagner and was the first to publish some excellent French translations of his works (*Quatre Poèmes d'opéra* and *Lettre sur la musique*). Both the lofty style and the nihilism of the two masters had a profound influence on him. It was then that he wrote his remarkable essay *Etudes et réflexions d'un pessimiste*, which he in fact just filed away in a drawer, so that his *Etudes et réflexions* was not published until after his death. We are told that it was written, repeatedly revised, and corrected between 1861 and 1869. Since Challemel-Lacour went into politics after his return to France in 1865, he could not have his essay published because his overly explicit views would have given away his secret—the secret of a fervent and calculated man of action. For example:

> One cannot help but acknowledge the special grandeur of the pessimist who is not paralyzed by foreseeing the results of his action. Fortunately, a few such pessimists join forces in all revolutions, including our own. They are never found in positions of leadership, because they loathe the rhetoric that is indispensable to such positions, and because they do not share in the general intoxicated rapture. But such figures, who work in the half-light and rarely emerge from it, because when they do, they are victimized—such figures, who are all too often neglected by history and who are both haughty and intelligent—are those to whom I most willingly give my attention.
>
> I like such skeptics as Chamfort, who act according to their principles. Chamfort had proclaimed the revolution and became its champion. But he had learned too much about life (if one learns nothing, what is the point of living?) to believe that a pure and triumphant revolution would fulfill the cherished dreams of his friends. When he saw the turn it was taking, when he saw that lovely girl, who was thought to be pregnant with a new world, fall from the hands of her master into those of flunkeys and scullery boys—when he saw her thus sterilized and tainted, and on

the way to becoming a barrack-room mattress—he felt neither the surprise which is typical of simpletons, nor the discouragement that comes from lack of foresight. He remained what he was; he continued to want what he had always wanted; he did not give up his love of the impossible; and although he tried to kill himself, he did so not in the manner of Cato, but like a fastidious man whose nostrils were repelled by the foul stench of prisons.

That sums up the man. Secretive, scornful, contemptuous of his friends—perhaps especially of his friends —Challemel-Lacour was the Chamfort of the Third Republic. That child of the Revolution of 1848, whom Schopenhauer had purged of all enthusiasm and all faith, remained ambitious, fervently vindictive, and repelled by that class of French Notables to which his family had belonged, but did no longer. His hatred of them was matched only by his hatred of the Church, of that ancient Catholicism cluttered with miracles and dogmas. The purpose and goal of the embittered and violent *normalien* was to destroy all that, both Notables and bishops (just as the Revolution had destroyed the prominent figures and the princes), and on those ruins to remake and build the foundations of a new France, within a framework of popular and educational institutions, led and inspired by the common people, the intellectuals, and the academics. Directly after his return to France, with the Empire beginning to decline, Challemel-Lacour had realized that Gambetta was, by nature, a fine politician, that he could be useful and influential. He had therefore helped him and maneuvered him into the forefront.

Ambition filled his life as a disillusioned old man. He wanted to be an ambassador, to follow in the footsteps of men like Broglie and La Rochefoucauld, and he did take over their positions in London. But the records of the misdemeanors of his family, which were revealed by his enemies, made a most unfortunate impression on English society, which was then very particular and quick to close its doors, so that Challemel-Lacour was forced to return to France. From then on, he managed once and for all to forget his principles and the solemn oath he had pronounced in his twenties; he aspired to the highest positions in government and society; in a famous speech in the Senate he offset the bad effects of the violently anticlerical speeches he had made in 1875; he got himself elected to the presidency of the Senate and then to the French Academy, replacing Renan, and in his acceptance speech, expressed the reservations on Renan's skepticism and moral nihilism that were anticipated by those who had elected him: the Right had voted for him. He died in 1896.

It was perhaps not altogether pointless to have made special mention of "one of those figures who are all too often neglected by history," of that "infallible oracle" so greatly admired by Juliette Adam.

Editor's Notes

Chapter 1

1. Jules Grévy (1807–91), an austere doctrinaire republican of 1848 vintage from the Jura, succeeded MacMahon as the second President of the Republic following the 1877 crisis of the *Seize Mai*, thereby consolidating the republicans' hold on the new regime; elected to a second seven-year term in 1885, he was forced to resign two years later as a result of a scandal involving the sale of decorations by his son-in-law, Daniel Wilson.

Félix Faure (1841–99) succeeded to the presidency following Casimir-Périer's resignation in 1895, and died in office at the height of the Dreyfus Affair; it was on the day of his funeral that Paul Déroulède made an abortive attempt to carry out a rightist *coup d'état*.

2. Gabriel Hanotaux, *Histoire de la France contemporaine, 1870–1900*, 4 vols. (Paris, 1908), remains a standard work on the period by a distinguished statesman sympathetic to Gambetta and the Opportunists.

3. Jacques Bainville (1879–1936), a royalist historian and prominent member of the *Action Française*, author of the most popular history of the Third Republic.

4. 1876 would be more accurate, since the elections were held in February 1876.

5. The official Paris residence of the Presidents of the Republic since 1873.

6. The election was actually held on February 8.

7. A prominent Liberal publicist, Lucien-Anatole Prévost-Paradol (1829–70) was the author of *La France nouvelle* (1868). He was Daniel Halévy's uncle.

8. Two of Louis Philippe's sons, they were the uncles of the orphaned comte de Paris, the Orleanist pretender to the throne.

9. Supporters of the restoration of the Bourbon line in the person of the comte de Chambord, grandson of Charles X.

10. The elections to the Assembly were held according to a system of multiple elections whereby a candidate could be returned by several constituencies at the same time but would have to choose after the elections which one he would represent.

11. Gaston Crémieux (1838–71), a radical lawyer who was instrumental in launching the Marseilles Commune; despite Thiers's efforts to save his life, he was executed by a general who, it was said, had not forgotten that famous insult.

Chapter 2

1. The terrace was all that remained of this royal palace on the western outskirts of the capital which was burned down by the Prussians during the siege of Paris.

2. The French counterpart of the London *Times*, *Le Temps*, founded by Nefftzer in 1861, became the Third Republic's most serious and authoritative daily.

3. French infantry troops noted for their valor; the name is derived from an Algerian tribe who constituted its first recruits in 1831.

4. It was near this town outside Orléans that the Army of the Loire was defeated by the Germans on December 2, 1870; Joan of Arc had beaten the English at the same spot during the Hundred Years' War, in 1429.

5. I.e. the bishop of Orléans.

Chapter 3

1. Louis Bonald (1754–1840) and Joseph de Maistre (1753–1821), the two leading legitimist political theorists during the Restoration, who advocated an alliance of Throne and Altar in opposition to the egalitarian ideas bequeathed by the Revolution.

2. An international secret society that originated in Italy after the fall of Napoleon and was dedicated to overthrowing all European monarchies in order to replace them with liberal and democratic institutions; the name is derived from its symbol of black charcoal kindling to a bright flame.

3. A state prison located on what is now the boulevard Diderot.

4. Jules Simon (1814–96), a republican professor dismissed from his post for refusing to take the loyalty oath to the Second Empire; elected to the *Corps législatif* in 1863 and again in 1869, he became a member of the Government of National Defense and subsequently premier under the Republic.

Jules Favre (1809–80), a republican lawyer, first elected to the *Corps législatif* as deputy from Paris in 1858; member of the Government of National Defense, he was responsible for negotiating the Treaty of Frankfurt; resigning from the Foreign Ministry in July 1871, he ended his career as a senator.

Ernest Picard (1821–77), elected as one of the first republicans—"the Five"—to the *Corps législatif* in 1858; serving as Minister of Finance in the Government of National Defense, he assisted Favre in negotiating peace, and later became one of the leaders of the Left Center in the Assembly.

5. A large public park on the western outskirts of Paris adjacent to the Bois de Boulogne.

Chapter 4

1. Paul Thureau-Dangin (1837–1913), author of a standard history of the July Monarchy.

2. Henri Wallon (1812–1904), distinguished Greek scholar and member of the French Academy, who shifted from royalism to a Conservative republican position; it was his famous amendment, adopted by a majority of one in January of 1875, that broke the constitutional deadlock and formally established the Republic.

3. Elected local bodies at the departmental level.

4. Notre Dame de Fourvière, the church dominating Lyons and site of an annual pilgrimage associated with the martyrdom of Saint-Pothin, first bishop of Lyons and primate of Gaul.

5. *Le Journal Officiel*, the official government publication reporting parliamentary debates.

The End of the Notables

Chapter 5

1. Edouard Lockroy (1840–1913), who, as a Paris deputy to the National Assembly, had tried in vain to prevent a clash between the Commune and Versailles; he wrote for *Le Rappel* after being briefly imprisoned for his Communard sympathies, and later represented the Radicals in various coalition cabinets.

2. Pius IX's Syllabus of Errors (1864), which condemned the ideas of progress and liberalism as modern heresies, aroused the indignation not only of the non-Catholic world but of Liberal Catholics as well.

3. John Lemoinne (1815–92), for many years editor of that Liberal newspaper, became a senator and a member of the French Academy.

Chapter 6

1. Charles Maurras (1868–1952), founder of the royalist *Action Française*, was the most outspoken and persistent critic of parliamentary democracy as represented by the Third Republic, which he relentlessly condemned as "the Slut."

2. Well-to-do-district on the Left bank, stretching from the Invalides to the French Academy, where many members of the aristocracy, both legitimist and Orleanist, had their residences.

3. The comte de Chambord's château in Austria.

4. General Charles Bourbaki (1816–97), who commanded the Army of the East during the Franco-Prussian War and was known for his loyalty to the Bonapartists.

5. The die-hard legitimists known as *Chevau-légers*—a term derived from the name of the street in Versailles where they had their headquarters.

6. National Audit Office, roughly comparable to the U.S. Bureau of the Budget.

7. Eugène Rouher (1814–84) served as Napoleon III's Minister of State, 1863–69. He was regarded as the champion of the authoritarian Empire as opposed to such Liberals as Emile Ollivier; and elected deputy from Corsica in 1871, he was the leader of the thirty-odd Bonapartists in the Assembly.

8. General Auguste Ducrot (1817–82) distinguished himself during the Franco-Prussian War both at the Battle of Woerth

Editor's Notes

and the siege of Paris, but had rallied to the royalists after the fall of the Empire.

Chapter 7

1. A working-class district in the 20th *arrondissement*, the east end of Paris.

2. The lower, popularly elected assembly in the Second Empire's bicameral Parliament.

3. It was in a famous speech in Bordeaux, once a bastion of royalism, that Louis Napoleon, having concluded a triumphant tour of the provinces, proclaimed the restoration of the Empire in 1852.

4. Juliette Adam, née Lamber (1836–1936), was the wife of Edmond Adam, who had been mayor of the 18th *arrondissement* and then *Préfet* of Police in the Government of National Defense. A staunch republican propagandist and a champion of *Revanche*, she presided over a salon which attracted the leading dignitaries of the Third Republic.

5. A Radical program on which Gambetta was returned to the *Corps législatif* by Belleville in 1869. It called, among other things, for the election of all civil servants, the suppression of standing armies, the abolition of all privileges and monopolies, and the separation of Church and State.

6. Auguste Scheurer-Kestner (1833–1899), elected to the Assembly by the Haut-Rhin, resigned in protest against the annexation of Alsace, but was subsequently returned by the Seine; he later became political editor of Gambetta's paper, and is chiefly remembered for having taken the initiative in forcing the government to reopen the Dreyfus Case in 1897.

Chapter 8

1. Political editor of *Les Débats*, Jean-Jacques Weiss (1827–91) later became its drama critic; the quotation is from his *Combat constitutionnel*.

2. Auguste Blanqui (1805–81), a veteran revolutionary advocating the dictatorship of the proletariat, spent most of his life in prison; he was elected to the Commune by the 18th *arrondissement*, but was unable to take his seat.

223

The End of the Notables

3. The passage cited is from Louis Veuillot, *Paris pendant les deux sièges*, (Paris, n.d.), p. 174.

Chapter 9

1. Charles Maurras.

2. I.e. Germaine de Staël (1766–1817), daughter of Louis XVI's finance minister, Jacques Necker, was persecuted and exiled by Napoleon for her liberal views.

3. General Alfred Chanzy (1823–83) commanded the Second Army of the Loire during the Franco-Prussian War; appointed Governor of Algeria in 1873, he subsequently served as ambassador to Russia.

4. General Nicolas Changarnier (1793–1877), a resolute monarchist, whose dismissal as Commander of the National Guard and of the Paris garrison by Louis Napoleon in 1851 had marked the first step toward the establishment of the Empire.

5. Antoine Berryer (1790–1868), the great orator of the legitimist party.

6. Jules Guesde (1845–1922) was to introduce a Marxist element into the French Socialist movement running counter to the tradition of gradual social reform associated with Jean Jaurès.

7. Literally *blockheads, jerks*, but here also a pun on the people who made the pilgrimage to Lourdes.

Chapter 10

1. Louis-Charles-Elie Decazes (1819–86), son of Duc Elie, Louis XVIII's Prime Minister, had shifted to the Orleanist side and, together with Broglie, Pasquier, and MacMahon, was to dominate "the Republic of the Dukes" following the fall of Thiers. Appointed Foreign Minister in Broglie's first cabinet in 1873, he remained in charge of foreign affairs in seven successive cabinets until 1877.

2. Jules Méline (1838–1925) became a champion of agricultural interests under the Republic, reversing the Second Empire's free-trade policy by introducing the Méline tariff in 1892.

3. Cf. Jean Bouvier, "Des Banquiers devant l'actualité politique en 1870–71," *Revue d'Histoire Moderne et Contemporaine* 5 (April–June 1958): 137–51.

4. Like all members of the propertied class, Thiers had reacted to the social menace of the June Days by supporting the Falloux Law of 1850, granting religious congregations the right of opening secondary schools.

5. This Renaissance palace on the Left Bank became the seat of the Senate after 1879.

6. It was by refusing to withdraw from this island that England had violated the Peace of Amiens, thus providing Napoleon with a convenient pretext for resuming war in 1803.

7. The peace treaty had allowed the French to retain Belfort in return for a German victory parade in Paris.

Chapter 11

1. Only a small square and street, tucked away in the elegant 16th *arrondissement*, were named after him.

2. Jean Cartier de Villemessant (1812–79) founded *Le Figaro* in 1854 as a satirical weekly which replaced *L'Evènement* in 1866 and became the most dazzling Parisian political daily. Later taken over by the Conservative perfumer François Coty, *Le Figaro* is still today the favorite paper of the upper *bourgeoisie*.

3. Eugène Sue (1804–57), best known for his romantic novels *Les Mystères de Paris* and *Le Juif errant*.

Chapter 12

1. A French parliamentary device which was to become the main source of ministerial instability under the Third Republic, and whereby any deputy could challenge the cabinet on any issue. It had to be followed by what amounted to a vote of confidence before the Chamber could proceed to the order of business for the day.